COMMUNITY CARE AND THE LAW FOR OLDER PEOPLE

RIGHTS, REMEDIES AND FINANCES

COMMUNITY CARE FOR OLDER PEOPLE

RIGHTS, REMEDIES AND FINANCES

Margaret Richards

JORDANS
1996

Published by
Jordan Publishing Limited
21 St Thomas Street
Bristol BS1 6JS

British Library Cataloguing in Publication Data
A catalogue record for this book is available from the British Library.

ISBN 0 85308 293 6

Typeset by Mendip Communications Ltd, Frome
Printed in Great Britain by Hobbs the Printers of Southampton

PREFACE

'... last Scene of all
That ends this strange eventful history,
Is second childishness, and mere oblivion,
Sans teeth, sans eyes, sans taste, sans everything'
(*As You Like It*, Act II, Scene 7).

This book is the outcome of the analysis, questioning and discussion which has gone on in the many professional development courses which I have presented to practitioners over the past five years. Long before the implementation of Part III of the National Health Service and Community Care Act in April 1993, a declining political commitment to the Welfare State, pitted against demographic factors implying a need for expansion, indicated that there was likely to be an increasing demand for new legal expertise in respect of the long-term care of vulnerable elderly people. And so it was.

Older people are not, of course, the only social group who are subject to community care policies, and an academically pure approach to the subject-matter might not have linked the application of the law so closely with one particular client group. But for legal practitioners, often in high street firms and battling against market forces which seek to diminish their client base and belittle their skills, the development of legal services for older clients is now of considerable importance. This book is mainly for them.

In writing the book, I have had two main objectives:

(i) to give practitioners an understanding of the complex and difficult policy issues in and around community care, together with some information about how the system works. Most lawyers who advise elderly clients have a background in private law, and the public law obligation to provide health and social care through the responsibilities vested in local authority social services departments or the National Health Service, is often unfamiliar territory. To achieve successful outcomes for clients requires, however, an understanding of how decisions are made, who makes them, and the financial and cultural context in which they are made;

(ii) to identify particular problems that practitioners are likely to encounter and provide the tools with which they can be addressed. In respect of the latter, the difficulty faced by those outside the public sector in accessing secondary legislation and quasi-legislative guidance on community care is an affront to our constitution. Chapter 1 contains what I hope are helpful suggestions as to ways and means of overcoming this problem. In addition, the absence of significant legal research and analysis in this area is a considerable handicap, and Chapter 1 also seeks to highlight useful sources of know-how of which practitioners may not be aware.

The focus of the book is the interface between health and social care; the responsibilities of the State to provide care for its frail elderly citizens; and the financing of both residential care and services delivered at home. Much of the material is complex and will be new to practitioners. To prevent the book from becoming too large and indigestible, housing issues have been covered, in outline, in one chapter only. Nevertheless, given the importance of good housing for the well-being of elderly people, and so for the success of community care policies, there is perhaps room for another book which can explore the complexities of law and practice in that area in more detail.

The book includes many case studies which analyse some of the practical problems which legal advisers face, particularly those arising out of the local authority's financial assessment for residential care.

The perspective throughout is that of the individual older client or, in Chapter 11, of the informal carer. For this reason, there is an emphasis on financial matters: the costs of care; the means test; and, of course, protecting assets. This emphasis accurately reflects, I think, clients' expectations of their legal advisers.

While I was writing this book, many changes in the law were either taking effect or pending. Trying to put together a state-of-the-art analysis turned out to be akin to shooting at a moving target. I have had to revise the text several times, even after delivering the 'final' manuscript. As a result, the book is up to date to April 1996. Having said that, I have incorporated many important changes, under the shadow of publication, with less time to reflect than I would have liked.

This comment applies especially to the increases in the upper and lower capital limits for residential and nursing care, which took effect in April 1996; the knock-on effects of which are likely to be significant. All calculations have been revised to take account of these changes and of the new 1996/97 benefit rates.

Although the new limits have been welcomed by, for example, the large charities concerned with care of the elderly, they are regarded more as a political fix than a comprehensive attempt to sort out funding for care. The underlying question of how far care for an increasingly elderly population should be seen as a collective responsibility, to be provided for through general taxation rather than private provision, urgently needs a more open and comprehensive public debate.

I have several debts to acknowledge. The first is owed to my fellow lecturer and former colleague, Norma Martin Clement, who has written Chapters 12 and 13 on remedies and housing and with whom I have shared ideas and information over a long period. The second is to my publishers, and particularly to Martin West, who has given me help and support throughout this project. The third is to my family, who, over the past year, have uncomplainingly put up with my distractedness and the mountains of paper generated by my research. Thank you all.

I would also like to acknowledge the inspiration and understanding which has come out of my involvement with St Anne's Shelter and Housing Action in Leeds, an organisation which aspires to, and achieves, community care in action.

This book is dedicated to my parents and, posthumously, to my parents-in-law, for whom community care was little more than a slogan.

All the opinions expressed in this book are personal, and the errors and omissions are mine alone.

MARGARET RICHARDS
Leeds
April 1996

CONTENTS

Preface   v
Table of Cases   xvii
Table of Statutes   xxi
Table of Statutory Instruments   xxv
Table of Directions and Guidance   xxvii
List of Abbreviations   xxxi
Glossary of Terms   xxxiii

PART I   THE LEGAL FRAMEWORK   1

Chapter 1   THE CLIENTS AND THE TASK   3
             1.1   Introduction   3
             1.2   Demographic factors   3
                    1.2.1   An ageing population   4
                    1.2.2   Health   5
                    1.2.3   Income and expenditure   5
                    1.2.4   Housing   6
                    1.2.5   Residential care   6
                    1.2.6   Information sources   7
             1.3   Client concerns   8
             1.4   Advice needs   8
                    1.4.1   Know-how   9
             1.5   The legal framework   10
                    1.5.1   Primary legislation   10
                    1.5.2   Regulations   10
                    1.5.3   Directions and guidance   10

Chapter 2   WHAT IS COMMUNITY CARE?   13
             2.1   Who needs community care?   13
             2.2   The development of community care policies   14
             2.3   Who delivers community care?   15
                    2.3.1   Local authorities   16
                    2.3.2   National Health Service   17
                    2.3.3   The independent sector   20
             2.4   Funding community care before the 1993
                    reforms   21
                    2.4.1   Joint finance   22
                    2.4.2   The perverse incentive towards
                             residential care   22
                    2.4.3   DSS funding for in-patient NHS care   23
                    2.4.4   'Reducing benefits'   24

	2.5	A new framework for community care	24
		2.5.1 The key changes	25
		2.5.2 The boundary between health and social care	28
		2.5.3 Better value for taxpayers' money: an end to the 'perverse incentive'	31
Chapter 3		COMMUNITY CARE PLANS	35
	3.1	Consultation	36
	3.2	Practice points	37
Chapter 4		WHAT ARE COMMUNITY CARE SERVICES?	39
	4.1	Introduction	39
	4.2	Community care services	40
		4.2.1 Part III of the National Assistance Act 1948	40
		4.2.2 Section 45 of the Health Services and Public Health Act 1968	41
		4.2.3 Section 21 of and Sch 8 to the National Health Service Act 1977	42
		4.2.4 Section 117 of the Mental Health Act 1983	43
		4.2.5 The Chronically Sick and Disabled Persons Act 1970 and the Disabled Persons (Services Consultation and Representation) Act 1986	43
	4.3	Practice points	46
	4.4	Examples of community care services	48
Chapter 5		ASSESSMENT OF NEEDS	51
	5.1	Introduction	51
	5.2	A needs-led approach	52
	5.3	The 'right' to assessment	53
	5.4	Relationship between assessment and service provision	54
		5.4.1 Unmet need	54
	5.5	The process of assessment	55
		5.5.1 Eligibility for assessment	55
		5.5.2 Information about assessments	56
		5.5.3 Levels of assessment	57
		5.5.4 The assessment of disabled people	58
		5.5.5 Waiting for an assessment	59
		5.5.6 How will an assessment be carried out?	59
		5.5.7 Participation	60

	5.5.8	Carers	60
	5.5.9	Collaboration with other agencies	61
	5.5.10	Confidentiality	61
	5.5.11	The result of an assessment	62
	5.5.12	The financial assessment	62
	5.5.13	Reviewing assessments	63
5.6	Practice points		63

Chapter 6   THE DECISION TO PROVIDE SERVICES   67

6.1	The duty to make a decision	67
6.2	Determining service provision	68
6.3	Service provision for the disabled	69
6.4	The extent of a local authority's obligation to provide services for the disabled	70
6.5	The care package	72
6.6	Choice	73
6.7	Practice points	74

Chapter 7   DISCHARGE FROM HOSPITAL   75

7.1	Introduction	75
7.2	Arrangements for discharge	76
7.3	Consultation with the patient	77
7.4	The decision on continuing care	77
7.5	The patient's right to refuse discharge to nursing home or residential care	78
7.6	New review procedures	79
7.7	Case study	81
7.8	Practice points	82
7.9	Flowchart of the review procedure	84

Chapter 8   CONTRACTS FOR CARE   85

8.1	Selection of providers		86
8.2	Contract types and purchasing arrangements		87
8.3	Relationship with health care contracts		88
8.4	Contractual terms and conditions		88
	8.4.1	Conditions	89
	8.4.2	Service specifications	89
8.5	Quality assurance		89
	8.5.1	R v Newcastle City Council ex parte Dixon (1993) 17 BMLR 82	90
	8.5.2	R v Cleveland County Council ex parte Cleveland Care Homes Association (1993) 17 BMLR 122	90
	8.5.3	Conclusions	91
8.6	Rights of service users		92

Chapter 9	**RESIDENTIAL CARE SERVICES**		95
	9.1	The previous regime	95
		9.1.1 Part III accommodation	95
		9.1.2 Schedule 8 to the National Health Service Act 1977	96
		9.1.3 The independent sector	97
		9.1.4 Residential care homes and nursing homes	97
		9.1.5 Quality standards	97
	9.2	The new regime: local authority responsibilities	98
		9.2.1 Ordinary residence	98
		9.2.2 The extent of the local authority's enhanced powers	99
		9.2.3 The gatekeeping role of the local authority	100
		9.2.4 Individual choice of home	101
		9.2.5 Paying for choice	102
	9.3	Residential care contracts	103
		9.3.1 Fees	103
		9.3.2 Standard terms and conditions	104
	9.4	Private residential care arrangements	105
	9.5	Healthcare services for residents	105
		9.5.1 Incontinence services	106
	9.6	Practice points	106
Chapter 10	**RESIDENTIAL CARE – QUALITY ASSURANCE**		109
	10.1	The Registered Homes Act 1984	109
	10.2	Quality standards	110
	10.3	The scope of the Registered Homes Act 1984	111
	10.4	Registration of residential care homes	112
	10.5	Registration of nursing homes	113
	10.6	Refusal of registration	113
	10.7	Small homes	114
	10.8	Dual registration	115
	10.9	Cancellation of registration	116
	10.10	The inspection process	117
		10.10.1 Inspection units	118
		10.10.2 Inspecting nursing homes	118
		10.10.3 Lay assessors	118
	10.11	Inspection and quality assurance	119
Chapter 11	**CARERS**		121
	11.1	Assessment	122
	11.2	Carers (Recognition and Services) Act 1995	123
	11.3	Respite care	125
	11.4	Charging carers for services	126

	11.4.1	Home-care services	126
	11.4.2	Respite care	126
11.5	Complaints by carers		126
11.6	Future indicators		126

Chapter 12	HOUSING AND COMMUNITY CARE		129
	12.1	Introduction	129
	12.2	Profile of the housing circumstances of the elderly population	130
	12.3	Housing policies and the elderly	130
		12.3.1 Housing and the National Health Service and Community Care Act 1990	131
		12.3.2 Homelessness	133
	12.4	Housing options for the elderly	134
		12.4.1 Staying put with necessary repairs	134
		12.4.2 Staying put with adaptations	135
		12.4.3 Moving to smaller mainstream accommodation	137
		12.4.4 Moving to specialist housing	138
		12.4.5 Moving in with the family	143
	12.5	Conclusion	146

Chapter 13	CHALLENGING COMMUNITY CARE DECISIONS		147
	13.1	Introduction	147
	13.2	The complaints procedure	148
		13.2.1 Who can complain?	149
		13.2.2 What can be complained about?	149
		13.2.3 The procedure for complaining	150
		13.2.4 Evaluation of the complaints procedure	153
	13.3	The local authority's monitoring officer	154
		13.3.1 The function of the monitoring officer	154
		13.3.2 Evaluation of the monitoring officer	155
	13.4	The local government Ombudsman	155
		13.4.1 The jurisdiction of the Ombudsman	155
		13.4.2 The mechanics of complaining to the Ombudsman	155
		13.4.3 Evaluation of complaining to the Ombudsman	156
	13.5	Default powers of the Secretary of State	156
		13.5.1 Scope of the default powers	156
		13.5.2 Evaluation of the default powers	156
	13.6	Judicial review	157
		13.6.1 The requirements for judicial review	157

		13.6.2	Alternative remedies precluding or delaying judicial review	158
		13.6.3	The grounds for judicial review	158
		13.6.4	Evaluation of judicial review as a remedy	160
	13.7		Tort action for damages	160
		13.7.1	Breach of statutory duty	161
		13.7.2	Common law duty of care in negligence	162
	13.8		Conclusion	163

PART II   PAYING FOR CARE   165

Chapter 14   THE NEW FUNDING ARRANGEMENTS   167
	14.1	Introduction	167
	14.2	Paying for residential care before 1 April 1993	168
	14.3	Paying for services delivered at home before 1 April 1993	169
	14.4	Charging policies from April 1993	170
	14.5	Paying for residential care after April 1993	170
	14.6	Preserved rights	171
	14.7	Paying for home care services after 1 April 1993	171
	14.8	Essential reference materials for the legal adviser	172

Chapter 15   THE LOCAL AUTHORITY'S MEANS TEST
FOR RESIDENTIAL CARE   173
	15.1		What is the legal basis of the means test?	173
	15.2		How does the means test operate?	174
	15.3		How is capital assessed?	175
		15.3.1	The new capital limits	175
		15.3.2	Method of valuation	176
		15.3.3	Ownership of assets	177
		15.3.4	Co-ownership of assets	177
		15.3.5	Disregarded capital	179
		15.3.6	Notional capital	180
		15.3.7	The resident's own home	181
	15.4		How is income assessed?	188
		15.4.1	Disregarded income	188
		15.4.2	Rental income	189
		15.4.3	Notional income	189
	15.5		The personal expenses allowance	190
	15.6		Married or unmarried couples	191
		15.6.1	Assessing one partner	191
		15.6.2	Assessing both partners	192
		15.6.3	Liable relatives	192

15.7	Calculating the local authority's charge	193
15.8	The residential allowance	193
15.9	Placements in local authority managed homes	194
15.10	Case studies: calculating residents' contributions	195
15.11	Enforcing payment of assessed contributions	196
	15.11.1 Section 22 of the HASSASSAA 1983	197
Chapter 16	**PRESERVED RIGHTS TO INCOME SUPPORT**	199
16.1	Why do 'preserved rights' cause problems for clients?	200
16.2	Can the local authority help?	201
16.3	Does the district health authority have any responsibility?	201
16.4	Are there any other options?	202
Chapter 17	**PAYING FOR NON-RESIDENTIAL SERVICES**	205
17.1	Section 17 of the HASSASSAA 1983	205
17.2	Charging strategies	206
17.3	Welfare benefits and charging	207
17.4	Treatment of capital for charging purposes	208
17.5	Couples and non-residential charges	209
17.6	Inability to pay	210
17.7	Collecting charges	210
17.8	Practice points	210
Chapter 18	**PRESERVING ASSETS FROM THE STATE**	213
18.1	Professional issues	215
	18.1.1 The Law Society's guidelines on gifts of property	217
18.2	The notional capital rule	217
	18.2.1 Regulation 51 of the ISG Regulations 1987	218
	18.2.2 Reduction of notional capital	219
	18.2.3 Regulation 25 of the NA(AR) Regulations 1992	219
	18.2.4 What determines the application of the notional capital rule?	220
	18.2.5 Deprivation	221
	18.2.6 Purpose	221
	18.2.7 Timing	224
	18.2.8 Disregarded capital	225
18.3	Rights of local authorities to recover gifts from third parties	228
18.4	Setting aside dispositions under the Insolvency Act 1986	230

| | | 18.4.1 | Section 339 of the Insolvency Act 1986 | 230 |
| | | 18.4.2 | Section 423 of the Insolvency Act 1986 | 232 |

Chapter 19 USING WELFARE BENEFITS TO FUND RESIDENTIAL CARE   235

19.1 What benefits?   235
    19.1.1 Income support premiums   236
19.2 Availability of disability benefits to those in residential care   238
    19.2.1 DLA (mobility component)   238
    19.2.2 Attendance allowance and DLA (care component)   238
    19.2.3 Means testing of attendance allowance and disability living allowance (care component)   240
19.3 Example   241
19.4 Practice points   242

Appendix   243
Bibliography   251
List of Useful Addresses   257
Index   259

TABLE OF CASES

References are to paragraph numbers.

Akbarali v Brent London Borough Council; Abdullah v Shropshire County
Council; Shabpar v Barnet London Borough Council; Shah (Jitendra) v
Barnet London Borough Council; Barnet London Borough Council v Shah
[1983] 2 AC 309, [1983] 2 WLR 16, [1983] 1 All ER 226, HL   9.2.1
Associated Provincial Picture Houses Ltd v Wednesbury Corporation [1948] 1
KB 223, [1947] 2 All ER 680, [1948] LJR 190, CA   13.6.3

Bardrick v Haycock; Same v Vernon; Same v Robinson (1976) 31 P&CR 420,
CA   12.4.5
Blyth v Blyth (No 2) [1966] AC 643, [1966] 2 WLR 634, [1966] 1 All ER 524,
HL   4.2.5

Caparo Industries v Dickman [1992] 2 AC 605, [1990] 2 WLR 358, [1990] 1
All ER 568, HL   13.7.2
Chief Adjudication Officer v Harris (1994) 15 April, (unreported)   19.4
Chief Adjudication Officer v Kenyon (1995) *The Times*, 17 October   19.2.2
Chief Adjudication Officer v Palfrey (1995) *The Times*, 17 February,
CA   15.3.4, 15.3.7, 18.2.8
Cocks v Thanet District Council [1983] 2 AC 286, [1982] 3 WLR 1121, [1982]
3 All ER 1135, HL   13.7.1
Coombs v Hertfordshire County Council (1991) 89 LGR 774, [1991] COD
515, (1992) 4 Admin LR 185   10.6
Council of Civil Service Unions v Minister for the Civil Service [1985] AC 374,
[1984] 1 WLR 1174, [1984] 3 All ER 935, HL   13.6.3

Harrison v Cornwall County Council 90 LGR 81, (1992) 156 LG Rev 703,
(1991) *The Times*, 1 August, CA   10.3

Isle of Wight County Council v Humphreys (1991) 90 LGR 186, [1992] COD
308, (1991) *The Times*, 27 December   10.6

Kumar (A Bankrupt), Re, ex parte Lewis v Kumar [1993] 1 WLR 224, [1993]
2 All ER 700, [1993] 2 FLR 382, ChD   18.4.1

Lloyds Bank plc v Rosset and Another [1991] 1 AC 107, [1990] 2 WLR 867,
[1990] 1 All ER 111, HL   12.4.5

Midland Bank plc v Wyatt [1995] 1 FLR 696, [1996] BPIR 288, [1995] Fam
Law 299, ChD   18.4.2

Peters v Chief Adjudication Officer, *see* Social Security Decision No
  R(SB)3/89

R v Avon County Council, ex parte M [1994] 2 FLR 1006, [1995] Fam Law
  66, QBD   9.2.4, 13.2.3, 13.2.4, 13.6.3
R v Canterbury City Council, ex parte Gillespie (1986) 19 HLR 7   12.4.3
R v Cleveland County Council ex parte Cleveland Care Homes Association
  (1993) 17 BMLR 122, [1994] COD 221, (1994) 158 LG Rev 641   8.5.2
R v Devon County Council ex parte Baker; R v Durham County Council ex
  parte Curtis [1995] 1 All ER 73, 91 LGR 479, [1993] COD 253, CA   10.11, 13.6.2,
                                                                           13.6.3
R v Ealing District Health Authority ex parte Fox [1993] 1 WLR 373, [1993] 3
  All ER 170, [1993] COD 478   4.2.4
R v Ealing London Borough Council ex parte Leaman (1984) *The Times*, 10
  February   4.2.5
R v Gloucestershire County Council ex parte Mahfood and Barry (1995) *The
  Times*, 17 June, DC   2.5.3, 4.2.3, 4.3, 5.5.13, 6.4, 6.7, 7.8, 13.1, 13.6.3, 13.6.4, 13.7.1
R v Hereford & Worcester County Council ex parte Chandler (CO/1759/91)
                                                                               4.2.5
R v Lancashire County Council ex parte Ingham, (1995) 5 July, DC, Lexis   4.2.5, 6.6
R v London Borough of Tower Hamlets ex parte Ferdous Begum, *see* R v
  Oldham Metropolitan Borough Council, ex parte Garlick; R v Bexley
  London Borough Council, ex parte Bentum; R v London Borough of
  Tower Hamlets, ex parte Ferdous Begum
R v Mid-Glamorgan County Council ex parte Miles (1994) Legal Action
  January, 21   5.3, 13.2.1
R v Newcastle-upon-Tyne City Council ex parte Dixon (1993) 17 BMLR 82,
  (1994) 158 LG Rev 441, (1993) *The Times*, October 26   8.5.1, 8.5.2, 8.5.3
R v North Yorkshire County Council ex parte Hargreaves (1994) 30
  September, QBD, Lexis   1.5.3, 11.3, 13.2.3, 13.2.4
R v Northavon District Council ex parte Smith [1994] 2 AC 402, [1994] 3
  WLR 403, [1994] 3 All ER 313, HL   12.3.1
R v Oldham Metropolitan Borough Council, ex parte Garlick; R v Bexley
  London Borough Council, ex parte Bentum; R v London Borough of
  Tower Hamlets, ex parte Ferdous Begum [1993] AC 509, [1993] 2 WLR
  609, [1993] 2 All ER 65, HL   12.3.2
R v Royal Borough of Kingston-upon-Thames, ex parte T [1994] 1 FLR 798,
  QBD   13.6.2
R v Secretary of State for Social Services ex parte Hincks (1980) 1 BMLR 93,
  CA   2.3.2
R v Wandsworth London Borough Council ex parte Beckwith [1996] 1 WLR
  60, [1996] 1 All ER 129   2.5.1, 9.2, 13.6.3, 15.9

Shah v Barnet London Borough Council, *see* Akbarali v Brent London
  Borough Council; Abdullah v Shropshire County Council; Shabpar v
  Barnet London Borough Council; Shah (Jitendra) v Barnet London
  Borough Council; Barnet London Borough Council v Shah
Social Security Decision No CIS 62/1991   18.2.6
Social Security Decision No CIS 81/1991   18.2.8

Social Security Decision No CIS 231/1991   18.2.8
Social Security Decision No CIS 562/1992   18.2.8
Social Security Decision No CIS 242/1993   18.2.7
Social Security Decision No R(SB)25/83   15.3.3
Social Security Decision No R(SB)40/85   18.2.6
Social Security Decision No R(SB)3/89 sub nom Peters v Chief Adjudication
  Officer [1989] Fam Law 318, CA   15.3.3
Social Security Decision No R(SB)9/91   18.2.7
Steane and Another v Chief Adjudication Officer and Another [1995] TLR
  687, (1995) *The Times*, 19 December, CA   19.2.2

Tanner v Tanner [1975] 1 WLR 1346, [1975] 3 All ER 776, (1975) Fam Law
  193   12.4.5
Tribe v Tribe [1995] 3 WLR 913, [1995] 4 All ER 236, [1995] 2 FLR 966, CA 18.4.2

Waldron, Re [1986] QB 824, [1985] 3 WLR 1090, [1985] 3 All ER 775, CA   13.6.2
Warwickshire County Council v McSweeney (1988) (unreported)   10.6
White and Others v Chief Adjudication Officer and Another [1993] TLR 439,
  (1993) *The Times*, 2 August, CA   2.4.3, 14.2, 16.3
Wyatt v Hillingdon London Borough Council (1978) 76 LGR 727, CA   13.7.1

X (Minors) v Bedfordshire County Council; M (A Minor) and Another v
  Newham London Borough Council and Others; E (A Minor) v Dorset
  County Council; Christmas v Hampshire County Council; Keating v
  Bromley London Borough Council [1995] 2 FLR 276, [1995] 3 WLR 152,
  [1995] 3 All ER 353, HL   13.7, 13.7.1, 13.7.2

TABLE OF STATUTES

References are to paragraph numbers.

Access to Health Records Act
1990   5.5.10
Access to Personal Files Act 1987   5.5.10,
13.2.3

Carers (Recognition and
Services) Act 1995   4.4, 11.1, 11.2,
11.3, 11.4.1
s 1(1)   11.2
(3)   11.2
Children Act 1948   2.3.1
Children Act 1989   12.3.1, 13.6.2
Chronically Sick and Disabled
Persons Act 1970   1.5.1, 2.3.1, 4.1,
4.2.5, 4.3, 5.5.4, 12.4.2, 13.6.4
s 1   4.2.5, 4.4
s 2   4.2.5, 4.3, 4.4, 6.3, 6.4, 6.7, 12.4.2,
13.1, 13.6.3, 13.7.1, 14.3
(e)   12.4.2
s 3   12.3.1
Community Care (Residential
Accommodation) Act 1992   9.2.2,
13.6.3

Data Protection Act 1984   5.5.10
Disabled Persons (Services,
Consultation and
Representation) Act 1986   1.5.1, 2.5.1,
4.2.5, 5.5.4
s 1   4.2.5, 5.5.7
s 3   4.2.5, 5.5, 5.5.7, 5.5.13
s 4   4.2.5, 4.4, 5.5.4, 6.3, 11.1
s 8   11.1

Education Act 1993
s 168   5.3

Health and Social Services and
Social Security Adjudications
Act 1983   1.5.1, 2.4, 2.4.1

s 17   4.3, 11.4.1, 14.3, 17.0, 17.1, 17.2,
17.3, 17.7
(1)   17.1
(3)   17.1, 17.5, 17.6
(4)   18.4
s 21   15.4.3, 18.3, 18.4.1
(1)   18.3
(7)   18.3
s 22   15.3.7, 15.11.1, 18.3,
18.4.1
(3)   15.11.1
(5)   15.11.1
s 24   15.11.1
Health Authorities Act 1995   7.6
Health Services and Public
Health Act 1968   1.5.1, 2.3.1
s 43(3)   8.0
s 45   4.1, 4.2.2, 4.2.3, 4.4, 11.2, 14.3
s 65   4.2.2
Housing Act 1985   1.5.1, 15.3.7
Pt II   12.4.2
Pt III   12.3.2
Pt IV   12.4.4
ss 21, 22   12.4.3
s 58(2A)   12.3.2
s 59(1)   12.3.2
s 92   12.4.3
Sch 5, paras 10, 11   12.4.4
Housing Act 1988   12.4.4, 12.4.5
Sch 1, para 10   12.4.5

Insolvency Act 1986   15.11, 18.3
s 339   18.4.1
s 423   18.4.2

Landlord and Tenant Act 1985
ss 18–30   12.4.4
s 26   12.4.4
Landlord and Tenant Act 1987
ss 41–44   12.4.4

Law of Property Act 1925
  s 30   15.3.7
Leasehold Reform, Housing and
  Urban Development Act 1993
  s 87   12.4.4
  s 106   12.4.4
Local Authority Social Services
  Act 1970   2.3.1
  s 7   1.5.3, 5.5, 6.3, 8.0
    (1)   1.5.3
  s 7A   1.5.3
  s 7B   13.2, 13.2.1
    (1)   13.2.2
    (2)   13.2.1
    (3)   13.2
  s 7C   13.5.1
  s 7D   13.5.1, 13.5.2, 13.6.2
Local Government Act 1972
  s 195   9.1.1
Local Government Act 1988   9.1.1
  s 17   8.0
Local Government and Housing
  Act 1989   12.3, 12.4.2
  Pt VIII   12.4.1
  s 5   13.3.1
  s 112   12.4.1
  s 114(1)(a),(b)   12.4.2
     (3),(4)   12.4.2
     (6)   12.4.2
  s 115   12.4.1
  s 131   12.4.1

Mental Health Act 1983   1.5.1, 9.1.2
  Pt II   7.5
  s 1   4.2.1
  s 117   4.1, 4.2.4, 4.2.5, 14.3
    (2)   4.2.4

National Assistance Act 1948 1.5.1, 2.3.1,
    2.4, 2.5.1, 2.5.2, 4.1, 5.6, 9.1.5,
                 9.2.2, 15.9
  Pt III   2.5.1, 4.1, 4.2.1, 4.2.5, 9.1.1, 9.2,
    10.3, 10.10, 10.10.3, 12.4.4, 14.2,
    14.5, 15.1, 15.8, 15.9, 16.0, 18.3,
         19.1, 19.2.2, 19.2.3
  s 1   9.1.1
  s 21   1.5.3, 2.5.1, 2.5.2, 4.2.1, 4.2.2,
    4.2.3, 4.3, 4.4, 5.3, 8.5.1, 9.1.1, 9.2,
    9.2.2, 9.2.3, 9.3, 9.3.1, 9.4, 11.2, 11.3,
    13.6.3, 15.2, 15.9, 15.11, 18.3, 19.2.2,
                       19.4

  s 21(1)   4.2.1, 4.2.3, 9.2
    (a)   19.2.2
    (b)   9.1.1
    (4)   9.1.1, 9.2
  s 22   9.1.1, 9.3.1, 14.2, 15.1,
                    18.4.2
    (1)   15.3.7
    (2)   15.2
    (3)   15.9
    (4)   15.5, 15.6.1
    (5)   15.1
    (5A)   11.4.2, 17.8
  s 23   15.9
    (3)   15.9
  s 24   9.1.1, 9.2.1
    (3)   5.3, 9.2.1
    (6)   9.2.1
  s 26   2.5.1, 8.5.1, 9.1.1, 9.1.3, 9.2,
    9.2.2, 9.2.4, 13.6.3, 15.1, 15.2,
         15.3.7, 15.11, 19.2.2
    (1)   9.1.1
    (2)   9.3.1, 15.3.7, 15.7
    (3)   15.2
    (1A)   9.2.2
    (1B)   9.2.2
    (1C)   9.2.2
    (1D)   9.2.2
    (1E)   9.2.2, 9.3.2, 10.4
    (3A)   9.3.1, 9.3.2
    (4)   11.4.2
    (5)   9.3.2
  s 26(A)   9.2.4
  s 26A   9.2.2, 16.2
    (1)   16.4
    (3)   16.2
  s 29   4.2.1, 4.2.2, 4.2.5, 4.3, 4.4, 5.2,
       5.5.4, 8.2, 11.2, 13.7.1, 14.3
    (1)   12.4.2
  s 42   9.2.5, 15.6.3, 17.5
  s 43   15.6.3, 15.11
  s 46   2.5.1
  s 47   9.4, 10.9
  s 56   15.11, 18.4
National Health Service Act 1946   2.5.1
National Health Service Act 1977   1.5.1,
          4.2.3, 4.2.4, 4.3, 9.1.2
  s 1   2.3.2, 7.5
  s 3   2.3.2, 4.3, 4.4, 7.5, 7.8, 9.1.2
    (1)   2.3.2, 2.5.2, 7.4
    (e)   4.2.3

National Health Service Act
1977—*cont*
s 21   4.1, 4.2.3, 9.1.2, 11.2
s 22   4.2.3
s 23   2.3.2, 2.4.3, 7.1, 16.3
s 28   11.3
s 28(A)   2.4.1
s 28A   2.3.3, 8.3, 16.3
Sch 8   4.1, 4.2.3, 4.2.4, 4.3, 9.1.2, 9.1.4,
        9.2, 11.2, 14.3
    paras 1, 2   4.2.3
    para 3   4.2.3, 4.4
National Health Service and
Community Care Act 1990   1.5.1,
    1.5.3, 2.2, 2.5.2, 4.1, 4.2.2, 4.2.5,
    5.3, 5.5.4, 5.5.5, 8.5.2, 9.1.5, 9.2.1,
    11.0, 11.1, 12.3, 12.3.1, 13.6.3,
    14.1, 16.0
Pt I   2.3.2, 2.5
Pt II   2.3.2, 2.5
Pt III   2.0, 2.3.2, 2.5, 2.5.1, 4.1, 9.0,
    9.1.1, 9.1.3, 9.2, 10.0, 10.4, 14.2
s 42   2.5.1, 4.2.1
    (7)   8.0
s 43   16.2
s 44   15.1
s 46   2.5.2, 3.0, 4.2.5
    (2)   3.1
        (c)   12.3.1
        (e)   12.3.1
        (f)   3.1
    (3)   4.1, 12.3.1
s 47   2.5.1, 2.5.3, 4.1, 4.2.3, 4.2.5, 4.3,
    4.4, 5.1, 5.3, 5.5.3, 5.5.4, 6.0, 7.2, 7.3,
    11.1, 11.2, 13.2.2, 13.6.2, 13.7.1, 14.3,
    14.4, 14.5, 15.3.7, 16.4, 18.3
    (1)   5.3, 5.5.1, 6.0, 6.3, 6.4, 13.7.1,
           13.7.2
        (a)   5.5.13, 11.2
        (b)   6.1
    (2)   5.5.4, 6.0, 6.3
    (3)   6.1, 12.3.1
    (4)   5.5.9
    (5)   5.5, 5.5.5
s 48   10.10
s 50   5.5.1, 11.5, 13.2
    (7A)(1)   8.0
s 66   4.2.3
Nursing Homes Registration Act
1927   9.1.5

Pensions Act 1995   15.6.1
Poor Law 1832   9.1.1

Registered Homes Act 1984   1.5.1, 8.5.1,
    8.5.2, 9.1.5, 9.2.2, 9.3.2, 10.0, 10.1,
    10.3, 10.4, 10.7, 10.8, 10.11,
    12.4.4, 15.8
Pt I   9.2.2, 10.3
Pt II   9.2.2, 10.3
s 1   9.2.2, 10.10
s 2   10.4
s 3   10.4, 10.5
s 5(3),(4)   10.6
    (5)   9.2.2
s 9   10.6
    (1)   10.6
ss 10, 11   10.9
s 12   10.4
    (4),(5)   10.9
s 13   10.9
s 15   10.9
    (1)   10.6
s 17   10.4, 10.10
s 20(1)   10.3, 10.4
ss 21, 22   10.3, 10.5
s 23   10.5
s 25   10.6
    (1)   10.5
s 28   10.9
s 30   10.9
s 35   10.10
Registered Homes (Amendment)
Act 1991   9.2.2, 10.7
Rent Act 1977
Pt VI   12.4.4
s 71(4)   12.4.4

Social Security Contributions and
Benefits Act 1992   1.5.1
ss 64–67   12.4.4, 19.1
s 70   11.2
ss 71–76   19.1
s 73   17.3
    (14)   17.3, 19.2.1
s 106   15.6.3
s 134(1)   15.2
s 135(3)   16.4
Supplementary Benefits Act 1976
Sch 3   9.1.1

Trustee Act 1925
s 32   15.3.3

TABLE OF STATUTORY INSTRUMENTS

References are to paragraph numbers.

Access to Personal Files (Social
Services) Regulations 1989, SI
1989/206 — 4.3, 13.2.3

House Renovation Grants
(Reduction of Grant)
Regulations 1994, SI 1994/
2711 — 12.4.1

Housing Benefit (General)
Regulations 1987, SI 1987/
1971
reg 7(1)(a) — 12.4.5
reg 10 — 12.4.4

Income Related Benefits
Schemes and Social Security
(Claims and Payments)
(Miscellaneous Amendments)
Regulations 1995, SI 1995/
2303 — 15.3.7, 18.2.8
Income Support (General)
Regulations 1987, SI 1987/
1967 — 1.5.2, 15.1, 15.3.4, 15.3.5, 18.1
reg 17(1)(bb) — 15.8
reg 18(1)(cc) — 15.8
reg 19 — 16.4
(1ZB) — 16.0
(1ZF) — 16.4
(1ZG) — 16.4
reg 21(3A) — 15.8
reg 45 — 15.3.1
reg 46 — 18.2.8
reg 48 — 15.4.2
reg 51 — 15.3.6, 18.2, 18.2.1, 18.2.3,
18.2.5, 18.2.7
(1) — 18.2.1, 18.2.2, 18.2.3, 18.2.4,
18.2.8
(1A) — 18.2.2, 18.2.8
(2),(3) — 18.2.1, 18.2.3, 18.2.8
(4) — 18.2.8

reg 51(6) — 18.2.8
reg 51A — 18.2.1, 18.2.3
reg 52 — 15.3.4, 15.3.7
reg 53(1A) — 15.3.1
(1B) — 15.3.1
(1C) — 15.3.1
(4) — 15.3.1
Sch 2, para 2A — 15.8
para 9 — 19.1.1
para 9A — 19.1.1
para 10 — 19.1.1
para 13 — 19.1.1
para 14ZA — 19.1.1
Sch 3, para 3(8) — 15.3.7
para 5A — 12.4.4
Sch 7, para 1 — 2.4.3
Sch 9, para 9 — 19.2.3
para 30A — 18.2.1
Sch 10 — 18.2.8
para 1 — 15.3.7
paras 3–5 — 18.2.8
para 10 — 18.2.8
para 24 — 18.2.8
para 26 — 15.3.7, 19.3

Local Authority Social Services
(Complaints Procedure)
Order 1990, SI 1990/2244 — 13.2

National Assistance (Assessment
of Resources) Regulations
1992, SI 1992/2977 — 1.5.2, 9.6, 14.8,
15.1, 15.3.1, 15.3.4, 15.3.7, 15.4,
15.4.1, 15.6.1, 17.4, 17.5, 18.1,
18.2.8
reg 15 — 19.2.3
(1) — 19.2.3
reg 16 — 15.3.2
reg 17 — 15.4.3, 15.7
(1) — 15.4.3

National Assistance (Assessment of
  Resources) Regulations 1992, SI 1992/
  2977—*cont*
  reg 15(4),(5)   15.4.3
  reg 20   15.2
  reg 21   15.3.3, 18.2.8, 18.3
  reg 22   15.3.2
       (4)   15.4, 15.4.2
  reg 23   15.3.2, 15.3.7
  reg 25   15.3.6, 18.2,
            18.2.3, 18.2.5, 18.2.6, 18.2.7,
                        18.2.8, 18.3, 18.4.2
       (1)   18.2.3
  reg 26   15.3.6, 18.2.3
  reg 27   15.3.4, 15.3.7
       (1)   15.3.4, 15.3.7
       (2)   15.3.4
  reg 28   15.4
  Sch 3   15.4.1
     para 12   15.4.1
  Sch 4   15.3.5, 18.2.8, 18.3
     paras 1,2   15.3.7
     para 6   15.3.5
     para 8   18.2.8
     paras 10, 11   18.2.8
     para 18   15.3.7, 15.11.1
     para 24   18.2.8
National Assistance (Assessment
  of Resources) (Amendment
  No 2) Regulations 1995,
  SI 1995/3054   15.3.5, 18.2.8
National Assistance (Charges for
  Accommodation) Regulations
  1992, SI 1992/1563   1.5.2
National Assistance (Sums for Personal
  Requirements) Regulations 1994, SI
  1994/826   1.5.2
National Assistance (Sums for
  Personal Requirements)
  Regulations 1996, SI 1996/97   15.5
National Health Service (General
  Medical Services) Regulations
  1992, SI 1992/635   2.3.2
  Sch 1, para 12(ii)   2.3.2
Nursing Homes and Mental
  Nursing Homes Regulations
  1984, SI 1984/1578   1.5.2, 10.2
  reg 10   10.10

Residential Accommodation
  (Determination of District
  Health Authority) Regulations
  1992, SI 1992/3182   9.2.2
Residential Accommodation
  (Relevant Premises, Ordinary
  Residence and Exemptions)
  Regulations 1993, SI 1993/477   1.5.2,
                                          9.2.2, 16.2
  reg 5   16.4
  reg 8   16.2, 16.4
       (2)   16.2
  reg 9   16.2, 16.4
Residential Care Homes
  Regulations 1984, SI 1984/
  1345   1.5.2,
                                                   10.2
  reg 10   10.2
       (1)   10.2
  reg 11   10.2
Rules of the Supreme Court
  1965, SI 1965/1776
  Ord 53
  r 3(2)   13.6.1
  r 4(1)   13.6.1

Social Security (Attendance
  Allowance) Regulations 1991,
  SI 1991/2740   19.1
  reg 7   19.2.2, 19.4
  reg 8   19.2.2, 19.2.3, 19.4
       (6)   19.2.2
Social Security (Disability Living
  Allowance) Regulations 1991,
  SI 1991/2890   19.1
  reg 9   19.2.2, 19.4
  reg 10   19.2.2, 19.2.3, 19.4
       (8)   19.2.2
Social Security (Hospital In-
  Patient) Regulations 1975,
  SI 1975/555
  reg 2   2.4.3
Social Security (Invalid Care
  Allowance) Regulations 1976,
  SI 1976/409
  reg 4   11.2

TABLE OF DIRECTIONS AND GUIDANCE

References are to paragraph numbers

Directions and Circulars

Circular 12/70: The Chronically
Sick and Disabled Persons Act
1970
para 5   4.2.5
Complaints Procedure Directions
1990   11.5, 13.2, 13.2.3
Direction 2(1)   13.2.3
       (3)   13.2.3
Direction 5(2)   13.2.3
Direction 6(1)   13.2.3
Direction 7(2),(3)   13.2.3
Direction 8(1)–(3)   13.2.3

DoE Circular 4/90: Assistance
with Minor Works to Dwellings
                                      12.4.1
DoE Circular 10/90: Housing
and Community Care   12.4.2
paras 15–17   12.4.2
para 19   12.4.2
para 23   12.4.2
paras 36–48   12.4.2
DoE Circular 12/90: Local
Government and Housing Act
1989, House Renovation
Grants   12.4.1
DoE Circular 10/92 *see* DoH
Circular LAC 92(12); DoE
Circular 10/92: Housing and
Community Care
DoE Code of Guidance (1994):
Homelessness – Code of
Guidance for Local Authorities
para 6.9   12.3.2
DoH Circulars HC(89)5/LAC
(89)7/LAC(90)13: Discharge
of Patients from Hospital   7.3, 10.10
DoH/SSI Practice Guidance
(1991): Purchase of Services   8.0, 8.2,
                                         8.4

DoH Circular LAC(91)12:
Community Care: Review of
Residential Homes Provisional
Transfers   2.5.1
DoH Circular LAC(91)16:
Secretary of State's Direction:
s 46 of the NHSCCA 1990:
Community Care Plans   1.5.3
DoH Circular LAC(92)12; DoE
Circular 10/92: Housing and
Community Care   12.0, 12.3.1
para 10   12.3.1
para 13   12.3.1
para 16   12.3.1
para 19   12.3.1
Annex   12.3.1
DoH Circular LAC(92)17:
Health Authority Payments in
Respect of Social Services
Functions   2.4.1
DoH Circular LAC(92)24: Local
Authority Contracts for
Residential and Nursing Home
Care   9.5
DoH Circulars LAC(92)27/LAC
(93)18: National Assistance Act
1948 (Choice of
Accommodation) Directions
1992 and 1993   1.5.3, 6.6, 8.5.2, 9.2.4,
                                      15.3.7
DoH Circular LAC(93)4:
Community Care Plans
(Consultation Directions) 1993   1.5.3,
                                         3.1
DoH Circular LAC(93)6: Local
Authorities' Powers to Make
Arrangements for People Who
are in Independent Sector
Residential Care and Nursing
Homes on 31 March 1993   1.5.3, 16.3
DoH Circular LAC(93)7:
Ordinary Residence   1.5.3, 9.2.1,
                                         9.6

DoH Circular LAC(93)10:
  Approvals and Directions for
  Arrangements from 1 April
  1993 Made Under Schedule 8
  to the National Health Service
  Act 1977 and Sections 21 and
  29 of the National Assistance
  Act 1948   1.5.3, 4.2.1, 4.2.3, 4.3, 4.4
  para 5   13.6.3
DoH Circular LAC(93)18 *see*
  DoH Circulars LAC(92)27/
  LAC(93)18: National
  Assistance Act 1948 (Choice of
  Accommodation) Directions
  1992 and 1993
DoH Circular LAC(94)1   14.7, 15.5
  para 18   17.0
DoH Circular LAC(94)12:
  Community Care Plans
  (Independent Sector Non-
  Residential Care) Direction
  1994   1.5.3, 3.0
DoH Circular LAC(94)16:
  Inspecting Social Services,
  including Inspection Units
  Directions   1.5.3, 10.10, 10.10.3
DoH Circular LAC(94)24: A
  Framework for Local
  Community Care Charters in
  England   1.5.3
DoH Circular LAC (95)5 *see* DoH
  Joint Circular HSG(95)8/LAC
  (95)5: NHS Responsibilities
  for Meeting Continuing
  Health Care Needs
DoH Circular LAC(95)7/LAC
  (95)21/LAC(96)9: Charging
  for Residential
  Accommodation Guide
  (CRAG)   1.5.3, 14.8, 15.1, 15.3.2,
              15.3.3, 15.3.7, 15.4.3, 18.2.4
  para 4.005   15.6.2
  para 5.005   15.5, 15.6.1
  para 6.002   15.3.2
  para 6.012   15.3.2
  para 6.042   15.4.1
  para 6.061   18.2.5
  para 6.062   18.2.6
  para 6.063   18.2.6
  para 6.064   18.2.7

  para 7.014   15.3.4, 15.3.7
  Annex D, para 2.2   18.3
DoH Circular LAC(95)17 *see*
  DoH Joint Circular HSG(95)
  39/LAC(95)17: Arrangements
  for Reviewing Decisions on
  Eligibility for NHS Continuing
  In-patient Care
DoH Joint Circular HSG(95)8/
  LAC(95)5: NHS
  Responsibilities for Meeting
  Continuing Health Care Needs   1.5.3,
      2.3.2, 2.5.1, 2.5.2, 4.3, 4.4, 6.2, 7.3,
              7.4, 7.5, 7.6, 9.5.1, 11.3, App
  Section C   7.9
  paras 1, 2   2.5.2
  para 10   2.5.2
  para 19   7.2, 7.3
  para 21   7.4
  para 27   7.5
  para 30   7.6
  paras 38, 39   2.5.2
  Annex A   7.4
  Annex A, para E   2.5.2
  Annex A, para F   11.3
DoH Joint Circular HSG(95)39/
  LAC(95)17: Arrangements for
  Reviewing Decisions on
  Eligibility for NHS Continuing
  In-patient Care   1.5.3, 7.6, 7.7, 7.8, 7.9
  para 4   7.6
  para 6   7.6
  para 18   7.6
  para 27   7.6
  para 33   7.6
DHSS Circular (71)19: Welfare
  of the Elderly   4.4

Ministry of Health/Local
  Government Circular 82/69   12.4.4

**Department of Health Guidance
Letters on Implementation**
EL(91)28: Continence Services
  and the Supply of
  Incontinence Aids   4.4
EL(92)13/CI(92)10:
  Implementing Caring for
  People, March 1992   1.5.3

EL(92)65/CI(92)30:
Implementing Caring for
People, September 1992   1.5.3
CI(92)34: Implementing Caring
for People: Assessment,
December 1992   1.5.3, 5.4.1, 5.5.3,
    5.5.5
    para 31   5.5.13
EL(93)I8/CI(93)12:
Implementing Caring for
People, March 1993   1.5.3
EL(93)I19/CI(93)35:
Community Care   2.5.1

General Guidance
'Care Management and
Assessment', Managers' Guide
(HMSO, 1991)   1.5.3, 5.5.2
    para 2.24   5.5.11
    para 2.43   5.5.7
'Care Management and
Assessment', Practitioners'
Guide (HMSO, 1991)   1.5.3, 5.5.1,
    5.5.3
    para 1.21   5.5.10
    para 2.3   5.5.1
    para 2.22   5.5.1
    para 3.16   5.5.6
    para 3.38   6.2
    para 3.54   5.5.11
    p 11   6.4
    p 58   5.5.3
    p 61   6.5
'Care Management and
Assessment', Summary of
Practice Guidance (HMSO,
1991)   1.5.3, 7.1
    para 4.3   8.4.1
    para 11   5.2
    para 17   5.4.1
'Community Care in the Next
Decade and Beyond', Policy
Guidance (HMSO 1990)   1.5.3, 5.5.4,
    7.1, 10.10.2, 13.2.3

para 1.9   2.5.2
para 2.20   5.5.4
para 3.1   17.8
para 3.16   11.1, 11.3
para 3.18   5.3
para 3.20   5.5.3
para 3.24   6.2
para 3.25   6.2, 11.3
paras 3.27–3.29   5.5.8
para 3.28   11.1
para 3.29   11.1
para 3.31   5.5.12, 14.4,
    17.0
para 3.35   5.5.10
para 3.49   5.5.9
para 3.54   5.5.13
para 4.20   8.4.2
para 6.17   13.2.3
Annex A, paras 3–6   13.2.3

'Getting the Message Across', A
Guide to Developing and
Communicating Policies,
Principles and Procedures on
Assessment (HMSO, 1991)   1.5.3

Mental Health Act Code of
Practice   4.2.4

Social Services Inspectorate
Guidance: (1991) The Right
To Complain: Practice
Guidance on Complaints
Procedures in Local Authority
Social Services Departments   13.2
    para 3.10   13.2.3
    para 4.5   13.2.3
    para 4.9   13.2.3
    Appendix A   13.2.3
Social Services Inspectorate
Guidance: (1992) Homes are
for Living In   10.2

LIST OF ABBREVIATIONS

AOG	Adjudication Officers' Guide
CLAE	Commission for Local Administration in England
CRAG	Charging for Residential Accommodation Guide, 1995
CSDPA 1970	Chronically Sick and Disabled Persons Act 1970
DoE	Department of the Environment
DoH	Department of Health
DP(SCR)A 1986	Disabled Persons (Services, Consultation and Representation) Act 1986
DSS	Department of Social Security
HA 1985	Housing Act 1985
HA 1988	Housing Act 1988
HASSASSAA 1983	Health and Social Services and Social Security Adjudications Act 1983
HSPHA 1968	Health Services and Public Health Act 1968
ICA Regs 1970	Invalid Care Allowance Regulations 1970
ISG Regs 1987	Income Support General Regulations 1987
LASSA 1970	Local Authority and Social Services Act 1970
LGHA 1989	Local Government and Housing Act 1989
MHA 1983	Mental Health Act 1983
NAA 1948	National Assistance Act 1948
NA(AR) Regs 1992	National Assistance (Assessment of Resources) Regulations 1992
NHBC	National House Building Council
NHSA 1977	National Health Service Act 1977
NHSCCA 1990	National Health Service and Community Care Act 1990
RHA 1984	Registered Homes Act 1984
SHACS	Sheltered Housing Advisory and Conciliation Service
SSCBA 1992	Social Security Contributions and Benefits Act 1992
SSI	Social Services Inspectorate
STG	special transitional grant

GLOSSARY OF TERMS

Care management The process of co-ordinating and arranging services for an individual person.

Care manager A person who carries out community care assessments, prepares the care plan, and co-ordinates and monitors service provision. The care manager has budgetary responsibility, but is not usually involved in providing particular services.

Carer A person, usually a family member, who provides care and support for someone without being employed to do so.

Community Health Council Patients' Watchdog which has a statutory duty to monitor the NHS and to recommend improvements in services.

Complaints procedure The process set up by all social services departments to deal with complaints.

Day care Non-residential care provided at centres within the community usually by the local authority or by voluntary organisations. Workers may be paid or unpaid.

Directions (and approvals) Delegated legislation by which central government targets the general statutory responsibilities of public authorities.

Domiciliary care Services provided in people's own homes, usually by the local authority, but increasingly by voluntary or commercial organisations.

Health Service Commissioner The Health Service Ombudsman.

Health Authorities Generally means District Health Authorities which purchase health services from NHS hospital and community trusts. As from April 1996, Health Authorities will incorporate District Health Authorities and FHSAs (Family Health Service Authorities).

Independent sector Voluntary, charitable, not-for-profit and commercial organisations.

Local authority	Generally means social services departments. In unitary authorities, social services and housing departments are within the same authority. Otherwise, social services departments are within the county authorities, whilst housing departments are part of the district councils.
Provider	Agency or individal outside the local authority from whom the local authority purchases services.
Residential accommodation	Used as a generic term referring to residential care homes and/or nursing homes.
Respite care	Short-term periods of care which relieve the immediate family carers; usually involves residential care, but may be organised at home. Both the NHS and social services departments have statutory responsibilities.
User	An older client in respect of whom services are provided or commissioned by a local authority.

PART I

THE LEGAL FRAMEWORK

'Community care is like a jigsaw puzzle, it is the combination of support and services for a person with care needs.' (B. Meredith, *The Community Care Handbook*, 1995)

Chapter 1

THE CLIENTS AND THE TASK

1.1 Introduction

This book is about legal rights and duties to receive or provide care and the costs of care. The perspective is that of the older client and her/his legal adviser. The focus is an area of public law, the scope and content of which is as yet relatively unexplored by the courts or by academic writers.

Many private client practitioners now perceive the need to integrate what might reasonably be regarded as a new specialism into their portfolios of services for older clients. They are often handicapped, however, in two ways:

(i) culturally, by relative unfamiliarity with or experience of the operation of the Welfare State and the delivery of welfare services by either the National Health Service or by social services departments of local authorities;

(ii) legally, by the paucity of doctrine and analysis of the relevant issues, and by the inaccessibility of the delegated legislation and quasi-legislative measures which determine the activities of the State in this area.

To address all practitioners' know-how and development needs is a tall order, but this book aims at least to take a step in the right direction. The agenda for this first chapter is to identify the essential tools on which practice development initiatives must rely. These fall under two heads:

(a) information about the client group and its needs, which will underpin both marketing strategies and professional development; and

(b) information about new professional skills which must be acquired and about the technical know-how on which successful growth and development must ultimately rest.

1.2 Demographic factors

Legal marketing is based on hard information about what services clients need and how they would like them to be delivered. Firms may consider ways and means of obtaining particular information about actual or potential older clients and new technology will assist in this. It will also be useful for firms to acquire a broader information base, covering, for example, GP services in their area; other community health provision; day centres; residential care and nursing homes; and respite care facilities. As suggested later in this book (for example in Chapter 7), firms may be well advised to identify relevant decision-makers in their area and to find out about the local politics of health and of care.

There is also a good deal of empirical research material available about the elderly population as a whole, from which, again, it will be possible to draw inferences to support professional development initiatives. Given the alarmist stories often quoted in the press about the 'demographic time bomb' and its consequences for the future of the NHS and the social security system, it will be useful at least to know what the real facts are. It is therefore proposed, first to summarise some of the information which is likely to point towards the development of certain types of legal services, and, secondly, to refer to a few useful access points from which practitioners can obtain further information.

This chapter, and indeed the book as a whole, is written on the assumption that the client group is defined by reference to people above pensionable age.

1.2.1 An ageing population

–   In 1993, the population of the UK was just over 58,000,000. More than 10,500,000 people (18% of the population) were over pensionable age.

–   By 2031, it is projected that the population will exceed 62,000,000 people and that 23% will be over pensionable age.

–   In 1993, 4,002,000 people were aged 75 or more and 982,000 people were aged 85 or more.

–   It is projected that by 2011 there will be 4,803,000 aged 75 or more and 1,468,000 aged 85 or more.

–   The number of people aged over 75 and their proportion of the population is projected to double within the next 50 years.

–   Women now comprise 60% of the entire elderly population and 74% of those aged 85 or more.

–   In the 21st century, the relative size of the elderly population will increase and relative changes in the patterns of marriage and family formation suggest that there may be more childless, or never/not currently married elderly people. This possibility carries serious implications for family caring.

–   There is evidence to show that the effects of the 'demographic time bomb' have been exaggerated. There are upward pressures on spending from the ageing population, but even if benefit levels became index-linked the total net effects on public finances over the next 50 years would add up to about 5% of GDP. This is no more than the increase due mainly to the recession of the early 1990s. Over the past 20 years, welfare spending has been a stable share of national income, smaller than in most other European countries.

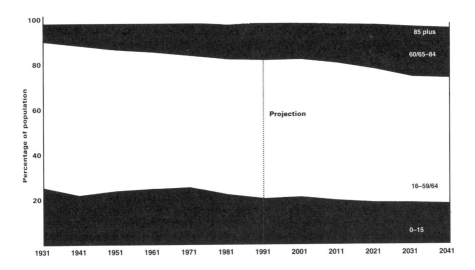

Figure 1. Age structure of the British population 1931–2041.
Britain already has a significant elderly population. Over the next 50 years the growth in those over 85 is most dramatic.
(From John Hills, *The future of welfare: A guide to the debate,* Joseph Rowntree Foundation, 1993.)

1.2.2   Health

– Numbers of disabled people and severity of disability increase steadily with age, becoming particularly marked over the age of 80; more than two-thirds of disabled adults are aged over 60.

– 67% of those aged over 75 have a long-standing illness, compared with 34% of people of all ages.

– About 5% of the population aged 65 or more suffer from dementia (mainly Alzheimer's disease). This proportion rises to 20% for the over 80s.

1.2.3   Income and expenditure

– The median income of pensioners is two-thirds that of non-pensioners.

– More than 50% of all pensioners live either in or on the margins of poverty, and one-third live at income support level.

– The DSS estimates that in 1992 between 23% and 35% of pensioners who were entitled to income support did not in fact claim it.

– In 1991, 60% of pensioners had occupational pensions, and the median income of occupational pensioners was 50% greater than that of other elderly people. Nevertheless, in 1989, 20% of occupational pensioners lived in households with income levels below £70 per week (1994 prices) for people living alone.

– Two-thirds of pensioners have some income from savings, but 40% receive less than £5 per week and 50% less than £10 per week.

– Between 1979 and 1991 pensioners' expenditure increased by less than their incomes.

– Pensioner households spend relatively more of their resources on housing costs, food and fuel than other households.

– By comparison with ten other 'wealthy' countries, including France, Germany, the USA, Australia and Sweden, average relative incomes of pensioners in the UK are the lowest.

1.2.4 Housing

– In 1993, 60% of all pensioner households were owner-occupiers and 6% of these had a mortgage. 29% were local authority tenants, 4% were tenants of housing associations or co-operatives and 5% were private tenants.

– Older private sector tenants occupy the worst housing.

– In 1993, 16% of men and 38% of women aged between 65 and 74 lived alone; 30% of men and 61% of women aged over 75 lived alone.

– In 1993, 69% of pensioner households had central heating compared to 82.5% of all households; 59.1% had a washing machine compared to 89.3% of all households.

1.2.5 Residential care

– More than 500,000 elderly people in the UK live in some form of institutional setting; the majority are in private nursing or residential care homes.

– 10% of single owner-occupiers could meet residential care fees from existing sources of income. Less than 1% of tenants in the same age group could do so.

– The value of a typical house could keep an older person in a residential care home for about 8 years, and in a nursing home for about 5 years. (1992 figures: the current position will be worse.)

– An estimated 40,000 houses per year are currently being sold to finance long-term care bills.

– Less than 20% of elderly owner-occupiers have substantial equity in their properties (see Figure 2).

– The amount of extra income which could be generated by a home income plan is limited to about £25 per week. Most home care packages would cost more than this, and such an amount would make little inroad into residential care fees.

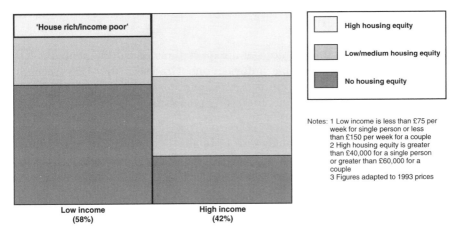

Figure 2. Incomes and housing equity.
Relatively few elderly people households currently fit the description 'house rich/income poor'. (From John Hills, *The future of welfare: A guide to the debate*, Joseph Rowntree Foundation, 1993.)

– To date, the marketing of private long-term care insurance has flopped. Possible reasons are:

- cost;
- belief in the Welfare State;
- antipathy to paying for something in respect of which tax and national insurance contributions have previously been paid.

A compulsory State insurance scheme for younger people is now advocated by the private insurance sector and by the public and voluntary sectors.

1.2.6   Information sources

The miscellany of selected information set out above is drawn from a number of sources, all of which are referred to in the Bibliography. For practitioners, the most accessible and up-to-date sources of demographic information are:

(i) Age Concern;

(ii) other voluntary agencies, for example the Alzheimer's Disease Society;

(iii) The Joseph Rowntree Foundation. The foundation is an independent, non-political body which funds programmes of research in the fields of housing, social care and social policy. It produces numerous publications including a series of short findings on social policy research;

(iv) The Family Policy Studies Centre;

(v) *Social Trends*, published annually by The Central Statistical Office, and available from HMSO, or in public libraries.

(For addresses, see List of Useful Addresses in the Appendix.)

1.3 Client concerns

Qualitative data on the opinions and expectations of elderly people is less accessible than demographic information. However, the DSS recently published a research report entitled *Managing Money in Later Life* (Finch and Elam, 1995) which offers some interesting perspectives. Key findings were as follows:

– Current pensioners strongly wish to retain their assets, not to run them down. This perhaps explains the deficit between income and expenditure referred to above. They are greatly concerned about diminishing savings.

– Most older people want to leave something to 'pass on' to their families, irrespective of whether families encourage or discourage them in this view.

– The need to retain sufficient resources to cover funeral costs is regarded as of paramount importance; there is an acute dislike of debt.

– Older people regard the State retirement pension as a universal right which they have worked and paid for. Income-related benefits are, however, considered to be a last resort.

– There is a wish to retain independence and a reluctance to depend on family support; older people are often reluctant to move house even in order to release capital.

In addition, a recent National Opinion Poll survey found that only 18% of respondents expected to have to pay towards their care in old age (PPP Lifetime Research 'Care in the Community. Two Years On', April 1995).

1.4 Advice needs

From the information above it is possible to draw inferences as to the range of legal services that older clients may want and/or need.

The list which follows offers suggestions for new services. It is taken for granted that practitioners will already be offering advice in the core areas of wills, probate, substituted decision making and tax planning:

– advice on income maximisation, perhaps by identifying entitlement to welfare benefits;

– advice on benefit claiming and benefit planning;

– advice and assistance in connection with hospital discharge (see Chapter 7);

– advice and assistance in connection with community care assessments – both 'needs' assessments and financial assessments (see Chapters 5 and 15);

- assistance in obtaining home care services, enforcing quality and asserting choice;

- advice and assistance in connection with entry into residential care;

- advice and assistance in connection with unsatisfactory care/abuse in residential accommodation;

- the provision of 'advocacy' services for clients who are incapacitated or in conflict with authority;

- assistance with financial planning for care;

- given the advent of new legislation on capacity, substituted decision-making on issues of personal care or consent to medical treatment;

- advice on new ways of funding care packages.

1.4.1 Know-how

The Bibliography refers to a number of general legal texts as well as to more specialist source material. Community care has received relatively little attention in the legal literature, and analysis of the new financial regime in particular is conspicuously lacking. The following distillation of accessible and current sources of know-how may be helpful.

(a) Age Concern offers a comprehensive information service on many issues relevant to elderly clients, and a subscription is very cost-effective. In particular, there is a factsheet service, with titles ranging from 'Legal Arrangements for Managing Financial Affairs', through 'Raising Income or Capital From your Home' to 'Local Authority Charging Procedures for Residential and Nursing Home Care'.

(b) Briefings by other charities, for example: Alzheimer's Disease Society; Counsel and Care for the Elderly; Carers National Association; Disability Alliance ERA.

(c) The Public Law Project. The Project published a valuable briefing: *Challenging Community Care Decisions* in October 1994.

(d) National Association of Community Health Councils.

(e) *Community Care* by Barbara Meredith (2nd edn, 1995). A very useful overview of community care policy and practice. It is written from a social work perspective, but identifies the important legal issues. Available from Age Concern, or from bookshops.

(f) *Child Poverty Action Group: National Welfare Benefits Handbook (1996/7)* and *Rights Guide to Non-Means Tested Benefits (1996/7)*. These are comprehensive and inexpensive guides to all the relevant benefits, written from the claimants' point of view.

(g) The Community Care Practitioners Group: This is a new special interest group which meets regularly, in London, to share information and know-how. Material is circulated even if members are unable to attend meetings.

1.5   The legal framework

The law on community care is complex. In order to assist practitioners, this section lists the most important sources of law, together with a number of quasi-legislative measures which are of considerable importance.

1.5.1   Primary legislation

National Assistance Act 1948;
Health Services and Public Health Act 1968;
Chronically Sick and Disabled Persons Act 1970;
National Health Services Act 1977;
Health and Social Services and Social Security Adjudications Act 1983;
Mental Health Act 1983;
Registered Homes Act 1984;
Housing Act 1985;
Disabled Persons (Services, Consultation and Representation) Act 1986;
National Health Service and Community Care Act 1990;
Social Security Contributions and Benefits Act 1992.

1.5.2   Regulations

Residential Care Homes Regulations 1984;
Nursing Homes and Mental Nursing Homes Regulations 1984;
Income Support (General) Regulations 1987;
National Assistance (Charges for Accommodation) Regulations 1992;
National Assistance (Assessment of Resources) Regulations 1992;
Residential Accommodation (Relevant Premises, Ordinary Residence and Exemptions) Regulations 1993;
National Assistance (Sums for Personal Requirements) Regulations 1994.

1.5.3   Directions and guidance

Directions have legislative force, but do not require Parliamentary approval. The Secretary of State for Health has express powers under most of the community care legislation to make directions or give approval in respect of the exercise of general powers contained in the primary legislation. For instance, the new responsibilities of local authorities to make arrangements for nursing home care (see **2.5.1**) were instigated by directions made under s 21 of the National Assistance Act 1948 (NAA 1948). In addition, the National Health

Service and Community Care Act 1990 (NHSCCA 1990) has added a new s 7A to the Local Authority Social Services Act 1970 (LASSA 1970). This states, in general terms, that every local authority shall exercise its social services functions in accordance with directions which may be given by the Secretary of State. Such directions must be in writing, and may be given to a particular local authority, or to authorities generally.

The Government has made it clear that it intends to use the new direction-making power to reinforce guidance on community care. It indicates that specific directions may be used to correct errors by local authorities, and that more general directions may serve to enforce Government expectations of local authorities as regards the implementation of community care policies.

As far as guidance is concerned, s 7(1) of the LASSA 1970 provides that local authorities shall act under the general guidance of the Secretary of State. Generally speaking, the term 'guidance' indicates something less compelling than 'directions', but s 7(1) makes it clear that local authorities are required to do more than 'have regard to' guidance. It may perhaps be regarded as offering assistance in reaching a decision, without compelling any particular decision. Given, however, that guidance is generally intended to be a statement of what the Government considers to be best practice it should inevitably determine a local authority's actions, to the extent that the divisional court has recently held that a decision which was contrary to policy guidance was unlawful (*R v North Yorkshire County Council ex parte Hargreaves* Lexis transcript, QBD, 30 September 1994).

Most guidance issued to local authorities is in the form of Circulars, but general guidance has also been published under s 7 of the 1970 Act, and executive letters are issued from time to time by the Department of Health or the Chief Inspectorate of Social Services.

The most important directions and guidance are listed below:

(a) Directions and Circulars
    DoH Circular LAC(91)16 Secretary of State's Direction: s 46 of the NHSCCA 1990: Community Care Plans.
    DoH Circular LAC (93)4: Community Care Plans (Consultation Directions) 1993.
    DoH Circular LAC(93)6: Local Authorities' powers to make arrangements for people who are in independent sector residential care and nursing homes on 31st March 1993.
    DoH Circular LAC(93)7: Ordinary Residence.
    DoH Circular LAC(93)10: Secretary of State's Approvals and Directions under ss 21(1) and 29(1) of the National Assistance Act 1948 and paras 1 and 2 of Sch 8 to the National Health Service Act 1977.
    DoH Circular LAC(92)27/LAC(93)18: National Assistance Act 1948 (Choice of Accommodation) Directions 1992 and 1993.
    DoH Circular LAC(94)12: Community Care Plans (Independent Sector Non-Residential Care) Direction 1994.

DoH Circular LAC(94)16: Inspecting Social Services, including Inspection Units Directions.

DoH Circular LAC(94)24: A Framework for Local Community Care Charters in England.

DoH Circular LAC(95)7: Charging for Residential Accommodation Guide (CRAG).

DoH Joint Circular HSG(95)8/LAC(95)5: NHS Responsibilities for Meeting Continuing Health Care Needs.

DoH Joint Circular HSG(95)39/LAC(95)17: Arrangements for reviewing decisions on eligibility for NHS continuing inpatient care.

(b) Department of Health guidance letters on implementation
EL(92)13/CI(92)10: Implementing Caring for People, March 1992.
EL(92)65/CI(92)30: Implementing Caring for People, September 1992.
CI(92)34: Implementing Caring for People: Assessment, December 1992.
EL(93)18/CI(93)12: Implementing Caring for People, March 1993.

(c) General guidance
'Community Care in the Next Decade and Beyond', *Policy Guidance* (HMSO 1990).
'Care Management and Assessment', *Managers' Guide* (HMSO, 1991).
'Care Management and Assessment', *Practitioners' Guide* (HMSO, 1991).
'Care Management and Assessment', *Summary of Practice Guidance* (HMSO, 1991).
'Getting the Message Across', *A Guide to Developing and Communicating Policies, Principles and Procedures on Assessment* (HMSO, 1991).

The importance of directions and guidance for those who advise on community care issues is belied by their relative inaccessibility. There is no current central database of Circulars and it is often difficult to obtain copies. A Parliamentary Question which was directed at the Secretary of State for Health asking for a list of Statutes, Statutory Instruments, Circulars, Advice Notes and Departmental Letters concerned with provision of community care, provoked the response that the cost of providing such information would be disproportionate (written answer, 4 May 1995). This issue is currently being pursued further.

Two useful resources are, however, as follows (see List of Useful Addresses in the Appendix):

(i) Department of Health Publications Unit (all Department of Health Publications which are identified by number can be obtained here);

(ii) HMSO Publications Centre.

Chapter 2

WHAT IS COMMUNITY CARE?

'Community care means providing the services and support which people who are affected by problems of ageing, mental illness, mental handicap or physical or sensory disability need to be able as independently as possible in their own homes, or in "homely" settings in the community' (*Caring for People*, 1989, Cm 849).

'Community care has laboured under the disadvantage of being a no-man's land, a sort of buffer zone between the main service sectors' (Twigg, 1988).

'Looking back, one is struck by the imprecision with which the term community care has been used, whether applied to elderly people or to other groups. Its meaning has been changed to suit new policies; its catchphrase character has obscured the complexities of care; it has invested a hotch-potch of policies and practices with a spurious sense of integration and consistency and because of its attractive connotations it has tended to escape close political scrutiny' (Parker, 1990).

These contrasting observations on community care suggest that there may have been – and may still be – a gap between rhetoric and reality; that the concept itself may be imprecise and that, from a legal perspective, it may therefore be difficult to allocate rights and responsibilities to those who need or those who deliver community care. The remainder of this book demonstrates in some detail that all this is true. This introductory chapter attempts to explain what community care is, or should be; who is or should be responsible for organising and delivering community care; how community care is funded; and how Part III of the NHSCCA 1990 has contributed to the development of a more clearly defined area of service provision.

2.1   Who needs community care?

As has been seen, the percentage of the population which is over 65, over 75 and over 85 is increasing, and the incidence of disability becomes relatively higher with advancing age. Most people at some time in their lives experience incapacity, but for many older people incapacity may be prolonged. It may involve physical or mental illness or impairment, and is frequently characterised by loss of mobility; impairment in sight or hearing; general physical frailty; confusion or dementia.

Apart from the elderly, policy makers have identified three other client groups who also suffer long-term incapacity: the mentally ill, the mentally handicapped and the physically handicapped. Clearly, there is substantial overlap between the four client groups.

People who are temporarily incapacitated may need hospital treatment and/or recuperative care at home before they can resume their normal lives. Where incapacity is prolonged there are likely to be day-to-day needs for support and help. Apart from intensive medical treatment these might include the provision of day centres; domestic assistance; personal and/or nursing care; equipment; access to transport; and, in some cases, sheltered accommodation or even full-time care given in a residential establishment.

2.2   The development of community care policies

Community care is often understood as the antithesis of institutional care, which was a hallmark of 19th-century social policy. This century, particularly since the Second World War, home-based care has come to be seen as preferable to placing people in institutions, and research evidence of institutional abuse and malpractice has supported this approach. The child care service, which was set up in 1948, led policy in this respect. Then, in 1957, the Royal Commission on the Law Relating to Mental Illness recommended a shift from hospital to community care for the mentally ill, and a massive closure programme was instituted in respect of the long-stay mental hospitals.

As regards older people, there was no real impetus towards community care until the early 1980s. The institutional population of older people has never been particularly large, although there is some evidence of inappropriate placements in hospital continuing care beds or in residential accommodation, when other options have not been available. Historically, the 'problem' of the older was seen as the relief of poverty, and this continued to be the main preoccupation of policy-makers until well into the 1970s. For years the provision and the resourcing of retirement pensions dominated the policy agenda, and the care needs of older people were largely ignored. This was partly because there was, and always had been, a network of informal care provided within families. Only when research began to highlight the implications of the 'demographic time bomb' (see Chapter 1), and the plight of older people living alone without family support and without services, did governments begin to address the care issue.

Translating general policy into clear objectives and eventual action took 20 years. Between 1970 and 1974, expenditure on personal social services rose by 12% each year, but the 1974 economic crisis reversed this trend and since then the policy of successive governments has been largely directed towards reducing public expenditure and pushing back the frontiers of the State. In this financial climate, community care was seen as a highly desirable objective. In 1981, a White Paper (*Growing Older*) indicated that community care really meant care *by* the community and that the primary sources of support which enable older people to live independently should be informal and voluntary. Public services were seen as sustaining, developing, but never displacing 'the community'. The White Paper advocated strengthening primary (health) and social services in tandem with neighbourhood and voluntary support, whilst maintaining adequate NHS provision for acute care, together with residential care facilities for a minority of older people.

It did not, however, make specific recommendations about how the balance of care should change, and by the mid-1980s it was apparent that there had been a reduction in the numbers of older people in hospital geriatric wards but not much more. In particular, the decrease in reliance on hospital care had been more than offset by growth in the residential homes sector. This development raises an important question about the definition of community care which the NHSCCA 1990 has not resolved. Although community care policies have always been anti-institutional, it has never been made explicit whether community care means care given at home, within *the community*, or whether it includes care delivered in a residential setting – in hostels, community hospitals, or care homes within *the community*. This is a fundamental ambiguity. Throughout the 1970s, local authorities consistently spent around 30% of their local social services budgets on residential care. Between 1981 and 1986 there was a 29% increase in the numbers of older people in residential accommodation, far in excess of the overall increase in the number of over 65s in the population.

An influential report by the Audit Commission, published in December 1986 (*Making a Reality of Community Care*), commented on the dangers of creating a new pattern of care based on residential homes, rather than a more flexible mix of services. Adopting the first definition of community care, it emphasised that 'community services are usually more effective, since they meet people's needs better; and they are more efficient, since they achieve more for the same amount of money' (para 14). More recent research shows, however, that the shift from residential care to care *in* the community has not really been achieved, although there has been a huge decline in hospital use by older people (see Chapter 6).

It may be that residential care is still the only realistic option for very older, very dependent people. To be credible as community care, however, a residential placement must be a positive choice (Wagner, 1988) and it must also be 'home' for the resident.

2.3 Who delivers community care?

Service provision emanates from four sources:

   (i) local authorities;

   (ii) the National Health Service;

        } statutory sector

 (iii) the independent sector, which encompasses voluntary or not-for-profit agencies, and commercial enterprises;

(iv) informal carers.

This chapter will consider the respective roles of the statutory and independent sectors. Chapter 11 looks at the demography of informal care and at the legal position of carers.

2.3.1 Local authorities

Local authorities' responsibilities for providing services for older people derive, historically, from the Poor Law. When the National Assistance Act 1948 abolished the Poor Law, the only statutory responsibility then allocated to the new local authorities was the provision of residential accommodation for the elderly. In addition, however, local authorities were forced to make use of much of the former workhouse infrastructure. No fresh start was made as, for example, with the provision of the new children's departments under the Children Act 1948.

Over the years statutory responsibilities were added, but it was not until 1968 that the Health Services and Public Health Act gave local authorities a general responsibility for promoting the welfare of older people in their areas, and a specific duty to introduce a home help service. Only in the 1970s were local authorities empowered to provide more general domiciliary services for the older, although a few authorities had previously derived powers from local Acts of Parliament. In 1970 the Local Authority Social Services Act created new social services departments, which carried clear statutory responsibilities for the welfare of four client groups:

the elderly;
the disabled;
children and their families;
the mentally disordered.

The Act was intended to improve social services provision, but also to assist and encourage families, and the community itself to promote 'welfare through community'. At the same time, the home nursing service, and some other services for which local authorities had previously been responsible were transferred to the NHS.

Since 1970 there has been a good deal of legislation requiring or enabling local authorities to provide services for older and disabled people, and this is analysed in more detail in Chapter 4. In particular, the Chronically Sick and Disabled Persons Act 1970 (CSDPA 1970) was considered to be a landmark in social provision. Generally speaking, however, until April 1993, when the community care reforms were implemented, social services departments saw themselves essentially as providers of services rather than, for example, as commissioners and planners of services provided by other agencies. This was partly because the legislation itself was so framed, but also because, for political and historical reasons, that mantle had always fitted the local authorities.

In April 1993, a major cultural change was initiated which has required social services departments to take stock of their existing philosophies of care and revise their previous attitudes towards effective service provision.

2.3.2 National Health Service

Section 1 of the National Health Service Act 1977 (NHSA 1977) requires the Secretary of State for Health to promote a comprehensive health service.

Section 3(1) states:

'It is the Secretary of State's duty to provide ... to such extent as he considers necessary to meet all reasonable requirements—

(a) hospital accommodation;

(b) other accommodation for the purpose of any service provided under this Act;

(c) medical, dental, nursing or ambulance services;

(d) ...

(e) such facilities for the prevention of illness, the care of persons who have suffered from illness and the after-care of persons who have suffered from illness as he considers are appropriate as part of the health service ...'

The 1977 Act allowed many of these statutory functions to be delegated to the district health authorities. In addition, the new organisational model created by Parts I and II of the NHSCCA 1990 gave district health authorities overall responsibility for assessing the health needs of their populations, for allocating resources, and for commissioning appropriate services within the NHS internal market. From 1 April 1996, new health authorities have combined the responsibilities of the former district health authorities and family health service authorities.

Acute services

Acute care services are usually delivered in hospital. In the past, patients entered hospital for surgery or treatment of acute conditions and would generally expect to remain there for the immediate post-operative/ recuperative period before returning home, or, if necessary, moving to a residential establishment for a more extended period of convalescence.

However, over the last ten years this picture has changed dramatically. Since 1982 there has been a 25% decrease in the overall numbers of acute care hospital beds, and a 200% increase in day admissions. For the elderly as a patient group, the available beds have been reduced by one-third, and the length of stay in hospital by a corresponding one-third. In June 1994 the Secretary for State for Health announced that 40% fewer hospital beds would be needed in the future.

The implications of these changes for older patients and their carers is alarming. As the focus shifts more towards delivery of even acute services in the community, there is little evidence that adequate support services will be available for those who are most vulnerable, and a good deal of evidence that parallel policies relating to the discharge into the community of the mentally ill are not meeting patients' needs because the infrastructure of support has not been put in place.

Legal advisers may see these changes in NHS practice forcing discharge of older clients from hospital before the social care and financial implications have been fully grasped, and there will be a need for advocacy services or even legal intervention on behalf of such clients. This issue is discussed more fully in Chapter 7.

Continuing in-patient care

Although the Secretary of State for Health has a clear responsibility under s 3(1) of the NHSA 1977 to provide after-care facilities for those who have suffered from illness, it is well known that few hospital beds are now available for chronically sick, frail or mentally impaired patients. Since 1990 there has been a 30% cut in these services, and some health authorities now no longer maintain continuing care beds at all.

Section 23 of the NHSA 1977 gave district health authorities power to discharge their s 3 duties by purchasing beds from the independent or voluntary sectors. In the past, these 'contracted' beds in private nursing homes have been an important part of NHS provision, and the White Paper on Community Care emphasised the continuing role of the NHS:

> 'Health Authorities will need to ensure that their plans allow for the provision of continuing residential health care for those highly dependent people who need it' (para 4.21).

It is nevertheless clear that some health authorities have become reluctant to allocate resources to this kind of in-patient care and, as will be seen, have taken the opportunity afforded by Part III of the NHSCCA 1990 to shift responsibility for such provision to local authorities. This development raises considerable financial implications for some older patients, which will be explored more fully in Chapter 7.

In a recent, highly publicised report on the failure of the NHS to offer continuing care to the victim of a catastrophic stroke, the Health Service Commissioner found that the health authority under investigation neither provided continuing hospital care for people with neurological conditions, nor made contractual arrangements with nursing homes in the independent sector. It was, apparently, the health authority's policy to spend 'no' resources on patients in this category. The Commissioner ordered the authority to refund to the patient's relatives the substantial sums which they had been obliged to spend on private nursing home fees (HSC: 'Failure to provide long-term NHS care for a brain-damaged patient', HMSO, 1994).

The courts have not, up to now, generally been prepared to review cuts in service provision driven by pressure on resources (*R v Secretary of State for Social Services ex parte Hincks* (1980) 1 BMLR 93 (CA)). It may, however, be arguable that failure to make *any* provision under s 3(1) of the NHSA 1977 would be unlawful. New *Guidance* on NHS responsibilities for meeting continuing care needs (HSG(95)9; LAC(95)5; discussed at p 29 and Chapter 7) supports that approach.

Community health services

Within the NHS, community health services meet the health care needs of people living at home, or in residential care homes or nursing homes, who do not require the centralised services of hospitals. The main users are children, older people and people with physical disabilities, learning disabilities or mental health problems. One-third of all NHS expenditure is deployed in the community.

Since the creation of the NHS internal market in 1991, funds have been devolved to what are now the combined health authorities to commission community health services, and in many areas community health trusts have been set up to co-ordinate the provider function. From April 1996 the merging of the district health authorities and family health service authorities into single, unified purchasing authorities, within which GPs have considerable influence, marks a further move towards a primary care-led NHS.

Community health services include:

– GP services;

– dental services;

– optical services;

– pharmaceutical services;

– community nursing and health visiting services;

– special therapeutic or para-medical services, such as occupational therapy, physiotherapy, speech therapy and chiropody.

GPs must provide 'appropriate personal medical services' (NHS (General Medical Services) Regulations 1992). Since 1991, GP fundholders have been able to purchase a range of such services, including community nursing services, from their devolved budgets. Other GPs rely on district health authorities to commission medical services.

As regards all patients aged 75 or over, there is a specific duty for a GP to hold at least an annual consultation, and to offer to make a home visit in order to assess whether there is a need for 'personal medical services'. Such services include 'giving advice, as appropriate, to enable patients to avail themselves of services by a local social services authority' (NHS (General Medical Services) Regulations 1992, Sch 1, para 12(ii)). This provision indicates that GPs are intended to provide a link between the agencies responsible for community care. Recent research evidence reveals, however, that many GPs have little real understanding of their patients' needs for services, or of what services may be available to them ('The role of the GP and primary health care team', DoH 1994; *Getting the message across,* Leeds Community Health Council, 1995).

Although it regulates the role of the GP, the law does not purport to define 'community health services' or to specify in detail what the range of such services might be. Section 3 of the NHSA 1977 refers only generally to 'medical' and 'nursing' services and implicitly leaves district health authorities to set priorities and allocate resources. The section does not, for example, make any reference to nursing specialisms, therapeutic services or para-medical services which, in practice, are an important part of community health provision.

Guidance refers to 'grey areas' of provision where 'health' and 'social care' seem to overlap and where either district health authorities or social services departments, or both agencies, may have responsibilities. Such services include washing, dressing, bathing, lifting, incontinence laundry and mobility rehabilitation. Overlapping responsibilities may appear to offer benefits for patients. In fact, however, the opposite is true. Recent evidence suggests that the inability to attribute clear and exclusive legal responsibility for service provision leads to buck-passing between agencies and sometimes to a failure to deliver services at all. In addition, serious financial implications for older clients arise out of the fact that national health services are free of charge, whereas social care services must be charged out to users.

A report by Age Concern cites two examples of 'grey' areas, leading to gaps in services:

> 'Mr A cares for his mother who has mental health problems and is incontinent. He was told that his mother does not require a medical bath and that, as social services do not do bathing, he would have to find private help'.

> 'Mrs B, who has had a stroke, can wash herself but cannot manage a bath without assistance. She is sometimes incontinent and would like an occasional bath. Her husband is in poor health and cannot help her and she is not considered in need of a medical bath. She, therefore, cannot be bathed at all'.

> (*The Next Steps, Lessons for the Future of Community Care,* Age Concern 1994, p 41.)

Problems like these reflect enormously on the quality of life of older clients and their carers, and legal advisers must be prepared to address them. Remedies available to the individual are discussed in Chapter 13. Increasingly, however, service users are using political channels and the media to air their grievances. Advisers too may find it useful to develop their skills in this area (see *Independent on Sunday,* 21 May 1995).

2.3.3 The independent sector

The independent sector is to be contrasted with the 'statutory' sector, previously discussed. It can be further divided into two sub-sectors.

(a) the private sector, which consists of companies and individuals who provide services for profit;

(b) the voluntary sector, which consists of charities and 'not-for-profit' organisations. Although these sub-sectors may appear disparate, in creating the new 'market' in social care, the Government did not distinguish between them. They are both 'independent' providers of services.

The private sector

In the past, private sector companies have been active in providing residential care, and some large public limited companies such as Takare, Crestacare and Goldsborough now operate in this field, alongside smaller companies, or individual providers. The 'perverse' financial incentive towards residential care (see p 20) probably accounted for some of this development.

The voluntary sector

Many national or local charities provide community care services. They obtain funding from sponsorship, donations, legacies, public sector grants (under, for example, s 28A of the NHSA 1977) trading subsidiaries and by charging for some services. Most charities rely, to some extent, on voluntary staff, many of whom are nevertheless highly trained.

Housing associations are 'not-for-profit' organisations. Like charities they are run by voluntary committees, and some of them provide housing or residential accommodation for people with special needs, such as frail older people, or people with learning disabilities. Nowadays, all housing associations have to raise a large percentage of their funds in the marketplace (for example from building societies or corporate investors) and by charging their residents. They do not have shareholders, however, and are not permitted to distribute profits.

2.4　Funding community care before the 1993 reforms

Local authority services for children, older people, the disabled and the mentally ill are funded principally through the revenue support grant, which is made available by central government from general taxation. Allocation of the grant between authorities is based on the Government's 'standard spending assessment', which is matched to demographic factors in each area. This funding is topped-up with council tax, raised locally, and with fees charged by local authorities for some services.

Social services departments are high spenders within local authorities, but the division of resources between different client groups is always a difficult exercise, informed ultimately by the political agenda of the day. The Government purports to allow local authorities complete discretion over their resources, but it has restricted their capital investment and has regularly capped the amounts available to high spending authorities from local taxation.

Social services departments spend considerable amounts of money on services for older people. In 1992, residential care services accounted for 50% of all local authority spending on social services. The NAA 1948 requires social services departments to charge residential care users to the full extent of their ability to pay. The Health and Social Services and Social Security Adjudications Act 1983 permits charges to be made in respect of all domiciliary services, apart from social work help and advice. Many such charges have increased massively since April 1993 (see Chapter 17).

NHS funds for hospital and community health care are devolved from central government through the purchasing budgets of health authorities and GP fundholders. There is no general power to charge patients for any NHS services; NHS care is still free at the point of delivery. A few peripheral charges (for example prescription fees) are specifically authorised.

2.4.1   Joint finance

Since 1973, health and local authorities have been obliged to co-operate in the exercise of their respective functions, and joint consultative committees were established in 1974 to advise both authorities on planning and service development.

Subsequently, s 28(A) of the NHSA 1977 (amended by HASSASSAA 1983) permitted health authorities to make payments to local authorities, housing associations and voluntary organisations in respect of personal social services and housing. Since that time, the Government has regularly made funding available for 'joint finance' projects, and has specified that it should be targeted towards new and innovative day, domiciliary and respite services in order to support the general development of community care (LAC(92)17). In all cases, payments must be recommended by the appropriate joint consultative committee.

2.4.2   The perverse incentive towards residential care

The Audit Commission Report published in 1986 (*Making a Reality of Community Care*) observed that the effect of 30 years of community care policies had largely been to shift people, and expenditure, from hospitals to residential homes. The Commission concluded that the 'perverse incentive' exerted by the Government's social security policies was mainly to blame for this (para 87).

From the early 1980s, means-tested supplementary benefit (and from 1988, income support) was available to meet the full fees of residential care homes or nusing homes for people on low incomes and with limited capital assets. Individuals could arrange their own placements, without an assessment of need on the understanding that benefits would be available if their own resources were, or became, insufficient. The system was open to financial opportunism; the guaranteed subsidy from the DSS encouraged entrepreneurs to set up residential establishments and pushed up the level of fees.

At length, in 1986, the Government imposed a statutory ceiling on benefit payments for residential care. From then on, home fees slowly rose above benefit levels, particularly in the south of England, and 'topping up' payments made by residents' families became an essential part of the financial arrangements. There was still, however, no test of need, notwithstanding that the Audit Commission had commented:

> 'in short the more residential the care, the easier it is to obtain benefits, and the greater the size of the payment ... very large sums of public money are being paid to people living in private homes without there being any mechanism (other than means testing income) for ensuring that the benefits are appropriate ... perversely, money is available for some of the high cost institutional options, while the low cost options are starved of finance' (*Making a Reality of Community Care*, Audit Commission 1986, paras 89 and 96).

By 31 March 1993, these large sums of public money amounted to some £2.5bn per year.

2.4.3 DSS funding for in-patient NHS care

Residential care arrangements may have attracted enhanced DSS funding, but benefit payments for hospital in-patients have always been modest. In the 1996/7 benefit year, for example, a hospital patient can claim only £15.30 per week income support to cover personal expenses. This amount is reduced to £11.75 after 52 weeks in hospital (Income Support (General) Regulations 1987, Sch 7, para 1). The reasoning is that NHS care is free of charge and that to pay substantial benefits to patients would be to make double provision for one particular need.

The legal position appears to be the same where health authorities use statutory powers (eg s 23 of the NHSA 1977) to purchase nursing home beds in the independent sector in pursuance of community care policies (reg 2 of the Social Security (Hospital In-Patient) Regulations 1975). In *White v Chief Adjudication Officer* (1993) *The Times*, 2 August, a group of older and mentally infirm patients had been discharged from an NHS hospital into a privately owned nursing home under a contractual arrangement between the health authority and the home proprietors. The Court of Appeal, overturning a previous decision of the Social Security Commissioner, ruled that the individuals concerned were still to be regarded as placed in 'hospital'. Consequently, they could not claim the enhanced rates of income support then available to other nursing home residents, which had, of course, been an essential consideration for the health authority in setting up the scheme.

The same issue came before the courts more recently when, following a similar contractual arrangement between a health authority and a housing association, six elderly people suffering from Alzheimer's disease were refused the nursing home rates of income support. Since this decision meant that the arrangement was no longer financially viable, the housing association gave the residents notice to quit their nursing home accommodation. There followed a six-day sit-in by relatives and friends which was ended by an injunction ordering the health authority to continue to provide nursing care (*Alzheimer's Disease Society Newsletter*, July 1995).

Before 1993, community care schemes such as those described above were an important part of the long-stay hospital closure programme, and DSS funding was relied on. The decision in *White v Chief Adjudication Officer* (above) was a major setback for such initiatives. Since April 1993, less DSS money has been available through the benefits system, and funding has been made available to local authorities to purchase nursing home care. Schemes entered into after April 1993 are likely, therefore, to draw on revenue funding from local authorities and to rely less on benefits.

2.4.4 'Reducing benefits'

As will be seen, the creation of a new funding structure for community care was fundamental to the reforms proposed by the Griffiths Report in 1988 and by the Government White Paper in 1989. The intention was to cut drastically the availability of means-tested benefits for residential care, and to require local authorities to act as guardians of public expenditure. Legal advisers must be aware, however, that DSS funding is still an essential, and often problematic element in the community care world. Older clients who have 'preserved rights' to income support may face grave financial difficulties (see Chapter 16), and it will be important for some clients needing social care to claim disability benefits, such as attendance allowance. Clients will be looking for good benefits advice and, where necessary, help with claiming.

2.5   A new framework for community care

Following the Audit Commission's highly critical report on community care in 1986, Sir Roy Griffiths (then deputy chairman of Sainsburys, and the Government's adviser on health services) was asked to review the use of public funds in implementing community care policies, and to advise on how resources might be more effectively deployed.

His conclusions (*Community Care: Agenda for Action*, 1988) were taken up in the White Paper which followed in 1989 (*Caring for People*, Cmnd 849) with the significant exception of his strongly expressed view that resources for community care should be 'ring-fenced' and thus protected from competing claims from other interest groups. Griffiths highlighted in particular the need to allocate more specifically responsibility and accountability for the provision of community care; he saw clarification of the respective roles of health and social services authorities as essential.

The White Paper put forward six key objectives (para 1.11):

  (i) to promote the development of domiciliary, day and respite services to enable people to live in their own homes wherever feasible and sensible, and to encourage the targeting of home-based services on those people whose need for them is greatest;

(ii) to ensure that service providers make practical support for carers a high priority;

(iii) to make proper assessment of need and good case management the cornerstones of high quality care. Packages of care should then be designed in line with individual needs and preferences;

(iv) to promote the development of a flourishing independent sector alongside good quality public services. Social services authorities should be 'enabling' agencies. It should be their responsibility to make maximum possible use of private and voluntary providers, and so increase the available range of options and widen consumer choice;

(v) to clarify the responsibility of agencies and so make it easier to hold them to account for their performance;

(vi) to secure better value for taxpayers' money by introducing a new funding structure for social care. Social security provisions should not provide any incentive in favour of residential and nursing home care.

In pursuit of these objectives the White Paper outlined an implementation plan which would involve a number of changes in the funding structure, organisation and delivery of community care. Some of these changes would require legislation. The Government originally intended to introduce new legislation on community care in tandem with provisions creating a new infrastructure for the NHS, and the National Health Service and Community Care Bill went through Parliament in 1990. Parts I and II reconstruct the NHS; Part III addresses care in the community. Parts I and II were brought into force in 1991 but, for political reasons, Part III was phased in more gradually, with the most important changes taking effect from April 1993.

2.5.1 The key changes

Service development
On 1 April 1993, local authorities became both facilitators and gatekeepers of community care policies. Part III of the NHSCCA 1990 created a 'market' in social care, as in health. In the new marketplace, the local authority's role is to purchase or commission services, rather than to provide its own services. In NHS parlance, the purchaser and provider functions in the social care field are now largely split. In theory, the effect of this change was to allow 'enabling' local authorities to unlock the enterprise of the independent sector and so encourage the development of more imaginative and effective community care services.

The Government has also passed over to local authorities the major financial responsibility for community care services. The huge commitment of DSS funds to residential care, via the benefits system, has ceased, and local authorities now have equivalent transferred funding available to them to enable them to implement their community care programmes (see **2.5.3**).

This very significant cultural and financial shift has not occasioned much new law. There was, on the whole, no need to give local authorities added responsibilities to provide services, or to enable them to commission services from others as comprehensive powers and duties were already in existence (see Chapter 4).

The one important new responsibility is in s 42 of the NHSCCA 1990, which amends the NAA 1948 by extending the local authority's obligation to provide residential accommodation for elderly or infirm adults to include a duty to make nursing home placements for people who are sick (ss 21 and 26 of the NAA 1948). The NAA 1948 originally delineated the social care obligations of local authorities and the NHSA 1946 created a comprehensive health service for the sick. The amendments to the NAA 1948 can be seen as creating a 'second health service' – which is operated by social services departments and is means tested (Clements, 1994). They lead directly to the new DoH *Guidance* on NHS responsibilities for continuing care, which endorses the withdrawal of continuing in-patient provision for most older people and effectively transfers responsibility for providing non-acute nursing care to social services departments. (For further discussion see **2.5.2** and Chapter 7.)

One major problem for local authorities is to allocate their limited resources in the target areas identified by the White Paper, namely home-based services for those in greatest need. Substantial guidance has been issued by central government to assist them with service planning and prioritisation (see Chapter 1). Section 46 of the NAA 1948 requires them to prepare and publish annual community care plans, in consultation with all major providers of care services, service users and carers. These plans should state objectives and priorities for community care and the local authority's targets for meeting them. They should also be used to 'manage the market' by giving information about the kinds of services the local authority wishes to purchase ('Community Care' EL(93)119/CI/(93)35).

Community care assessments

Section 47 of the NHSCCA 1990 requires local authorities to assess people who may be in need of community care services and to determine whether assessed needs call for the provision by them of such services. It builds on a narrower duty to assess disabled people under the DP(SCR)A 1986. Assessment is discussed in detail in Chapter 5 and service provision in Chapter 6.

Section 47 reflects the concerns expressed by the Audit Commission in 1986, and by Sir Roy Griffiths in 1988, that public spending was being skewed towards residential care placements, made without assessment of need, and that more cost-effective home-based services were being starved of investment.

Assessment is now the cornerstone of the community care reforms because it unlocks service provision. The assessment process raises many questions for local authorities, both practical and philosophical. In particular, who defines 'need'? What is to be the distinction between 'wants' and 'needs'? What happens where 'needs' exceed resources?

The mixed economy of care

Local authorities are now expected to be arrangers and purchasers of care services, rather than monopolistic providers (White Paper, para 3.1.3). This posits a fundamental change in social services culture and ethos. The 'helping' role of social services is subordinated to the 'case management' approach, which requires managers to contract for, monitor and evaluate services which are to be delivered largely by others.

Before April 1993, most independent sector activity was concentrated on residential care (see p 22). Home-based services were provided almost exclusively by local authorities themselves. The expectation now is that a case management approach on the part of local authorities will stimulate competition and encourage diversification in the independent sector.

The contracting mechanisms which are used in the new marketplace are discussed in Chapter 8. In some respects, the 'contract culture' is more amenable to commercial providers of services than to voluntary organisations. The latter have concerns about the legal and financial implications for them of the contracting process, and are not always happy to be locked into a contractual relationship which may pre-empt their independence and power to innovate. The reliance of many voluntary agencies on volunteer staff creates problems in meeting tight service specifications. Contracting also involves extra expense for smaller voluntary providers, and already there are indications that agencies are having to make a choice between combining forces or going out of existence.

The Government acknowledges that some important voluntary sector activities such as development work, advocacy and education are not suited to the contractual approach, and that the old grant-based funding should still be available for such activities. In practice, however, such funding is increasingly uncertain.

There are now indications that larger providers of services, which are able to offer economies of scale, are beginning to dominate the market, particularly in the residential sector. In time, this development may produce a reduction in the variety and flexibility of services available.

As yet, local authorities are not required to put community care services out to tender, and it is envisaged that the statutory sector will continue to provide a core of services where there are gaps in the marketplace. Hitherto, for example, the independent sector has shown little interest in developing residential care in some inner city areas, especially in London, and local authorities have always made substantial provision of Part III accommodation under s 21 of the NAA 1948. DoH Circular LAC(91)12 seems to expect that local authorities will continue to make this provision where necessary (but note the recent decision of the House of Lords in *R v Wandsworth Borough Council, ex parte Beckwith* [1996] 1 All ER 129). However, since present funding arrangements require local authorities to spend most of their community care budgets on independent sector services (see **2.5.3**), their options for direct provision will inevitably be limited.

2.5.2   The boundary between health and social care

Although the White Paper emphasised the continuing importance of community health provision, it made no proposals for altering the statutory responsibilities of the NHS. It did, however, assert the importance of joint planning and joint working with local authorities, and observed that statutory provision for joint finance and for joint consultative committees was already in place. To move forward from there, local authorities in their 'lead' role must prepare and publish community care plans (NHSCCA 1990, s 46) and district health authorities must also prepare plans outlining their own proposals for securing community care services (White Paper, para 5.12).

The *Policy Guidance* commented that the overall objective for those responsible for community care should be to provide a 'seamless' service for users,

> 'in which the boundaries between primary health care, secondary health care and social care do not form barriers seen from the perspective of the service user' (para 1.9).

Commentators have observed that the White Paper signally failed to predict likely developments in the NHS, and was mainly concerned to delineate the boundary between personal social services and the social security system, in line with the previous Audit Commission recommendations (Wistow 1994; see **2.2**). Since 1990, there has in fact been further withdrawal of NHS funding from convalescent and continuing in-patient care, and hospital care is now in the process of being redefined solely in terms of acute, high-tech intervention.

In fact, the 'grey' area between health and social care remains unclarified by the 1990 Act and the service remains anything but seamless. There is no doubt, however, that the new emphasis on the role of local authorities has given a hidden incentive to health authorities to divest themselves of some of their financial responsibilities in favour of local authorities. In particular, as observed in **2.5.1** the extension of local authority responsibility under the NAA 1948 to arrange residential accommodation for the elderly has been treated as relieving the NHS of its responsibility to provide continuing nursing care.

The debate over nursing care

Nursing care is at the heart of the grey area. Although, technically speaking, the NHS is responsible for all nursing services, wherever delivered (NHSA 1977, s 3(1)), the amendments to s 21 of the NAA 1948 require social services departments to purchase nursing home services out of their community care budgets and to charge users according to their ability to pay. These amendments may be perceived as a 'Trojan Horse' bringing NHS continuing care patients into the social services' camp, and so signalling the end of a comprehensive, free national health service.

Publication of the NHS Commissioner's Report in 1993 (see p 18) unleashed public concern about the direction of events, which has led to pressure on the NHS Executive to clarify the responsibilities of the NHS for meeting continuing health care needs. After an extended period of consultation, important new *Guidance* was published in February 1995 (HSG(95)8; LAC (95)5).

NHS responsibilities for meeting continuing health care needs

The new *Guidance* emphasises that the NHS is responsible for arranging and funding a full range of services to meet the continuing physical and mental health needs of older people and others (para 1). Both the district health authorities and local authorities, however, have responsibilities for 'arranging and funding services to meet people's needs for continuing care' (para 2).

The *Guidance* (at para 10) purports to identify the range of services for which the NHS is, or may be, responsible. These are:

- specialist medical and nursing assessment;

- rehabilitation and recovery;

- palliative health care;

- continuing in-patient care under specialist supervision in hospital or in a nursing home;

- respite health care;

- specialist health care support to people in nursing homes or residential care homes or the community;

- community health services to people at home or in residential care homes;

- primary health care;

- specialist transport services.

There is, however, no unequivocal commitment to any particular level of provision. Rather, the guidance is full of references to local planning, based on the needs of local populations and demographic trends.

Continuing in-patient care

Where patients require continuing care, either in hospital or in nursing homes, all health authorities should arrange and fund an adequate level of service to meet their needs on a short-term or long-term basis (Annex A, para E). The *Guidance* sets out four eligibility criteria:

(i) where the complexity or intensity of patients' medical, nursing care or other clinical care or the need for frequent not easily predictable interventions requires the regular supervision of a consultant, specialist nurse or other NHS member of the multi-disciplinary team (in most cases interventions might be weekly or more frequent);

(ii) where patients require routinely the use of specialist health care equipment or treatments which must be supervised by specialist NHS staff;

(iii) where patients have a rapidly degenerating or unstable condition which means that they will soon require specialist medical or nursing supervision;

(iv) where patients have finished acute treatment or inpatient palliative care, but their prognosis suggests that they are likely to die in the very near future.

Such patients should be able to choose between remaining in NHS funded accommodation, and returning home with appropriate support.

The *Guidance* also states that health authorities, in collaboration with local authorities, must produce local eligibility criteria for continuing health care, which will reflect the particular needs of their local population. Presumably, local criteria would elaborate on the conditions set out above, or possibly extend them. Clearly, it would not be appropriate to restrict further what is stated in the guidance to be an 'integral' part of NHS responsibilities. In addition, local policies should state how continuing in-patient care will be purchased, and give details of arrangements for contracting beds in the independent sector.

Future developments

By 29 September 1995, all district health authorities were required to develop draft local policies and eligibility criteria for continuing health care. These were then made available for public consultation and were finally put in place by 1 April 1996. From that date, the new unified health authorities will be expected to report annually to the NHS Executive on their planned and achieved levels of spending and activity on continuing health care (*Guidance* paras 38 and 39).

The *Guidance* also lays down new procedures for the discharge of patients from hospital. These are reviewed, in some detail, in Chapter 7.

Clarification of NHS responsibilities is both timely and necessary, but the new *Guidance* carries worrying implications for older people.

(i) Not only will NHS resources for continuing care be rationed in future, but also priorities will be set at local level, inevitably giving rise to discrete inequities in provision. In one area, a chronically ill elderly client may receive long-term in-patient care in an NHS hospital, while in another area, a client with similar needs may be placed by the social services department in a nursing home and will have to pay for the bed.

(ii) The emphasis placed in 'specialist' care suggests that basic nursing care for chronically, but not acutely ill patients, is no longer to be regarded as part of a 'comprehensive' national health service.

(iii) The *Guidance* does not rule out the possibility that local eligibility criteria for continuing care may be based on means. In areas where there is a large elderly population it may be considered appropriate to allocate resources on the basis of socio-economic groupings or property values.

2.5.3   Better value for taxpayers' money: an end to the 'perverse incentive'

One imperative in April 1993 was to curtail the perverse effects of funding residential care through the DSS. The strategy adopted was to transfer from central government to local authorities resources equivalent to the enhanced benefit provision previously allocated by the DSS for people in residential care homes and nursing homes. Income support payments for residents were then capped at the levels available to claimants living in their own homes in the community.

It is now intended that people with limited resources wishing to enter care homes or nursing homes will first have to ask social services departments to assess their needs under s 47 of the NHSCCA 1990. If they do not 'need' residential accommodation, there will be no State help with fees. If need is established, the local authority makes a financial assessment by applying a new means test, and, based upon this, residents are asked to contribute towards the cost of their residential placement.

The theory is that the local authority is meeting the costs of 'care' but that a resident meets his own day-to-day living expenses and his overheads in the same way as if he were still living in the community. If his resources are insufficient, he may claim a basic level of income support to top up. In practice, the cost of care will be the difference between the resident's own resources, including income support, and the fees charged by the residential establishment.

The local authority transparently has a gatekeeping role which hinges on the s 47 assessment. Residential care is no longer an option for people who are not wealthy unless they have need for it. 'Need' is defined by the gatekeeper (see Chapter 5). The wealthy retain, of course, their freedom to make their own care arrangements. It must be remembered that residential care is only one of many service options which the local authority may consider for an elderly person whom it has assessed. Community care policies require home-based services to be provided, both as an alternative to residential care, and as a means of enabling the residential option to be postponed. The assessment of need is the gateway to all service provision, not just residential care, and the process is subject to many tensions, which are explored in Chapter 5.

The major underlying problem, however, is how far the transferred funding is adequate to meet the costs of residential care (or alternatives to residential care) which, before April 1993, were the responsibility of central government and now are the responsibility of local authorities. Since 1993, community care funding has been allocated as follows:

(i) In 1993/94, £565.4m was transferred to local authorities by way of a 'special transitional grant' (STG). Of this, £399m (the 'transfer element') represented what the DSS calculated it would have spent on maintaining residential placements under the old system.

(ii) In 1994/95, the STG was £735.9m with a transfer element of £651.8m.

(iii) For 1995/96, the STG is £647.6m, with £517.7m transfer element.

(iv) In each of 1994/95 and 1995/96, the previous year's STG was incorporated into the Government's standard spending assessment for local authorities, so that the baseline for the following year's revenue support grant increased by the amount of the previous year's STG.

(v) Every year since 1993 the Government has specified that 85% of the new transfer element in the STG plus 85% of previous years' transfer elements must be spent on commissioning services in the independent sector.

(vi) The Government has announced that, for the financial year 1996/97, a further £418m will be made available for community care, in addition to the previous three years' STGs. It is not yet clear what proportion of this money will be designated as the new STG and therefore ring-fenced for community care. The Government has expressly declined to adopt the Griffiths recommendation that community care funding should be permanently ring-fenced, and 1996/97 will be a transitional year, after which the present arrangements will cease. Thereafter, resources for community care will become subject to the annual local authority spending round where, for example, children's services will compete with services for older people for a share of the money available.

(vii) The method of distributing the STG between local authorities has altered since 1993. In the first instance, 50% of the transfer element was allocated according to the actual national pattern of income support spending on residential accommodation. The other 50% was allocated according to the Government's normal standard spending assessment formula. The following year, however, the entire transfer element was distributed according to the standard spending assessment formula. The effect was that some local authorities, with high populations of older people and large numbers of residential establishments, took a considerable cut in resources in 1994/95.

The jury is still out on the question of adequacy. In 1994, 25% of local authorities reported funding problems, and there is evidence that eligibility criteria for services have been tightened up as a result (Wistow 1994). Up to now, the Department of Health has not carried out independent monitoring of demand for community care services or of spending patterns. There is, however, plenty of anecdotal evidence of services under financial pressure and legal challenges are now being pursued against some local authorities which have withdrawn services (note, for example, *R v Gloucestershire County Council, ex parte Mahfood and Barry* (1995) *The Times,* 17 June). A further concern is the likely extent of the financial burden that the reduction of NHS long-term care provision will place upon local authorities.

Chapter 3

COMMUNITY CARE PLANS

'The availability of information ... on services and care package arrangements is crucial in empowering users regarding service choice. The lack of available information on services was voiced consistently by user and carer groups' (*Implementing Caring for People*, DoH, 1994).

One of the cornerstones of the new community care regime is the requirement under s 46 of the NHSCCA 1990 for local authorities to prepare, and publish annually, plans for the provision of community care services in their areas.

The Government intends that community care plans should lay down indicators against which local authorities' performance can be monitored and assessed. Initially, local authorities were expected to:

– assess the needs of the populations which they served;

– describe existing services and set out strategic objectives for care in the particular community;

– specify how the activities of health authorities, housing authorities and the voluntary sector would be co-ordinated;

– describe how consumer choice would be increased and how it was intended to promote a mixed economy of care;

– set targets for the improvement of domiciliary services;

– lay down quality assurance systems and complaints procedures;

– give information about the cost of services.

The first plans were required to be in place by 1 April 1992 to assist local authorities in preparing for implementation of the other community care reforms in April 1993. Late in 1992, the Government identified a number of key tasks which both health and local authorities were expected to address. The 1993 community care plans should have given notice of this new agenda by indicating:

– resources which would be devoted to community care in 1992/93 and 1993/94;

– services expected to be available;

– details of assessment arrangements;

– arrangements for the purchase of residential and nursing home care;

– charging policies and arrangements for financial assessment;

– arrangements for hospital discharge;

– details of agreements with housing authorities;

–   how client choice would be taken into account.

Again, in 1993, further targets were identified and further headings added to community care plans. The most significant of these were:

–   increasing the involvement of service users and carers;

–   developing assessment and care management systems;

–   developing a positive relationship with providers;

–   shifting the balance of resources towards non-residential care, and providing more respite care and support for carers.

Section 46 of the NHSCCA 1990 contains power for the Secretary of State to make directions in relation to the preparation and publication of community care plans. In 1994 the Department of Health issued a direction, with accompanying guidance, requiring local authorities to include in their community care plans a statement of their proposals for making arrangements to purchase independent sector non-residential community care services. (Circular LAC(94)12). The direction was an endorsement of the recommendation in the White Paper on community care that social services authorities should be accepting responsibility 'to make maximum possible use of private and voluntary providers, and so increase the available range of options and widen consumer choice' (para 1.11). In focusing on non-residential care services, the direction acknowledges that there is still much scope for growth in this sector, in line with the general objectives of community care policy. The Government intends to stimulate service development by requiring local authorities to communicate to providers and potential providers information which will enable them to develop innovative and flexible services to accommodate the needs of the local population.

3.1   Consultation

An effective consultation process is an essential part of community care planning. A major objective of the White Paper on community care is that service provision should be targeted so as to make the best possible use of limited resources. If consultation is not sufficiently thorough, the settling of priorities may become unbalanced, and the needs of the most organised and vocal groups within the community may be over-reflected at the expense of more vulnerable people.

Section 46(2) of the NHSCCA 1990 requires local authorities to consult health authorities; housing authorities (except in unitary authorities) and voluntary organisations when preparing or revising the community care plans. Section 46(2) does not require commercial providers to be included in the consultation process, but the Secretary of State has now issued directions under s 46(2)(f) to the effect that local authorities should consult with representative organisations (whether corporate or unincorporated) which give written notice of their wish to be included in the process. This means that, for example, associations of residential care home or nursing home providers may ask for consultation. Furthermore, the Secretary of State directs local authorities to include details of the consultation process in the community care plans themselves (Community Care Plans (Consultation) Directions, 1993). Statements issued by local authorities in pursuance of the non-residential care services direction of 1994, discussed above, are subject to this general consultation requirement.

3.2 Practice points

There is evidence that some community care plans have not been written in plain English and may be difficult for some people to understand. Given also that there is considerable recent research evidence of a lack of other sources of information as to, for example, the assessment process and the services available, it will be important for legal advisers to familiarise themselves with their local community care plans. There is a role for the legal adviser in providing an interface between the client and the community care system. Helping clients to understand how the system operates and how to access services they need will be a major part of client care for this group.

Chapter 4

WHAT ARE COMMUNITY CARE SERVICES?

4.1 Introduction

Part III of the NHSCCA 1990 has been described, accurately enough, as a 'raft of duties floating over the existing legislation making key amendments but repealing little' (Clements, *Legal Action,* July 1993). The policy objectives have already been discussed in terms of the creation of a coherent framework for the provision of services for adults within the context of a new market philosophy for social care. The 'amendments' made by the 1990 Act are indeed crucial to this, but the extent of the existing stream of provision is often not appreciated.

One of the key amendments referred to is s 47 of the NHSCCA 1990 which imposes a duty on local authority social services departments to assess the needs for community care services of people whom they have power to assist and who may be in need of such services. The content of the duty to assess and the assessment process are discussed in Chapter 5. 'Community care services' are defined in s 46(3) of the NHSCCA 1990 as services which local authorities may provide or arrange under any of the following:

– Part III of the National Assistance Act 1948;

– s 45 of the Health Services and Public Health Act 1968;

– s 21 of and Sch 8 to the National Health Service Act 1977;

– s 117 of the Mental Health Act 1983.

Apart from assessing need, social services departments have a duty under s 47 of the NHSCCA 1990 to decide whether or not to provide community care services. Patently, therefore, the 1990 Act is concerned with reinforcing statutory powers and duties which already exist. The framework is comprehensive. It emanates from the National Assistance Act 1948, one of the foundations of the Beveridge Welfare State, which abolished the 19th-century Poor Law and made new provision for income maintenance and social care services for disabled, sick and elderly people. Only Part III of the NAA 1948 remains in force, but it underpins all subsequent legislation in creating statutory powers and duties for (the then new) local authorities.

Most of such legislation is characterised by the creation of powers or qualified duties to be exercised by local authority social services departments. Qualified duties have to be regarded as subject to, for example, available resources and implicitly leave local authorities to allocate priorities appropriately. Some duties (for example, those in respect of disabled people created by the Chronically Sick and Disabled Persons Act 1970) are legally sharper and appear to be more susceptible to enforcement by individuals irrespective of resources. Recent case-law suggests, however, that there can be no absolute right to service provision. There is a more extensive discussion on this point in Chapter 6.

The primary responsibilities laid down by the various pieces of community care legislation are extensively written subject to a requirement for local authorities to act under directions made or approval given by the Secretary of State. The right to issue directions means that central government, through the Secretary of State, has the final say over which, out of a range of general responsibilities, a local authority will be obliged to carry out. Approvals are weaker; they indicate simply service areas to which local authorities should attach priority. It is inherently unsatisfactory that these legislative and quasi-legislative interventions are not readily accessible to those affected by them (see Chapter 1). The credibility of initiatives such as the introduction of Community Care Charters is undermined as a result.

4.2　Community care services

4.2.1　Part III of the National Assistance Act 1948

Section 21 of the National Assistance Act 1948
This section, which was amended by s 42 of the NHSCCA 1990, requires local authorities to arrange residential accommodation for people who 'by reason of age, illness, disability or any other circumstances are in need of care or attention which is not otherwise available to them' (s 21(1)). The function is subject to the approval of and directions made by the Secretary of State.

Various directions have been issued over the years and these are now consolidated as appendices to DoH Circular LAC(93)10:

(i) the Secretary of State now directs that the s 21(1) duty is owed to those ordinarily resident in the local authority area (see **9.2.1**). The duty also extends to providing temporary accommodation for other people not referred to in s 21(1) who are in urgent need of care in unforeseen circumstances. By contrast, the Secretary of State merely approves and empowers the making of residential arrangements for people with no settled residence;

(ii) the Secretary of State further directs local authorities to make arrangements for the care and after-care of people with a mental disorder, whether or not they have settled residence in a particular local authority area;

(iii) there is, finally, an approval of arrangements by local authorities to provide accommodation which will meet needs in respect of the prevention, care and after-care of illness. This last approval gives legal validation to the enormously important new area of activity for local authorities – making arrangements for nursing home care (see Chapter 9).

Section 29 of the National Assistance Act 1948

The responsibility covered here is the provision of a whole variety of services for disabled people ordinarily resident within the local authority area. Section 29(1) defines the client group as people aged 18 or over who are blind, deaf or dumb or who suffer from a mental disorder of any description, and other adults who are substantially and permanently handicapped by illness, injury, congenital deformity or such other disabilities as may be prescribed by the Secretary of State. Circular LAC(93)10 extends this definition to people who are partially sighted or hard of hearing. 'Mental disorder' means mental illness, arrested or incomplete development of mind, psychopathic disorder and any other disorder or disability of mind (s 1 of the MHA 1983).

As with s 21 of the NAA 1948, the Secretary of State may approve or direct certain types of provision. LAC(93)10 directs local authorities to make the following arrangements for people ordinarily resident in their area:

–   to provide a social work service and social work advice and support to people in their own homes and elsewhere;

–   to provide rehabilitative day care services plus occupational, recreational, social and cultural activities.

The Secretary of State has also approved, and so empowered local authorities to provide, such facilities as holiday homes; subsidised travel; and warden assisted housing schemes.

4.2.2   Section 45 of the Health Services and Public Health Act 1968

Section 45 of the HSPHA 1968 enables local authorities, subject again to directions or approval of the Secretary of State, to make arrangements for promoting the welfare of old people. The client group is intended to include those who are not substantially and permanently handicapped, and who could benefit from services which might help to postpone personal or social deterioration or breakdown. The Secretary of State has chosen only to approve provision rather than to issue directions, which means that this section is inherently weaker than ss 21 and 29 of the NAA 1948. Approval exists in respect of arrangements for domiciliary services such as:

–   provision of meals and recreation in the home and elsewhere;

–   identifying needs for services;

–   provision of advice and social work support;

–   home care assistance;

–   warden services.

There is also power to employ voluntary agencies as agents to deliver services and s 65 of the HSPHA 1968 links in with this by permitting grant aid. The NHSCCA 1990 has added the power to delegate all these functions to private sector providers.

4.2.3   Section 21 of and Sch 8 to the National Health Service Act 1977

The 1977 Act deals principally with health service provision. However, Sch 8 contains a list of responsibilities which s 21 specifically attributes to social services authorities. These consist of powers to make arrangements for the care of expectant and nursing mothers (para 1); for the prevention of illness; and for the care or after-care of people suffering from illness (para 2). As usual, they are subject to the Secretary of State's approval or directions. It is worth noting that, like the directions made under s 21(1) of the NAA 1948 (see p 38), para 2 appears to overlap with the duty of district health authorities (now unified health authorities) to provide after-care services (s 3(1)(e) of the NHSA 1977) (and see Chapter 7).

The Secretary of State has recently directed the provision of after-care facilities under para 2 for people suffering from mental disorder and has also approved arrangements for night-sitter services; recuperative holidays; facilities for social and recreational activities; and meals on wheels for house-bound people, where not provided under other legislation, for example s 45 of the HSPHA 1968 (Circular LAC(93)10).

Before April 1993, local authorities could discharge their responsibility under para 2 by making residential accommodation arrangements on behalf of the prescribed client group. This power is now repealed by s 66 of the NHSCCA 1990 and replaced by the new, extended powers in s 21 of the NAA 1948.

Paragraph 3 of Sch 8 imposes a clear duty on social services authorities to provide home help services for households where such help is required for adults suffering from illness; lying in; pregnant; elderly; or handicapped by illness or congenital deformity. This is linked with a power to provide laundry facilities for such households. The extent of the duty itself is to provide services 'on such a scale as is adequate for the needs of their area'. The generality of the language used means that it would be difficult to establish a specific duty owed to a particular individual. In practice, anyone requiring a home care service will now be subject to assessment of need under s 47 of the NHSCCA 1990, and to the local authority's determination on service provision (see Chapter 6). The priorities and eligibility criteria set by the local authority may reflect the language in para 3, but effectively the would-be service user will not be better placed than people who need other community care services (see *R v Gloucestershire CC ex parte Mahfood and Barry* (1995) *The Times*, 17 June, discussed at **6.4**).

When exercising any responsibilities under Sch 8, local authorities must co-operate with health authorities 'in order to advance the health and welfare of the people of England and Wales' (s 22 of the NHSA 1977). This is one of the provisions in the NHSA 1977 which aim to promote the 'seamless service' referred to in Chapter 2. It also establishes joint consultative committees to advise health authorities and local authorities on the planning and operation of services which are of common concern (see also Chapter 2, p 22).

4.2.4   Section 117 of the Mental Health Act 1983

This section applies to certain categories of mentally disordered patients who have ceased to be detained in hospital, or who leave hospital. It imposes a joint duty on district health authorities and social services authorities to provide after-care services for such patients in co-operation with voluntary agencies. There is some overlap with the provisions of the NHSA 1977 described above, but s 117(2) is more focused than Sch 8, and does require the local authority to consider the needs of individuals to whom the section applies. It is, therefore, more susceptible to enforcement by aggrieved clients. The Mental Health Act Code of Practice acknowledges this by setting out procedures for proper after-care arrangements, including appropriate consultations, record keeping, and establishment of a care plan.

In *R v Ealing District Health Authority ex parte Fox* [1993] 3 All ER 70, Orton J held that a district health authority (and also, therefore, a social services authority) has a duty under s 117 to provide after-care services, and acts unlawfully in failing to make practical arrangements for these before a patient is discharged from hospital.

4.2.5   The Chronically Sick and Disabled Persons Act 1970 and the Disabled Persons (Services Consultation and Representation) Act 1986

The statutory services discussed so far are unequivocally identified as 'community care services' by s 46 of the NHSCCA 1990. It is the view of the Department of Health that services provided under the Chronically Sick and Disabled Persons Act 1970 are also 'community care services' because they are provided in exercise of a local authority's functions under s 29 of the NAA 1948 (s 1 of the CSDPA 1970). This is an important point because the CSDPA 1970 and its 'partner' the Disabled Persons (Services, Consultation and Representation) Act 1986 are, in legislative terms, powerful measures, and the statutory framework of social care responsibilities would be considerably weakened if they were omitted from the scope of NHSCCA 1990. In the writer's view the Department of Health is correct in linking CSDPA 1970 with Part III of the NAA 1948, both on a straightforward interpretation of ss 1 and 2 of the CSDPA 1970 and because s 47 of the NHSCCA 1990 explicitly links the CSDPA 1970 and DP(SCR)A 1986 provisions into the new assessment of need. A recent decision of the Divisional Court in *R v Lancashire County Council, ex parte Ingham*, *Lexis*, 5 July 1995 supports this interpretation.

The Chronically Sick and Disabled Persons Act 1970

Section 2 of the CSDPA 1970 creates a duty in respect of the disabled or chronically sick. This is the client group already defined by s 29 of the NAA 1948. A local authority must arrange such of the services specified in s 2 as it is satisfied are necessary to meet the needs of a disabled person. As with s 117 of the MHA 1983, therefore, duties are apparently owed to individuals who, it seems, may seek to challenge shortcomings in the provision of services (see **6.4**).

The specified services are:

– provision of practical assistance within the home;

– provision of disability aids and equipment;

– assistance with adaptations to the home;

– provision of meals at home or elsewhere;

– provision of, or assistance in, getting a telephone or any special equipment necessary to use a telephone,

– provision of, or assistance in, taking advantage of educational or recreational facilities, both inside and outside the home, including provision of, or assistance with, incidental transport;

– provision of holidays.

Under s 1, local authorities must gather information about disabled people and publicise services available. They must then plan services in the light of the perceived needs of their population, and determine their own priorities within that framework. Section 2 is made subject to the general guidance of the Secretary of State, who has said that local authorities must 'assess the requirements of the individuals determined by them to be substantially and permanently handicapped as to their needs ... if they are satisfied that an individual is in need ... they are to make arrangements that are appropriate in his or her case' (Circular 12/70, para. 5).

Notwithstanding the guidance, however, the CSDPA 1970 is defective in that s 2 does not expressly require an assessment but merely that the local authority 'satisfies' itself as to the existence of need. This has been held to mean that the authority must 'make up its mind in each specific case' (*Blyth v Blyth (No 2)* [1966] 2 WLR 634). The duty to 'make arrangements' applies only where the local authority has made up its mind that services are needed and there is nothing in the section which directly requires the authority to do this. Consequently, there may be no legal peg on which to hang a request for services.

The Disabled Persons (Services Consultation and Representation) Act 1986

The *raison d'être* of this legislation is to reinforce the duties imposed by CSDPA 1970. In particular, under s 4, a local authority, when requested, must decide whether the needs of a disabled person call for the provison by it of any welfare services authorised by s 2 of the 1970 Act. The request may be made by an individual disabled person or by his or her carer, or by an 'authorised representative' who may be appointed by or on behalf of the disabled person under s 1 of this Act. The authorised representative may be the nearest relative or guardian where the disabled person is mentally disordered. Otherwise, friends or voluntary workers are likely to take on this role. Some voluntary agencies (eg Age Concern) provide advocacy services for disabled people (see below). Authorised representatives may not be paid out of public funds.

Section 4 of the DP(SCR)A 1986 is more focused than s 2 of the CSDPA 1970 in imposing a duty on the local authority to respond to a direct request for services by making a decision one way or the other. That necessitates an assessment, although the term is not used in s 4. As will be seen, s 47 of the NHSCCA 1990 extends the duty still further. Moreover, the draftsman has indicated quite clearly that if an assessment is carried out and results in the conclusion that services under the 1970 Act are required, then those services must be provided (but see **6.4**).

Section 3 of the DP(SCR)A 1986 has never been brought into force because of its resource implications. It requires the local authority, when carrying out an assessment of need, to provide an opportunity for the disabled person himself, or his authorised representative, to make representations as to his perceptions of his needs for services. This duty in effect initiates the provision of advocacy services for elderly and disabled people, which are given considerable emphasis in all the guidance on the NHSCCA 1990. There is a further duty to provide, on request, written details of the assessment.

Enforcement of service provision for disabled people
In the early 1970s the introduction of new services and new welfare benefits for the disabled was high on the political agenda following extensive research on the incidence and effects of disability carried out during the late 1960s. MPs who sponsored the CSDPA 1970 expected that the legislation would fill a serious gap in provision for disabled people and that services under s 2 would be available as of right.

Case-law has never unequivocally supported this expectation. The courts have always been extremely reluctant to allow private law remedies such as negligence or breach of statutory duty to lie against local authorities that fail to provide services. Public law proceedings have yielded only indirect authority that the duty in s 2 of the CSDPA 1970 is enforceable by an individual service user.

The underlying question which is fundamental to decision-making in respect of all public law responsibilities is how far may a local authority defend its failure to provide services for which there is an assessed need on the ground that its resources are insufficient? Until June 1995, however, this point had never been confronted directly in proceedings to enforce service provision under s 2 of the CSDPA 1970, although there was some authority to suggest that the s 2 duty could not be subordinated to the resource argument.

In *R v Ealing Borough Council ex parte Leaman* (1984) *The Times*, 10 February, Mann J ruled that a local authority which, as a matter of policy, no longer provided holiday facilities for the disabled as required by s 2 of the CSDPA 1970 was acting unlawfully. The policy had been set because resources were under pressure, but the court did not address the resource argument head-on.

Again, in *R v Hereford & Worcester County Council ex parte Chandler* (CO/1759/91), leave was granted for judicial review when the local authority failed to provide the applicant with a one-to-one full-time carer after an assessment had established his need for such provision. It appears from this interlocutory decision that, once a specific need is identified, the local authority must meet it, and not argue that it has insufficient resources to make the necessary arrangements. It appears, too, that needs must be met within a reasonable time, 'to delay the fulfilment of a client's expressed urgent needs as an administrative mechanism to control a budget cannot be acceptable' (Complaint No 91/c/3811).

This decision gave rise to a degree of optimism about the enforceability of s 2 rights, through public law proceedings, even in the face of arguments by local authorities that their resources are inadequate to meet every need. More recent developments have now indicated, however, that there are no 'absolute' duties within this area of public law, and that all service provision will be resource-led. This issue is discussed more fully in Chapter 6. Remedies against local authorities are reviewed in Chapter 13.

4.3   Practice points

(i) Services of particular importance to clients may be:

    –   Home helps/home care assistants
        The statutory responsibilities are in s 2 of the CSDPA 1970 and Sch 8 to the NHSA 1977. Persons eligible under the 1977 Act specifically include 'the aged'. Those eligible under the CSDPA 1970 must be disabled but may, of course, also be elderly.

        Neither Act places any ceiling on the type of help which may be provided. 'Cut backs' restricting the amount or type of housework undertaken by the home care services, without reference to need, may be challenged (*R v Gloucestershire County Council ex parte Mahfood and Barry* (1995), *The Times*, 17 June, see Chapter 6).

    –   Day centres
        Provision is made by s 29 of the NAA 1948 and by s 2 of the CSDPA 1970 (see also LAC(93)10).

– Respite care
Provision is made by s 21 of the NAA 1948. The NHS also has a responsibility for providing respite care (s 3 of the NHSA 1977) and this is further defined by the new *Guidance* on NHS responsibilities for meeting continuing health care needs (HSG (95)8; LAC (95)5).

(ii) There is no requirement that clients should be registered in order to be eligible for services. Under the CSDPA 1970, local authorities must keep a register of those covered by the definition of 'disabled' in s 29 of the NAA 1948. Registers, however, are intended only to facilitate the gathering of information and to assist in the planning of services (Circular LAC(93)10).

(iii) Clients who want services should be advised as follows:

– they should initially get in touch with the social services department directly, or through their GP;

– the local authority has a duty to assess their needs (s 47 of the NHSCCA 1990; see Chapter 4);

– the local authority must decide whether certain needs call for the provision of any services. The eligibility criteria set out in the community care plan should indicate what provision clients may expect, and it will be important to match the assessed needs against such criteria. All clients should insist on receiving a full written record of their assessment.

– where clients are disabled, the local authority will have a duty to provide services under CSDPA 1970. The decision in *R v Gloucestershire County Council ex parte Mahfood and Barry* (above) enables local authorities with limited resources to prioritise areas of need, but there will still be an effective presumption that some provision will be made. Once provided, services may not be rationed or withdrawn as long as the need exists (see Chapter 6).

(iv) Advisers should be aware of how to operate the local authority's complaints procedure. In general, a dispute over community services should be taken through the complaints system before referral to the Ombudsman or judicial review are contemplated (see Chapter 13). The first step in challenging the local authority will be to obtain a copy of the client's social services file (see Access to Personal Files (Social Services) Regulations 1989 (SI 1989/206)).

(v) Services will generally have to be paid for (see Chapter 17). There is evidence that charges for services provided at home are rising steadily and that there is no automatic exemption for people living on income support. Increasingly, clients may have problems in affording charges.

Advisers should be aware of the provision in s 17 of the Health & Social Services and Social Security Adjudications Act 1983 that such charges should be 'reasonable' (for further discussion see Chapter 17).

4.4 Checklist of community care services for elderly and/or disabled people

Service	Client Group	Duty/Power	Statutory Source
Residential Accommodation	Elderly and/or Disabled who are in need of care and attention not otherwise available to them	Duty	Section 21 of the NAA 1948 LAC(93)10
Day Centres and Activities	Elderly and Disabled	Duty	Section 29 of the NAA 1948 LAC(93)(10)
Meals at Home or Elsewhere	Elderly and Disabled Elderly	Duty Power	Section 2 of the CSDPA 1970 Section 2 of the CSDPA 1970
Home Help Services	Elderly and Disabled Elderly	Duty Power	Section 2 of the CSDPA 1970 Schedule 8, para 3 to the NHSA 1977
Aids, Equipment, Home Adaptations	Elderly and Disabled Elderly	Duty Power	Section 2 of the CSDPA 1970 Section 45 of the HSPHA 1968 DHSS Circular (71)19
Day Centres	Elderly and Disabled	Duty	Section 29 of the NAA 1948
Social Work Support	Elderly and Disabled Elderly	Power Power	Section 29 of the NAA 1948 Section 45 of the HSPHA 1968
Respite Care	General: Eligibility criteria relate to those with, e.g. complex or intense health care needs	Duty	Section 3 of the NHSA 1977 HSG(95)8; LAC(95)5
	As for residential accommodation	Duty	Section 21 of the NAA 1948 LAC(93)10

Service	Client Group	Duty/Power	Statutory Source
Assessment of Need	Elderly and Disabled Elderly	Duty Duty	Section 4 of the DP(SCR)A 1986 Section 47 of the NHSCCA 1990
Information about Services	Elderly and Disabled Elderly	Duty Power	Section 1 of the CSPPA 1970 Section 45 of the HSPHA 1968
Assessment of Carer's Needs	Informal Carers	Duty (from April 1996)	Carers (Recognition and Services) Act 1995
Incontinence Services	Elderly and Disabled	Qualified Duty	Section 3 of the NHSA 1977 Circular EL(91)28

Figure 3. The responsibility of different organisations in respect of care and accommodation services

Chapter 5

ASSESSMENT OF NEEDS

'Authorities will rightly be judged by the quality of this process above all else' (*Taking Care*, Audit Commission, 1993).

5.1 Introduction

In the White Paper on community care (Cm 849), the Government expressed approval of the principle that the provision of care at public expense should be preceded by a proper assessment of the individual's needs. Assessment is, therefore, an essential duty laid on social services authorities by s 47 of the NHSCCA 1990. It is a key part of service provision because it is the point at which authorities engage with individual clients, make decisions about specific services and commit resources to that end.

The Government's stated objective is that assessments should be 'needs-led'. Social services authorities should focus on the particular difficulties, in respect of which help is sought, but should take account of all individual circumstances, namely:

– people's capacities and incapacities;

– their preferences and aspirations;

– their living situations;

– the support available from relatives and friends;

– any other sources of help.

The information gained then provides the context for subsequent decisions as to what services (if any) should be provided. As will be seen (Chapter 6), a social services authority has no unequivocal obligation to provide services, but, if it does so, a needs-led approach dictates that any 'care package' must reflect the assessment. This approach to assessment represents a radical shift from the previous 'service-led' culture, which tended to fit people into an existing range of facilities. It meshes with the Government's view that separating the commissioning of services from their management and delivery will increase the range and flexibility of services and enable needs to be targeted more accurately.

5.2   A needs-led approach

Closer analysis reveals certain inconsistencies within this model.

(i) There is considerable emphasis in all the guidance on meeting need and on involving service users and their carers in the assessment process. The following extract from a Social Services Inspectorate Report is typical:

'It is vitally important that the assessment of need is managed on an individual basis and that the individual feels that he or she has been regarded as a unique person and is not just being fitted into existing services' (H. Laming, Chief SSI, 1993).

It is easy to infer, therefore, that assessments will be driven by users and that provision will be based on their perceptions of their own needs.

(ii) In fact, it is clear that the epithet 'needs-led' is apt to mislead. In the *Summary of Practice Guidance* (para 11), 'need' is defined as:

'... the shorthand for the requirements of individuals to enable them to achieve, maintain or restore an acceptable level of social independence or quality of life, as defined by the particular agency or authority.'

It is clear, therefore, that the assessor, not the service-user, will define need, so setting the framework for the assessment, and that the definition will be based on two considerations:

– the local authority's eligibility criteria, which will reflect its previous decisions on what types of service should be made available, in line with its statutory powers and responsibilities. This makes for circularity in the relationship between needs and services;

– the value judgments made by a professional assessor. Here research suggests that needs are often professionally categorised in a way which fails to procure the desired outcome from the users' and/or carers' perspectives (Assessment Systems and Community Care, SSI, 1991). In other words – the social worker knows best.

(iii) Ultimately, the more explicit the definition of need, the more informed will be public expectation of services. For this reason, local authorities should publish their needs eligibility criteria, and assessors should be seen to operate by reference to them.

(iv) It is also apparent that assessment is to be used as a means of targeting scarce resources, and indeed may be seen as part of a general rationing process. An enabling 'partnership-style' approach to assessment may be desirable, but the social services manager is also responsible for allocating a cash limited budget. Again, users' and carers' views may be indispensable, but only local authorities have purchasing power.

The Audit Commission has made it quite clear that a needs-led approach is intended to enable expenditure to be controlled: 'setting needs eligibility criteria is the most effective way of shaping a coherent approach to need while simultaneously containing expenditure ...' (*Taking Care*, Audit Commission, 1993).

Tensions between expectations and actual service delivery are almost inevitable. It is also worth noting here that certain community care legislation (eg s 29 of the NAA 1948) expressly prohibits the making of cash payments to individuals in place of arranging services, although there is much evidence to suggest that service users would prefer to budget for their own needs (see **8.6**).

5.3   The 'right' to assessment

The law underlines the tensions and inconsistencies referred to above. Section 47 of the NHSCCA 1990 makes assessment a necessary qualification for the provision of community care services. It creates a duty to assess need, and thereby categorises assessment itself as a preliminary service, which may or may not constitute a threshold for further services. It does not, however, create any new duties to provide other services.

This conceptual distinction between assessment and provision is also to be found in the Education Act 1993, which requires a local education authority to assess a child's special educational needs where it may be necessary to determine special educational provision for her/him, but obliges the authority to make a statement of those needs only where it in fact *is* necessary to determine such provision (s 168). There is no duty to make a statement of needs in respect of every child with special educational needs. Similarly, there is no duty under the NHSCCA 1990 to provide community care services for every person who is assessed as having a need for services.

Section 47(1) states:

> 'Where it appears to a local authority that any person for whom they may provide or arrange for the provision of community care services may be in need of any such services, the authority—
>
> (a)   shall carry out an assessment of his needs for those services; and
> (b)   having regard to the results of that assessment, shall then decide whether his needs call for the provision by them of any such services.'

Paragraph (a) contains what appears to be an unequivocal duty to assess need for community care services, which is owed to individuals. This breaks new ground. The preamble, however, limits the duty to assess to cases where the local authority has come to the conclusion that:

– there is an apparent need for services; and

– there are statutory powers (or duties) to provide services.

The duty is not, therefore, absolute.

(i) *Apparent need*

The local authority must perceive that an individual 'may' be in need of services. There is no requirement that the apparent needs must be urgent or immediate (*R v Mid-Glamorgan County Council ex parte Miles* (*Legal Action*, January 1994, p 21)). It is unlikely that any elderly client seeking assessment would fail to meet this criterion.

The *Policy Guidance* (para 3.18) requires local authorities to publish information about assessment, prepared in conjunction with other service providers, including health and housing authorities (see **5.5.2**).

(ii) *Is the local authority permitted to provide services for an individual?*

The duty to assess is also made subject to vires; s 47(1) refers to services which a local authority 'may' provide. When, therefore, will the local authority lack power to provide community care services, and so decline to carry out an assessment? Practically speaking, hardly ever. The only readily foreseeable limitation on a local authority's powers is the general restriction of its responsibility, throughout the legislation, to service users who are ordinarily resident in the local authority's area. The duty to provide residential accommodation for vulnerable people under s 21 of the NAA 1948, for example, is so restricted. Even then, however, s 24(3) of the NAA 1948 gives added power to dispense with residence qualifications, so that accommodation may be provided for non-residents who are in urgent need, and it would not, therefore, be legitimate to decline to assess such people's needs for services.

5.4 Relationship between assessment and service provision

The legislative framework allows local authorities to exercise considerable discretion as to what services they actually provide. This point is discussed more fully in Chapter 6.

The thrust of the new system is towards improving quality without dramatically increasing public spending, and there is a clear expectation that authorities will prioritise their expenditure by reference to a general review of need in their areas. Community care plans (see Chapter 3) will be important in communicating what these priorities are.

It is irrelevant to the duty to assess that a local authority has neither plans nor resources to allocate priority to meeting any needs which may be identified. It will, therefore, be unlawful to refuse an assessment of need merely because relevant services are not being provided, or to limit an assessment to situations where services are, or will be available (see Gordon, *Community Care Assessments*, Chapter 3).

5.4.1 Unmet need

Notwithstanding the distinction drawn in the legislation between assessment and service provision, many assessors will be uneasy about assessing, and recording, individual need for services which the local authority will not provide. This is quite understandable, bearing in mind that the *Practice Guidance* is misleading on this point, and seems likely to raise false expectations:

> 'Care management makes the needs and wishes of users and carers essential to the caring process. This needs-led approach aims to tailor services to individual requirements' (*Summary of Practice Guidance*, 1991, para 17).

Recent research by Age Concern indicates that practitioners are confused about recording unmet need, and that this has led to users having difficulty in obtaining information about the results of their assessments. There may have been reliance on the 'Laming' letter, issued by the Chief Inspector of the Social Services Inspectorate in December 1992, in which local authorities were warned to be cautious about recording the results of assessments, so as not to expose themselves to possible legal action if they could not provide services which clients were assessed as needing (Cl(92)34). More recently, however, the Government has said: 'We have made it clear to authorities that they should share the results of assessments with users so that they know where they stand' (John Bowis: House of Commons Written Answer, 16 July 1993, Col 689). Presumably, this means that it is better for users to be given unwelcome information, than no information at all.

5.5 The process of assessment

Section 47(5) of the NHSCCA 1990 states that the Secretary of State may give directions about how an assessment is to be carried out. Failing this, it will be subject to s 3 of the DP(SCR)A 1986 and 'shall be carried out in such manner and take such form as the local authority consider appropriate'. Section 3 requires local authorities to allow disabled clients, or their representatives, to make representations as to their needs before an assessment is carried out. It also provides that authorities must give written statements of their decisions as to needs, with reasons, and must explain decisions not to provide services to meet identifiable needs. Such requirements manifestly constitute best practice, but s 3 has not so far been brought into force. Similarly, the Secretary of State has not taken the opportunity to issue directions. Assessment procedures are, therefore, for each local authority to determine, subject, however, to a considerable amount of guidance issued under s 7 of the LASSA 1970, and also to the principles of natural justice.

5.5.1 Eligibility for assessment

People who appear to the local authority to need community care services are eligible for assessment (s 47(1)). Local authorities must respond to information received and approaches made by individual clients which reveal apparent need. Information published by a local authority should explain its strategies regarding vulnerable groups and should give details of the assessment process (see **5.5.2** below).

The *Practitioners' Guide* suggests that enquiries are likely to be received from potential service users, their carers, or other agencies, in the form of office visits, telephone calls or letters. The local authority's response should always be welcoming, informed and proactive (para 2.3). In practice, most people referred for assessment will fall into one of four categories (para 2.22):

(a) those for whom community living is no longer possible, or who are at risk (eg people with intensive personal care needs);

(b) those reliant on others for survival, requiring help with, for example, feeding or toileting;

(c) those reliant on others for support, requiring help with day-to-day household tasks such as cleaning or shopping;

(d) those whose functioning or morale is impaired, for example, as a consequence of a depressive illness.

The complaints procedure is available to individuals whose apparent need has 'come to the attention of the authority' and has not been addressed (s 50 of the NHSCCA 1990, and see Chapter 13).

5.5.2   Information about assessments

All the guidance emphasises that it is important for local authorities to inform the public of their assessment procedures. Publications should be written at the appropriate level, with sufficient detail, and should take account of special circumstances – for example different languages and cultures, or client groups whose mobility is restricted and who may be isolated and lack motivation to seek or use information.

The *Managers' Guide* lists the information on assessments which should be made available, namely:

– the range of needs for which the agency accepts responsibility;

– the aims, priorities and objectives of the agency;

– the types of services available and the needs for which they cater;

– the criteria determining access to resources;

– the referral, assessment and review procedures within and between agencies;

– the entitlements of users and carers to information, participation and representation, including provision for equal opportunities;

– the charging policies;

– the standards by which the agency will monitor its performance, including response times to referrals;

– complaints and feedback procedures.

The information should be available from social services departments or in public libraries.

5.5.3   Levels of assessment

The *Policy Guidance* states that 'assessment arrangements should normally include an initial screening process to determine the appropriate form of assessment'. Some people may need advice and assistance which do not call for a formal assessment, others may require only a limited or specialist assessment of specific needs, others may have urgent needs which require an immediate response. Procedures should be sufficiently comprehensive and flexible to cope with all levels and types of need presented (para 3.20).

Given the clear legal duty to carry out a s 47 assessment, it will be unlawful for a local authority to screen people out, without assessment, at a preliminary stage. It is clear, therefore, that a simple assessment must be part of the initial screening process and may or may not lead on to a more comprehensive assessment.

The *Practitioners' Guide* emphasises that the assessment process should be as simple, speedy and informal as possible. It should be based on the minimum level of enquiry needed to give a clear picture of need and form a basis for a decision to invest public resources. The *Guide* describes six levels of assessment which an authority might use, ranging from simple tests of need for people requiring basic provision, through to comprehensive multi-agency assessments. The initial screening process should indicate the appropriate level of assessment.

The *Guide* is not prescriptive as regards this model and, in practice, it appears that most local authorities use three levels of assessment:

'simple': where people require basic provision, such as bus passes, which are available from a single agency in well-defined circumstances;

'specialist': where, for example, people need straightforward packages of home-care services but various eligibility criteria will have to be taken into account;

'comprehensive': where people have multiple needs and are at risk of harm if services are not provided. Such assessments are likely to involve several agencies as will the ultimate provision of services under a care plan. They should be offered to individuals who, on preliminary screening, appear to be disabled (Circular Cl (92) 34, and see **5.5.4** below).

The *Practitioners' Guide* (p 58) gives suggested guidelines for a comprehensive assessment, indicating the range of information which should be gathered:

−   biographical details;

−   self-perceived needs;

–   self-care (ie how well the applicant can perform basic tasks and functions such as dealing with money, cooking, shopping, using the telephone and getting about);

–   physical health   ⎫ the   assessor   should   understand
    mental health, including memory ⎬ when it will be necessary to involve
                                                          ⎭ health professionals;

–   use of medicines (for instance by those with diabetes or chronic epilepsy);

–   abilities, attitudes and lifestyle;

–   race and culture;

–   personal history (for example, recent bereavement);

–   needs of carers;

–   social networks and support;

–   care services already received;

–   housing;

–   finance (ie whether a potential user is claiming relevant social security benefits, such as attendance allowance (but note **14.4**));

–   transport;

–   evaluation of risk which may be occasioned by environmental hazards (eg gas fires), health, or behaviour.

5.5.4   The assessment of disabled people

As stated above, a local authority must offer a comprehensive assessment to a person who appears to be 'disabled', irrespective of the scale of need that is actually presented. The reason for this is that s 4 of the DP(SCR)A 1986 requires an authority, on request by a disabled person, his carer or authorised representative, to decide whether his needs call for the provision of any services under the CSDPA 1970. To discharge this duty the local authority must carry out an assessment, and the duty to assess is, therefore, implicit. Section 47(2) of the NHSCCA 1990 extends the duty by removing the stipulation that it arises only on request.

The *Policy Guidance* goes on to emphasise the fact that there are no hard and fast rules for defining disability. The statutory definition in s 29 of the NAA 1948 is very broad, and the assessor, therefore, will have to have a 'clear understanding of the local authority's interpretation of a "disabled person" and ensure that staff implement the requirement for a comprehensive assessment consistently' (para 2.20). As with 'need' itself, the framework for service operation is still organisationally defined.

There is an argument that the assessment of need in respect of a disabled person is not necessarily the same as a s 47 assessment because welfare services under the CSDPA 1970 are not, technically, 'community care services'. This point has already been addressed in Chapter 4. Whatever the legal niceties this is probably a distinction without a difference, for it would be unacceptable if an assessment conducted under the 1990 Act were less comprehensive than an assessment under the 1986 Act.

5.5.5 Waiting for an assessment

The NHSCCA 1990 does not prescribe how quickly an assessment must be carried out. CI(92)34 (the 'Laming' letter) advises that the greater the apparent need, the more expeditious should be the assessment. There is also power under s 47(5) to provide services, as a matter of urgency, without a prior assessment of need.

There may be a danger that non-priority cases will stay forever at the bottom of the list. This is borne out by Age Concern's research indicating that priority is in fact being given to assessments on hospital discharge and that, in some areas, assessments in the community are subject to extreme delays, or are carried out in emergencies only (*Mapping the Change: No Time to Lose*, p 10). A recent consultation paper recommends that people should be entitled to expect that assessments will be provided within a reasonable time. The community care charters being promoted by the Secretary of State should spell out performance standards in respect of the time taken to start and complete the assessment; for the time taken to start service provision following assessment; and for the speed of delivery of services (*A Framework for Local Community Care Charters in England*, 1994, para B.2).

5.5.6 How will the assessment be carried out?

Those who carry out assessments must ensure that potential service users understand:

–   what is involved in the assessment process;
–   the likely timescale;
–   what authority the practitioner holds;
–   the possible outcomes;
–   the users' entitlement to information, participation and representation (*Practitioners' Guide*, para 316).

Assessments should take place wherever is most appropriate. For most older people this will be either at home, or in hospital when discharge is being considered (see Chapter 7). Where the assessment is concerned with the maintenance of a person at home it should take place in that setting.

If admission to residential care is under consideration, prospective residents should be given an opportunity to experience that setting before making a final decision. Care should always be taken to ensure that assessments do not expose individuals to unnecessary disruption.

Recent research highlights the obvious point that most assessments occur at times of heightened stress when users and carers are least able to take in new information or cope with new experiences. Despite all the requirements to provide information (see **5.5.2**), it was found that there was an over-reliance by assessors on verbally communicated information, and that many people had little recollection of an assessment after the event, apart from having been asked a range of questions.

Two very different styles of assessment emerged from the research. There was first the 'friendly chat' which elicited a positive response, but also gave rise to confusion about the nature and purpose of the exercise. Secondly, there was the 'qualifying test', which was usually received negatively, and with some resentment (*Getting the Message: Users' and Carers' Experiences of Community Care in Leeds*, March 1995).

This research suggests that many elderly people and their carers would benefit from the presence and support of a third party during the assessment (see **5.5.7**).

5.5.7   Participation

The guidance emphasises the importance of listening to service users and of enabling them to participate actively in the assessment process. Natural justice also requires involvement and may require that a service user be permitted to appoint a representative to put forward his case. It does not follow, of course, that views expressed by users or through their representatives will necessarily be acted on. The assessor should, however, record them.

The *Managers' Guide* nevertheless exhorts agencies to afford users 'a more powerful voice in expressing need and influencing services they receive' (*Managers' Guide*, para 2.43). This means encouraging and facilitating self-advocacy, and making sure that advocacy support is available for those who are in dispute with the local authority.

This emphasis on advocacy services reflects the statutory entitlement to representation, created by ss 1 and 3 of the DP(SCR)A 1986 (both still unimplemented). Some local authorities operate internal advocacy schemes, but there are difficulties in ensuring, and demonstrating, independence. Funding for new schemes is now being made available to a few voluntary agencies, but the development of advocacy skills requires training, and specialist agencies are few and far between.

5.5.8   Carers

The emphasis on participation described in **5.5.7** applies equally to carers. They must be listened to and, indeed, a comprehensive assessment should evaluate their role (see Chapter 11). There is no legal duty to look after an elderly relative, and it should never be assumed that a carer is willing to carry on caring.

Sometimes users and carers may be in disagreement, and frequently carers will also be users of services in their own right. Many elderly people care for partners whose disabilities only marginally exceed their own. The *Policy Guidance* emphasises that carers may request a separate assessment if they feel that they need community care services (paras 3.27–3.29). There is an extended discussion of carers' rights to assessment and services, and of relevant new legislation in Chapter 11.

5.5.9 Collaboration with other agencies

If, in the course of an assessment, it appears to the local authority that a person has health needs or housing needs, s 47(4) of the NHSCCA 1990 requires it to notify the district health authority or local housing authority and invite one or both of them to assist in the assessment. Where a patient is being discharged from hospital into the community, the district health authority will certainly be involved in the assessment process. (For hospital discharge procedures, see Chapter 7).

GPs should also be expected to make a contribution to assessments and, indeed, in many cases they may be responsible for the initial referral of a patient. Bearing in mind the relationship between GP and patient, however, it will usually be inappropriate for a GP to act as assessor – for example by carrying out a clinical examination.

The *Guidance* envisages that voluntary agencies too may have a role in providing expert advice in assessments, especially where needs are being assessed in relation to specific services – at alcohol centres, for example (*Policy Guidance*, para 3.49).

5.5.10 Confidentiality

Where needs are complex, several agencies may be involved in an assessment and confidentiality then becomes an issue. Formal case conferences will be unusual, and informal communication, perhaps by telephone, will be the norm (*Policy Guidance*, para 3.35). The *Practitioners' Guide* lays down some principles for ensuring confidentiality in the assessment process (para 1.21), viz:

– information should be used only for the purposes for which it is given;

– information about a user/patient should normally be shared only with the full and informed consent of that person;

– information should be shared on a 'need to know' basis;

– users and carers should be advised why, and with whom information about them has been shared;

– all confidential information should be rigorously safeguarded.

It should also be emphasised that the assessment procedure is subject to the general legislation which allows individuals access to information about themselves, for example:

Data Protection Act 1984;

Access to Personal Files Act 1987; ·

Access to Health Records Act 1990.

All service users are entitled to have access to their own assessments, which form part of their social services records.

5.5.11   The result of an assessment

The legislation does not expressly require that assessments should be recorded in writing and it may be appropriate for decisions 'in respect of simple needs' to be communicated orally (*Managers' Guide*, para 2.24). Natural justice, however, would generally require reasons to be given, where requested. This would necessitate a written assessment.

As already noted (see **5.4.1**), local authorities are expected to pass on to clients the full results of assessment, irrespective of whether the resources are available to meet the client's needs. The *Practitioners' Guide* indicates that a copy of the assessment should normally be shared with clients, representatives, and people who have agreed to provide a service. It will normally be combined with a written care plan (para 3.54; see Chapter 6). In practice, the following complaint seems not to be unusual:

> 'Whilst the outcome of the assessment was given and discussed, it was also made clear that the only document from social services would be a letter giving details of the attendant care provision ... This appears to be a most unsatisfactory way to conduct such assessments ...' (*Mapping the Change: No Time To Lose*, Age Concern, 1993).

The Consultation Paper on community care charters also suggests that users have a right to be told the outcome of the assessment and the reasons for any decisions (para B.1). There is no explicit reference to a written record, but the Secretary of State is being urged to issue specific guidance on this point. Legal advisers should always seek to ensure that clients are given full written records of all aspects of their assessments. These will be *essential* documents if clients seek to challenge assessments. Ultimately, as noted above, service users have statutory rights of access to their social services files and, consequently, to the assessments themselves.

5.5.12   The financial assessment

Social services departments perform a dual role in identifying need and managing resources, which engenders obvious conflict. Conflict is apparent when decisions about service provision are being made, but is even more manifest when users are being assessed as to means.

The *Policy Guidance* emphasises that the provision of services, whether or not the local authority is under a duty to provide them, should not be related to users' ability to pay. 'The assessment of financial means should, therefore, *follow* the assessment of need and decisions about service provision' (para 3.31). If decisions about services are allowed to become, or to seem, tainted by financial considerations they will be instantly challengeable. Financial assessments are discussed in detail in Chapter 15.

5.5.13 Reviewing assessments

The emphatic drafting of s 47(1)(a) of the NHSCCA 1990 appears to impose a continuing duty on local authorities to review their assessments from time to time and to reconsider initial assessments which are adverse to the user. Clearly, an individual may ask the local authority to review his or her assessment, but, additionally, CI(92)34 states:

> 'The clear plans of all users should be subject to regular review. For frail people in the community, frequent reviews and adjustments of their care plans are likely to be needed. Before any changes in services are made for existing users, they should be reassessed' (para 31).

This last point is now underlined by the decision of the Divisional Court in *R v Gloucestershire County Council ex parte Mahfood and Barry* (1995) *The Times*, 17 June, discussed in Chapter 6.

The unimplemented s 3 of the DP(SCR)A 1986 creates a right to have an assessment reviewed where a user is unhappy about its outcome. The *Policy Guidance* states (para 3.54):

> 'Decisions on service provision should be reached in discussion with users and carers and every effort should be made to ensure that the result is acceptable to them. A formal judicial appeal procedure would be foreign to such arrangements and it would not be appropriate to introduce one.'

Accordingly, the first step towards a review based not on change of circumstances but on dissatisfaction with the original assessment will be to invoke the complaints procedure (discussed in Chapter 13).

5.6 Practice points

(1) It will be apparent that clients may be able to challenge assessments in various circumstances. For example:

  – where the local authority refuses to carry out an assessment, or delays in doing so without good reason;

  – where the client disagrees with the priority given to an assessment;

- if the local authority adopts an initial screening procedure which prevents a client from obtaining an assessment or if it requires people to apply in writing for an assessment;

- if the local authority defines need restrictively, according to the services which it proposes to offer;

- if the local authority does not allow users to participate in assessments and, possibly, if some advocacy provision is not afforded to them, especially if there are communication or language difficulties;

- if the local authority conspicuously fails to observe established guidance on any point.

Legal advisers should also be aware of the means of challenging adverse decisions or bad practice and, in particular, should be familiar with complaints procedures. Chapter 13 elaborates on these and other remedies in some detail.

(2) Advocacy services offer some potential for lawyers developing their private client practice. Representation may be needed, not just in respect of assessments of need, but also when it comes to the means test, the care plan and, ultimately, complaints about services. Some clients will qualify for Green Form advice; for others advocacy will be a service which adds value to other services and can be appropriately charged out.

Lawyers have advocacy skills. Others have to acquire them, and may find the advocate's role difficult to adjust to. Practitioners already acting under powers of attorney or under the Court of Protection regime may find it quite natural to take on an advocacy role. To do so would in fact assist them to prepare for probable new legislation creating the role of a personal care attorney, following recent recommendations of the Law Commission (*Mental Incapacity*, Law Com No 231, 1995).

(3) Practitioners may sometimes be asked to advise clients whether they should request an assessment.

Example: Mrs Rose is 64. She is a widow, living alone, and has Alzheimer's disease. Her two daughters live some distance away. They are considering nursing home care for their mother.

Mrs Rose owns her house, which is worth about £70,000, and has £20,000 free capital. Her weekly income, from various sources, is £130.

(i) The inclination may be to arrange a private nursing home placement for Mrs Rose, perhaps near one of her daughters. Clearly, she will be required to fund her own care in the first instance (see Chapter 15). However, if Mrs Rose is assessed as needing nursing home care the local authority may determine that it will make the arrangements under the statutory responsibilities laid down in the NAA 1948, notwithstanding that, for the time being, Mrs Rose will be contributing the full fee (see Chapter 9).

(ii) The family may at this time be asking whether it is possible to mitigate the costs of care. Will the house have to be sold and the proceeds used to pay for the care bed? (See Chapter 15.)

(iii) Assessment is itself a service and Mrs Rose has a right to be assessed even if she decides to make private care arrangements. A professional assessment may be of some value to the family – for instance in choosing a suitable nursing home – or possibly in making arrangements for care at home. It will be unlawful for the local authority to refuse assessment; it may not anticipate the fact that Mrs Rose has moderate resources, and is therefore in a position to make her own arrangements.

(iv) It is to be expected that Mrs Rose's funds will run out within a few years, particularly if she enters a nursing home. It may, therefore, be important to establish whether the local authority will be prepared to take over the funding of any private placement which is chosen (see Chapter 9). An assessment would provide the opportunity for a 'partnership' arrangement with the local authority, which would prevent Mrs Rose from having to be moved at a later date.

(v) If home care is appropriate for the time being it may be sensible to tap into the local authority's care packages. Again, Mrs Rose would initially have to pay the full economic costs, but continuity of provision could be maintained, and the local authority would be responsible for care management, not the family.

(vi) The adviser should be alive to the possibility of a claim for the disability living allowance (DLA) care component or mobility component. These benefits would raise Mrs Rose's weekly income quite considerably and help to preserve capital. The adviser should also be aware of the consequences for the DLA (care component) where the local authority arranges the nursing home placement (see Chapter 19).

Chapter 6

THE DECISION TO PROVIDE SERVICES

'Authorities must define what they consider to constitute a need for services, in such a way that the most disadvantaged are included but which still allows for the Authority to balance its budget. Furthermore they must do so in a way that allows local flexibility and adjustment to tailor services to the particular needs of individuals as part of the assessment process. To do all of this will be no mean feat' (*Taking Care*, Audit Commission, 1993).

Assessments of need unlock the door to services but do not necessarily push it open. As has already been observed, the needs-led approach will be controlled by the purchasers of services and by the purse-strings, and in the present financial climate it cannot be assumed that assessment will lead to the provision of services. Section 47 of the NHSCCA 1990 only requires local authorities to make decisions about service provision, not to provide services; they must be expected to target their resources where need is greatest, and sometimes, therefore, services will not be made available and needs will be unmet.

Section 47(1) is concerned with a local authority's general response to an assessment of an individual's needs. Section 47(2) deals more specifically with the provision of services where the person who has been assessed is disabled.

6.1 The duty to make a decision

Once the assessment of need has been carried out, s 47(1)(b) of the NHSCCA 1990 comes into play. It states that the local authority:

'... having regard to the results of that assessment, shall then decide whether the user's needs call for the provision by them of any such [community care] services'.

The local authority must, therefore, make a decision about service provision and must also communicate this, with reasons, to the user. It has, however, a clear discretion to determine the scope of the provision that it will make and, in some cases, may determine that there will be no provision. Section 47(1)(b) does no more than emphasise that the creation of a qualified right to assessment has not altered the fact that the community care legislation creates powers and general responsibilities rather than specific duties which are owed to individuals. The local authority must now, as in the past, exercise its discretion in the light of the assessment, rationally, consistently and fairly, but taking into account the resources available to it.

Section 47(3) of the 1990 Act requires a local authority to take account of the likelihood of any provision being made by the district health authority or local housing authority when making its own decision as to services. The general responsibilities of housing authorities are discussed in Chapter 12 and the responsibility of the NHS for continuing in-patient care and community health services is considered in Chapter 2. Although there is considerable overlap in responsibility for care services between health authorities and social services departments, s 47(3) explicitly allocates the lead role to the local authority, giving health authorities an option to pursue other priorities, as described in Chapter 2. Shifting emphasis and responsibility away from the NHS in this way is likely to have far-reaching consequences, however, not least in terms of eroding a 'free' National Health Service.

6.2 Determining service provision

The *Policy Guidance* indicates (at para 3.24) that, since community care policies aim to preserve or restore normal living as far as possible, the following order of preference is implicit in determining service provision:

   (i) support for the user in his own home, including day and domiciliary care, respite care, the provision of disability equipment and adaptations to accommodation as necessary;

  (ii) a move to more suitable accommodation which might be sheltered or very sheltered housing, together with the provision of social services support;

 (iii) a move to another private household, to live with relatives or friends, or as part of an adult fostering scheme;

 (iv) residential care;

  (v) nursing home care;

 (vi) long-stay care in hospital.

It is accepted that care packages will include health provision, both primary and specialist, and housing provision as well as social services provision. The prioritisation relies ultimately on the availability of NHS resources for hospital care. In some health authority areas, however, no long-stay hospital beds are available. The new *Guidance* on continuing health care (HSG(95)8; LAC(95)5) confirms the contraction of NHS services in this area whilst purporting to clarify the responsibilities which the NHS will accept (for further discussion see Chapter 2 at page 27 and Chapter 7).

The *Policy Guidance* emphasises that the aim must always be to devise a cost-effective package of services to meet the users' care needs. However, local authorities also have a responsibility to act within the resources available, which 'will sometimes involve difficult decisions where it will be necessary to strike a balance between meeting the needs identified within available resources and meeting the care preferences of the individual' (para 3.25). Here, once again, the gap between 'needs' and 'preferences' is exposed.

Guidance for practitioners explains how policy statements or eligibility criteria are to be used to bridge the gap between assessed needs and what the local authority can be expected to provide ('Care Management and Assessment', *Practitioners' Guide*, para 3.38).

Such criteria should target resources in terms of:

– levels of risk, for example abuse or lack of support;

– tasks of self-care, for example feeding and toileting;

– needs of carers, for example respite care;

– other elements deemed necessary to a minimum quality of life, for example social contact.

Even with the acknowledged constraints, the expectation in the White Paper was that the needs assessment process would encourage practitioners to develop individualised rather than stereotyped responses to needs. Policies should, therefore, be flexible enough to allow this to happen. Over-rigid eligibility criteria may be reviewable. On the other hand, policies should be followed, because they create legitimate expectations so far as the public is concerned.

6.3 Service provision for the disabled

Section 47(2) of the NHSCCA 1990 runs as follows:–

'(2) If at any time during the assessment of the needs of any person under sub-section (1) it appears to a local authority that he is a *disabled person*, the authority—

(a) shall proceed to make such a decision as to the services he requires as is mentioned in Section 4 of the Disabled Persons (Services Consultation and Representation) Act 1986 without his requesting them to do so under that Section;

(b) shall inform him that they will be doing so and of his rights under that Act.'

Section 4 of the DP(SCR)A 1986 referred to in (a) above, states that a local authority must decide whether the needs of a disabled person call for the provision of services under s 2 of the CSDPA 1970. This duty arises on request by a disabled person, or by his/her carer or authorised representative. Section 47(1) of the NHSCCA 1990 goes further in making unconditional the duties to assess and to take decisions about service provision.

Under s 2 of the CSDPA 1970 itself, the local authority has to be satisfied 'that it is necessary in order to meet the needs of [an individual] for that authority to make arrangements to provide any or all of the services specified in the section'. Once the authority is satisfied both as to the needs and as to the necessity of making arrangements to meet such needs, then, 'it shall be the duty of that authority to make those arrangements'. Once assumed, that duty is stated to be subject to guidance issued by the Secretary of State under s 7 of the LASSA 1970.

It seems clear that s 47(2), like s 47(1), requires a local authority only to make a *decision* as to what, if any, services it should provide and that individuals whose needs have previously been assessed cannot expect provision unless it is *necessary* to meet those needs. It is fair to say, however, that until recently it had generally been assumed that because of the drafting of s 2 of the CSDPA 1970 itself, there was in fact a duty owed to individual disabled people rather than to the community at large, which might be directly enforceable. Such duty could not be qualified by the application of eligibility criteria or, in particular, by the argument that resources were inadequate to meet all assessed needs.

Decisions of the High Court on judicial review lent credence to this assumption (see p 45). In fact, neither ruling directly addressed the question whether lack of resources will afford a defence to a local authority which is challenged after failing to provide services following an assessment of need. In June 1995, however, the Divisional Court confronted this and related issues. Its decision is of considerable importance for local authorities, and will be reviewed here in some detail.

6.4 The extent of a local authority's obligation to provide services for the disabled

In *R v Gloucestershire County Council ex parte Mahfood and Barry* (1995) *The Times*, 17 June, five elderly and disabled people sought judicial review of the local authority's decision to withdraw services which it had previously provided under s 2 of the CSDPA 1970. The county council argued that, because of cuts in Government provision for community care, it no longer had the resources to meet the needs of the five applicants or, indeed, of perhaps 1,500 other people in a similar position. The applicants maintained, however, that individual need is the only criterion for service provision under s 2 of the CSDPA 1970, and that the duty to meet need is absolute and specific, and is not tempered by shortage of resources or the competing needs of others.

McCowan LJ expressed some sympathy for the applicants' contention, but concluded that their interpretation of s 2 would be 'impractical and unrealistic', given that any local authority faces an impossible task unless it can have regard to the size of its financial cake in order to determine how fairest and best to cut it. Nevertheless, the court granted declaratory relief to the applicants because the county council had acted unlawfully in cutting services without reassessing their needs.

The points of law which come out of this decision may be summarised as follows:

(i) It is clearly confirmed that s 47(1) of the NHSCCA 1990 creates entitlement to an assessment of need. Nevertheless, a local authority 'is right to take account of resources both when assessing needs and when deciding whether it is necessary to make arrangements to meet those needs'. These judicial remarks suggest that the very scope of an assessment may be restricted where resources are limited and in this respect go beyond the published guidance, which makes a distinction between the initial consideration of all relevant individual needs and the subsequent determination of resource provision based on whether or not the needs identitifed in the assessment meet the local authority's published eligibility criteria for services (see, for example, 'Care Management and Assessment', *Practitioners' Guide*, p 11). In fact, McCowan LJ seems to be suggesting that it would not in future be unlawful for a local authority to assess a person's needs only for the particular services which the local authority actually provides or for those services which the local authority has the resources to provide. The difficulty with such an interpretation is that assessments would cease to be objective and the old service-led ethos would be resurrected.

(ii) As indicated above, the local authority's decision as to service provision may be justifiably influenced by available resources. It will, therefore, be appropriate for eligibility criteria to be laid down to enable objective decisions to be taken as to which of an individual's needs will be eligible 'for provision within a limited budget'. Such criteria will therefore operate as rationing devices. Local authorities should, however, take care to ensure that they are reasonable, objective and consistently applied.

(iii) Whilst it is implicit in the Divisional Court's ruling that not all needs will be met, there will nevertheless be 'situations where a reasonable authority could only conclude that some arrangements were necessary to meet the needs of a disabled person and in which it could not reasonably conclude that a lack of resources provided an answer'. The suggestion here is that an assessment of risk in the individual case will have to be part of the decision as to services. For the legal adviser this aspect of the decision raises interesting questions: how far, for example, can highly restrictive eligibility criteria protect a local authority against a charge of acting unreasonably? What risks will require action to be taken? Given McCowan LJ's suggestion that it would, for example, be unreasonable not to provide assistance for people who are at 'severe physical risk' in their own homes, how far does his ruling reflect on community care policies to do with maintaining independence and personal choice?

(iv) Once a local authority, having considered its resources, has decided that it is necessary to provide a particular service to meet assessed needs, an absolute duty is then owed to the individual to make that provision, regardless thereafter of the availability of resources.

(v) Lack of resources alone cannot justify a withdrawal or reduction of services, and a reassessment of a service user's needs will be a prerequisite before any decision to reduce services is taken. It would appear to be lawful to carry out any reassessment in the light of revised eligibility criteria which take into account new resource constraints, but the local authority would also have to be satisfied that a reduction in services would not leave the user at severe risk.

(vi) It will be tempting, but probably unlawful, for local authorities to seek to make savings by reducing high-cost care packages. Given that the aim will always have been to target resources at those most in need, it is unlikely that any revision of eligibility criteria would justify reducing complex packages. Unless the service user's assessed needs have diminished, which will be unlikely, or the local authority can persuade other agencies to undertake particular tasks, or the service user is prepared to consider other service options (for example, day care or respite care) then a decision to reduce services will be transparently cost-led and so unlawful.

6.5 The care package

Following the decision as to services, the *Guidance* envisages that the local authority will set up, fund and monitor a care plan ('Care Management and Assessment', *Practitioners' Guide*, p 61 (note the case study example in the Appendix). Where individual needs are complex, a care manager, usually based in the social services department, will be responsible for devising a package of services. Budgets are normally devolved to care managers and will be used to commission services, both internal and external to the local authority (see Chapter 8). The on-going responsibility of the care manager will be to harmonise inter-agency inputs and monitor the quality of service. Managing commissioning budgets requires the development of new skills, including cash-flow management, and it is not intended, therefore, that care managers should be directly involved in service delivery. Consequently, many social services departments have now effected an internal split between purchaser and provider functions.

The Consultation Paper on community care charters suggests that service users should be entitled to expect a written care plan, giving details of services and providers and of a contact point to which to refer problems. It should include a statement of how and when the assessment and care plan will be reviewed (para B.4). Performance standards are also proposed. For instance, with home care services, users and carers should expect:

–   to be informed as precisely as possible when services will arrive;

–   that cancellations and disruptions will be kept to a minimum;

–   that notice of changes will be given in good time (para C.1).

6.6 Choice

Choice is the selling point of the community care reforms. Community care plans should identify how they intend to increase consumer choice; assessments should 'enable users and carers to exercise genuine choice'; care management systems should seek to promote 'individual choice and self-determination'. The supermarket analogy is defective, however, for where the fulfilment of an individual's choice is dependent on the allocation of limited resources by a publicly accountable body, and on the outputs of commissioning arrangements between that body and third party providers, the meaning of the term is fundamentally altered. As a result, the early research now shows some disillusionment with the actual outcomes.

For instance, the 'choices' of users and carers may be in conflict. Whose choice takes priority where maintaining the user's independence restricts the carer's capacity to choose? (see Chapter 11). Again, in some areas, local authorities' charging policies for home-based services are having the effect that the only real choice may be not to have expensive services. The Age Concern research refers to 'pressure which new charging policies, cuts in local services and targeting of services bring in placing the costs of care squarely on the shoulders of many who can least afford to pay' (*Mapping the Change: No Time to Lose*, p 16).

The Secretary of State has not issued directions or specific guidance on choice in respect of domiciliary services. There are, however, two directions on choice of residential accommodation (LAC(92)27 and LAC(93)18) which are considered in detail in Chapter 9. They cover the choices available once a local authority has agreed, after assessment, to arrange a residential placement. It remains to be seen how far it is possible for users to opt 'for' residential care rather than for a domiciliary package, when the latter would be cheaper, or indeed whether a very disabled person may choose to remain at home, whatever the cost of support. Some local authorities, for example, now operate, 'normal limits' policies which set a 'normal' ceiling on the cost of domiciliary packages, equivalent to the gross cost of arranging suitable residential placements. The Divisional Court has recently held that where a frail elderly person 'needs' 24-hour care, a local authority is entitled to offer only a residential placement rather than a domiciliary package where that would be a more efficient use of its resources (*R v Lancashire County Council ex parte Ingham*, 5 July 1995).

In theory, no one can be forced to accept a community care service that he or she does not want. In practice, budgetary issues may pre-empt choice. Furthermore, it appears that some elderly people assessed as needing residential care are seeking to remain at home because, under the statutory means test, which is confined to residential placements, the value of their homes will be taken into account. In response to this, at least one local authority is considering imposing legal charges on property in order to recover the full economic costs of home-care services (*Guardian*, 23 December 1994).

If choice exists at all the key to it must be information about available services, available resources and priorities, plus the ability to exert some influence on the assessment process. Many elderly people will need to call upon a 'more powerful voice' to help in this, and as noted already, there will be a role for the legal adviser.

6.7 Practice points

At the time of writing there is growing evidence of budgets coming under pressure and of cutbacks in existing services. Age Concern finds that day and domiciliary services have taken the brunt of social services expenditure cuts, and that some disabled older people are having services – such as home cleaning – reduced or withdrawn, notwithstanding their 'entitlement' under s 2 of the CSDPA 1970. Facilities are being effectively rationed via delays in provision and by more stringent charges. In addition, some services formerly delivered free of charge as part of a community health package – bathing for example – are being redefined as 'social care'.

The legal adviser will increasingly be faced with such problems. Some cases will be susceptible to legal challenge through the complaints procedures and, eventually, perhaps by judicial review. Following the *Gloucestershire* case, withdrawal of existing services for disabled people would certainly fall into this category. In other cases, these remedies will not be feasible because of the time and expense involved in pursuing them, and the only option will then be to fall back on the traditional lawyers' skills of negotiation and persuasion. To do this effectively, practitioners will need to obtain access to the community care plans and become familiar with the published guidance. They may also find it necessary to learn how to work through political channels.

Finally, for many clients who wish to remain at home rather than enter residential care, the best way forward may be to negotiate informal or private care arrangements to bridge any gap which the local authority is unable to fill out of its available resources.

Chapter 7

DISCHARGE FROM HOSPITAL

'Hospital discharge ... has been recognised by many as a key indicator of progress with Community Care changes' (*Taking Care*, Audit Commission, 1993).

An elderly person is admitted to an NHS Trust Hospital following a stroke. Since 1982 there has been a 25% decrease in the number of acute care hospital beds, and throughput time between admission and discharge has been reduced by one-third. It is highly likely, therefore, that discharge of this patient will be considered as soon as her condition has stabilised, and almost certainly while she still needs continuing care and support. There are various options. The patient may be discharged into a nursing home either for a period of rehabilitation or on a permanent basis. Alternatively, she may be discharged home, with support from social services and from the community health service. Hopefully, informal care will be available from a partner or other relative. If not, it will be important that the support services are on hand immediately to prevent deterioration in the patient's condition, and subsequent re-admission to hospital.

7.1   Introduction

Hospital discharge is a critical interface between the systems of health and social care, and the processes involved are certain to test joint planning arrangements between health authorities and social services departments. In addition, problems which have arisen in connection with discharge have exposed a fault line between community care policies and the 'new' NHS. In particular, the consequences of accelerated discharge from acute care beds have not been fully addressed. Indeed, the White Paper on community care makes only passing reference to discharge procedures, and the *Policy Guidance* is silent on the fact that elderly people now leave hospital more infirm and more dependent than in the past.

Such developments carry serious implications for informal carers who will continue to deliver most 'community care'. In addition, however, since discharge from hospital usually involves a shift in service responsibility for a patient from the NHS to social services, discharge is now beginning to highlight just how far the boundary between health and social care, or, more accurately, between 'free' care and care which must be purchased, has shifted over the past few years.

The patient in the example above can no longer expect to have the option of a long-stay hospital bed, funded by the NHS. Although the White Paper commented that 'health authorities will need to ensure that their plans allow for the provision of continuous residential health care for those highly dependent people who need it' (para 4.21), in fact provision of continuing care and psycho-geriatric beds in hospitals has been cut by over 30% since 1990 (Alzheimer's Disease Society Research 1993). The trend is continuing; between April 1993 and April 1994 long-stay provision was cut further from a national total of 56,000 beds to 51,000 beds (Laing & Buisson, 1995). In addition, health authorities have been cutting back on contractual arrangements made under s 23 of the NHSA 1977 to fund beds in private nursing homes (see post).

Experience suggests that elderly patients would often benefit from legal advice before they are discharged from hospital, but that this advice either may not be available or may not be perceived as necessary. This chapter will, therefore, address the following issues:

(1) Hospital discharge procedures: The practice guidance and what clients and their advisers should expect.

(2) How far it may be possible to influence the allocation of responsibility between the NHS and social services departments, for the benefit of individual clients.

7.2   Arrangements for discharge

Guidance to district health authorities and local authorities on the management of hospital discharges has always emphasised the importance of maintaining effective procedures to ensure that patients do not leave hospital without adequate arrangements being made for their support in the community. The key to successful discharge is said to be 'good joint planning at all stages'.

NHS consultants, in consultation with nursing staff, are responsible for deciding when a patient no longer needs acute care. Where a patient is likely to need intensive long-term support, a decision about discharge should be taken only after an appropriate multi-disciplinary assessment of his or her needs has been conducted under s 47 of the NHSCCA 1990. Technically, the duty to initiate and co-ordinate the assessment lies with the social services department (see Chapter 5). New DoH *Guidance* (HSG(95)8; LAC(95)5) emphasises, however, that patients should be referred to a consultant with specialist responsibility for continuing care who will, in practice, conduct the assessment in consultation with nursing and specialist NHS staff, the patient's GP, community health services and social services staff. Where a patient has no accommodation, or where his housing is no longer suitable for his needs, housing authorities and housing providers should also be involved in the assessment (para 19).

7.3   Consultation with the patient

As explained in Chapter 3, all the published guidance on s 47 assessments emphasises the importance of consulting with patients or carers, and their right to express choices. The new *Guidance* on hospital discharge emphasises that patients, their families and their carers should be given adequate information to enable them to understand the discharge process and to take sensible decisions about continuing care.

In particular, it allocates responsibility to social services staff to provide written information about the likely cost to a patient of any option which he or she is asked to consider and, where appropriate, details of social security benefits which may be available in those circumstances. Previous guidance (HC(89)5 and LAC(89)7) was far less explicit on this point. The new *Guidance* makes it clear, however, that patient choice does not enter directly into the decision as to whether NHS care should continue or whether responsibility for making continuing care arrangements, and for funding those arrangements, is to pass to social services and the patient's family. The *Guidance* states only that 'the assessment should take account of the views and wishes of the patient, his or her family and any carer' (para 19).

7.4   The decision on continuing care

Following the assessment, the patient's consultant will consider the available options, in consultation with nursing staff and other members of the multi-disciplinary team. The new *Guidance* lists the following options (para 21):

(a)   continuing in-patient care arranged and funded by the NHS;

(b)   a period of rehabilitation or recovery arranged and funded by the NHS to prepare for discharge arrangements breaking down;

(c)   discharge from NHS in-patient care to a placement in a nursing home or residential care home arranged and funded by social services or by the patient and his or her family;

(d)   discharge home, or to other accommodation, with a package of social and health care support.

For most patients, the likely options will be (c) or (d).

As described in Chapter 2, district health authorities have a qualified duty to provide continuing care under s 3(1) of the NHSA 1977. The new *Guidance* now purports to lay down general eligibility criteria for such care, which are clearly expected to determine whether or not the NHS will accept responsibility for a given patient (para 21). When considering a discharge from hospital, the consultant, in consultation with members of the multi-disciplinary team, must address whether the patient needs continuing in-patient care, either in hospital or in a nursing home, arranged and funded by the NHS.

There are four tests:

'(i) the patient needs on-going and regular specialist clinical supervision (in the majority of cases this might be weekly or more frequent) on account of:

   – either the complexity, nature or intensity of his or her medical, nursing or other clinical needs;

   – or the need for frequent not easily predictable interventions;

(ii) the patient requires the routine use of specialist healthcare equipment or treatments requiring supervision of NHS staff;

(iii) the patient has a rapidly degenerating or unstable condition which will require specialist medical or nursing supervision;

(iv) the patient has received acute treatment or in-patient palliative care in hospital or hospice, his or her prognosis is such that he or she is likely to die in the very near future, and discharge from NHS care would be inappropriate (Annex A).'

The *Guidance* indicates, however, that local policies and eligibility criteria should be prepared, reflecting the needs of the local population and the resources available to the health authority. They must incorporate the general criteria set out above, but presumably will contain amplification of the conditions justifying in-patient care and details of available arrangements.

In practice, however, there will be an expectation that a significant majority of people who require continuing in-patient care are likely to have their needs met in a nursing home setting through a social services placement. They will have to meet their own care fees, insofar as they are able to do so. Unfortunately, the *Guidance* is not wholly transparent as regards where the financial burdens of most care arrangements will rest.

7.5 The patient's right to refuse discharge to nursing home or residential care

The new *Guidance* states, quite unequivocally, that, where a patient has been assessed as not requiring NHS continuing in-patient care, he or she does not 'have the right to occupy indefinitely an NHS bed' (para 27). Bearing in mind the requirement under s 1 of the NHSA 1977 to provide a 'comprehensive' health service, and the general responsibilities of the Secretary of State for Health laid down in s 3 of the NHSA 1977, that proposition may not be legally sustainable. The *Guidance* then goes on to state, correctly, that any patient who is not sectioned under Part II of the MHA 1983 may refuse to be discharged into a nursing home or a residential care home.

In these circumstances, social workers, in conjunction with hospital and community-based staff, and with the patient, his family and carers, must explore 'alternative options'. If these are not acceptable, it may be necessary to discharge the patient home with a package of health and social care – for which the social services department may make a charge. In fact, it is difficult to see what 'alternative option' there might be, apart from discharge to the patient's own home, or to the home of a carer. There is no suggestion, for example, that the hospital consultant would at this point reconsider a decision not to authorise NHS continuing care. The *Guidance* also does not confront the possibility that a home-based package may be more costly than a residential placement. The implication of the reference to the social services' charge is that, once the hospital bed has been freed, the local authority, not the NHS, will have to deal with funding problems.

The vaguely threatening tones of para 27 of the *Guidance* seem to carry a warning for patients, or their advisers, who might otherwise consider blocking beds in an effort to extract a commitment from the NHS to fund nursing home placements. In practice, given the importance of throughput times for NHS performance targets, a refusal to accept a discharge may be a useful means of putting pressure on a health authority. Whether, however, it will be appropriate to use such a tactic on behalf of frail, possibly confused elderly clients, will be very debatable.

7.6 New review procedures

The *Guidance* creates, however, a new and more attractive option for challenging decisions about discharge from hospital. Paragraph 30 states that patients, their families, or carers, may ask the health authority to review a decision on eligibility for NHS continuing in-patient care. Further *Guidance* (*Arrangements for Reviewing Decisions on Eligibility for NHS Continuing In-patient Care* HSG(95)39; LAC(95)17) sets out details of the new review procedures which came into operation on 1 April 1996 (see the flowchart at **7.7**). This coincides with the creation of new Health Authorities, which, under the Health Authorities Act 1995, replace district health authorities and family health service authorities.

HSG(95)39 emphasises that the review procedure is to be seen in the context of 'high quality discharge policies'. It is intended as an additional safeguard for those patients who are assessed as ready for discharge from NHS in-patient care but who require on-going continuing support from health and/or social services, and who consider that the health authority's eligibility criteria for NHS continuing in-patient care (whether in a hospital or in some other setting such as a nursing home) have not been correctly applied in their case (para 4).

Where a patient is unhappy with the written continuing care plan, issued as part of the discharge arrangements, the patient or a carer should contact the person named in the plan as having initial responsibility for dealing with the patient's concerns over the discharge. Such person will conduct what is effectively an internal review of the decision. If there is no satisfactory resolution, the patient must be given information about the formal review procedure (see **7.8**) and, on request, will be put in touch with advocacy services. The patient or carer may then ask the designated officer in the health authority for a review.

Review panels are now being set up consisting of an 'independent' chairman and single representatives of the health authority and local authority. The health authority has discretion not to convene a panel where, for example, the patient falls well outside the eligibility criteria, or where the review is being used to challenge aspects of treatment or the content of the eligibility criteria. Panels will have only two functions:

(i) to check that proper procedures have been followed in reaching decisions about the need for NHS continuing in-patient care; and

(ii) to ensure that the health authority's eligibility criteria for NHS continuing in-patient care have been properly and consistently applied (para 6).

Panels will have access to existing documentation on the case, including the patient's record of assessment. They should also have access to the views of the patient and any carers, professionals involved, and 'any other relevant bodies or individuals' (para 27). Independent clinical advice will be available to the panel to explain the original clinical judgments and their relationship with the health authority's eligibility criteria, but not to provide a second opinion on clinical diagnosis, management, or prognosis for the patient.

The *Guidance* appears to rule out a hearing as such. Parties are encouraged to put their views in writing or to request an interview with the designated health authority officer. At that stage, a patient may have a representative to speak on his or her behalf. The health authority officer may then be asked to attend review panel meetings, although his or her role in such circumstances is not explained in the *Guidance*. Given that the review panel will, in most cases, be engaged in interpreting the eligibility criteria, it is disconcerting that the *Guidance* leaves no room for direct advocacy or, indeed, for written representations to be made direct to the panel.

Ultimately, the role of the panel is advisory, although the 'expectation is that its recommendations will be accepted in all but very exceptional circumstances' (para 33). The *Guidance* gives no hint as to what these circumstances might be, but it is reasonable to infer that financial considerations would govern a health authority's rejection of a panel recommendation. In all cases, the health authority must communicate the outcome of the review to the patient, in writing, and with reasons.

The *Guidance* stipulates that the health authority should aim to ensure that the review procedure is completed within two weeks – understandably, because it also states that patients should remain in NHS funded accommodation while the review is being conducted (para 18). This probably means that hospital discharge will be delayed, with resultant bed blocking, although patients could be moved to nursing homes, accompanied initially by NHS funding. Legal advisers will have to act quickly in preparing written or oral submissions to the health authority officer, and it will be difficult within this timescale to obtain a clinical opinion on the patient's continuing care needs. The nature of the 'independent' clinical advice which will be accessible directly by the review panel therefore becomes an issue. Since this advice is not meant to provide a second opinion on diagnosis or prognosis, which may well be what is in dispute, it may often be important for patients to obtain a further opinion, and for this reason the time-limit gives cause for concern.

7.7 Case study

Kathleen Jones is 83. She has been suffering from Alzheimer's disease for some years, and has been cared for at home by her husband who is 81. She was admitted to hospital eight weeks ago after suffering a stroke, which has left her paralysed down the left side and seems to have affected her speech. Her condition is now stable and the hospital consultant wishes to plan her discharge.

(a) Alzheimer's disease affects one in four people over the age of 80, and is a devastating condition. The disease is long term, progressive and irreversible, and the emotional and physical strain on carers is very high. Nevertheless, Alzheimer's patients are unlikely to meet the eligibility criteria for continuing NHS in-patient care laid down in the new DoH *Guidance.*

(b) How will the added disability caused by the stroke affect the care prognosis for Mrs Jones? Will she need the 'specialist clinical supervision' referred to in the new eligibility criteria? Does she have complex or intense clinical needs? This seems unlikely, in that local eligibility criteria may require, for example, that she fulfil *all* the following:

– she is frequently doubly incontinent;

– she requires constant observation to prevent harmful deterioration or injury to herself or others;

– she is unable to initiate purposeful movements even with aids;

– she needs feeding by technical means;

– her physical condition is poor, requiring active intervention supported by technical means.

(c) The likely outcome is that the NHS consultant responsible for Mrs Jones will recommend her discharge from NHS in-patient care into a nursing home under arrangements made by the social services department. Unless, therefore, Mrs Jones and her husband have very ample resources, they may now face the prospect of rapid impoverishment.

(d) Mr Jones may wish to reject the nursing home option and take his wife home. In these circumstances the social services department will put together a package of health and social care for Mrs Jones 'within the resources available'. Community health services will be available free of charge but Mrs Jones will be charged for the care element of the package. It is foreseeable that the cost to the local authority of a home care package will exceed the cost of a nursing home bed and that it may only be prepared to fund the equivalent of a residential placement (see p 73). If the charges to Mr and Mrs Jones are unaffordable they may have to forego services.

7.8   Practice points

(i) For some clients, the discharge from hospital has crucial long-term financial implications which may also affect the quality of care that they receive. Legal advice at this stage can be invaluable. Practitioners may wish to consider educating their clients in this respect.

(ii) The role of the legal adviser will be to ensure that clients have understood the terms on which they are to be discharged from hospital and that the financial implications of discharge have been explained and digested by clients and their families. If a client is unhappy about the arrangements being put forward, other steps may need to be considered.

(iii) A client may instruct his or her legal adviser to make representations to the person named in the written care plan. If, for example, the procedures laid down in the new *Guidance* have not been followed, or if the decision has not been properly explained, the plan may be challenged. Crucially, however, HSG(95)39 does not suggest what the possible outcomes might be. It refers to the possibility of 'agreement', but it is difficult to envisage a health authority reversing a decision not to fund a continuing care placement because, for example, the patient was not fully aware of the relevant eligibility criteria. It may be predicted, therefore, that any agreement may be peripheral to the client's main concern.

(iv) The client may want to ask the health authority to review the decision. The independent panel must meet and make its recommendation within a fortnight of the request, so the legal adviser must prepare the case quickly and effectively. The adviser must be thoroughly familiar with the local community care plan and with the local eligibility criteria for NHS continuing in-patient care. Information about the culture and previous practice of the independent panel will be helpful.

(v) There will be no right of appeal against a decision made by a health authority on the recommendation of the review panel. Given the duty to provide NHS care contained in s 3 of the NHSA 1977, it is, however, possible that the eligibility criteria themselves may be susceptible to judicial review if, for example, they are considered to be too narrow, or that the hospital discharge process, including the reviews, may be challenged if it is not seen as operating fairly. However, the recent decision in *R v Gloucestershire CC ex parte Mahfood* (see Chapter 6) casts a shadow over all decisions about care, by linking the performance of statutory responsibilities with available resources.

7.9 Flowchart of the review procedure

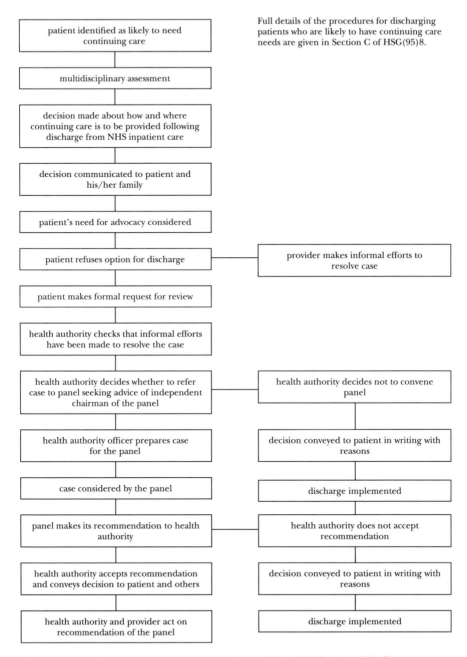

Full details of the procedures for discharging patients who are likely to have continuing care needs are given in Section C of HSG(95)8.

patient identified as likely to need continuing care

multidisciplinary assessment

decision made about how and where continuing care is to be provided following discharge from NHS inpatient care

decision communicated to patient and his/her family

patient's need for advocacy considered

patient refuses option for discharge — provider makes informal efforts to resolve case

patient makes formal request for review

health authority checks that informal efforts have been made to resolve the case

health authority decides whether to refer case to panel seeking advice of independent chairman of the panel — health authority decides not to convene panel

health authority officer prepares case for the panel — decision conveyed to patient in writing with reasons

case considered by the panel — discharge implemented

panel makes its recommendation to health authority — health authority does not accept recommendation

health authority accepts recommendation and conveys decision to patient and others — decision conveyed to patient in writing with reasons

health authority and provider act on recommendation of the panel — discharge implemented

Figure 4. Overall process for review procedure (HSG (95)39; LAC (95)17).

Chapter 8

CONTRACTS FOR CARE

'The Government will expect Local Authorities to make use wherever possible of services from voluntary "not for profit" and private providers insofar as this represents a cost effective care choice. Social Services Authorities will continue to play a valuable role in the provision of services, but in those cases where they are still the main or sole providers of services, they will be expected to take all reasonable steps to secure diversity of provision' (*Caring for People* 1989, Cm 849, para 3.4.3).

All local authorities must commission non-local authority services. They have done so, to an extent, for many years (in particular, residential care services) but the requirement to spend 85% of the special transitional grant on services provided outside local authorities themselves (see Chapter 2) dictates a far more substantial engagement with the independent sector.

The model for delivery of community care services presented in the White Paper emphasises a 'mixed economy' of care, with local authorities seeking out and purchasing services from a range of providers in the voluntary and private sectors. Authorities are also encouraged to develop an internal purchaser–provider split, separating the care management/commissioning role from service provision in order to secure the desirable range and diversity of services. The White Paper does not envisage the end of local authority run services, but rather a more market-orientated approach to some types of services which the 'market' itself may not be able to provide, for example services for people with high levels of dependency or particularly challenging behaviour (para 3.4.11). Nevertheless, the funding constraints mean that there may be an incentive to transfer local authority services to the independent sector. There has been explicit encouragement to do this with residential homes, both in order to benefit fully from the STG funding and also to release capital for the development of home care services (*Taking Care*, Audit Commission, 1993).

Statutory underpinning for the new purchasing role of the local authority is as follows:

(i) Section 43(3) of the HSPHA 1968, amended by s 42(7) of the NHSCCA 1990 allows local authorities to contract with voluntary or commercial organisations for the provision of services for elderly people.

(ii) Section 50(7A)(1) of the NHSCCA 1990 requires local authorities to exercise their social services functions in accordance with directions. Section 7 of the Local Authority (Social Services) Act 1970 also requires social services departments to act under the *general* guidance of the Secretary of State. The Government has published both policy guidance and practice guidance on the contracting process and on the substance of the contracts themselves.

(iii) Contracts for services are within the definition of 'Contracts for Public Works' in s 17 of the Local Government Act 1988, and local authorities must engage only on a commercial basis.

At the present time, the vast majority of local authority contracts are with providers of residential care, and a number of issues specifically applicable to such contracts are dealt with in Chapter 9. The remainder of this chapter will concentrate on the law and guidance relevant to all community care contracts. Further reference to the DoH/SSI Practice *Guidance 'Purchase of Services'* (1991) may be helpful.

8.1   Selection of providers

Community care contracts are not at present subject to compulsory competitive tendering. Local authorities may invite tenders, or may negotiate directly with providers. There is no obligation to act fairly in selecting contractual partners.

Tendering has advantages in that it may increase choice, allow new providers to enter the marketplace, permit tight specifications, and allow for clearer decisions on value for money. There are also disadvantages, however, in that the complexity of tendering requirements may exclude smaller providers offering a less structured and perhaps more personal service. In addition, price tends to become the dominant issue in the tendering process.

Direct negotiation is likely to be less costly and may enable local authorities to seek out specialist suppliers, or to deal more easily with known and trusted suppliers, particularly in the voluntary sector. On the other hand, such arrangements tend to reduce competition and to restrict consumer choice. Consultation with consumers can help to overcome this hurdle.

Authorities may also choose to set up new organisations by creating 'tailor-made' schemes or facilitating management/worker buy-outs. If the social services department is the sole supplier of a particular service, or if no service exists at all, the department can put out a 'request for proposals', allowing organisations with relevant expertise to come forward.

The old system of funding voluntary agencies through grant aid is not eradicated either. In practice, however, contracts will become the norm and will usually offer voluntary agencies more security than does grant funding. Voluntary agencies which rely on local authority funding face various dilemmas in becoming part of the contract culture. Not only is contracting a complex and expensive business, but agencies may also have concerns that their traditional independence and ability to innovate is likely to be overridden by their reliance for funding on contracts which reflect the local authority's priorities.

8.2 Contract types and purchasing arrangements

A local authority is free to use whatever contractual mechanisms it considers appropriate. The *Guidance* points out that the type of contract chosen must depend on the nature and comprehensiveness of the service. Essentially there are three broad categories of services:

Domiciliary care;
Day and residential care;
Advice and counselling.

Each service can be delivered at different levels of intensity, calling for different degrees of precision in the agreements themselves. For example, low intensity domiciliary care implies cleaning once or twice a week, and would be appropriately commissioned via a service agreement providing flexibility, or even a grant arrangement. High intensity day care, on the other hand, implies specialist social and other therapies for people with severe disabilities. Here a service contract with detailed specifications and explicit conditions would be appropriate or, alternatively, a partnership arrangement in which providers having input would share responsibility. Interestingly enough, the *Guidance* foresees local authorities 'pump priming' new projects to meet user-led demands for services, perhaps across a whole client group. These would then become privatised in the sense that providers would eventually sell their services directly to consumers. As resources for community care become increasingly stretched, the local authority's role in some areas may be simply to stimulate the market, because there are advantages for users in buying their own services rather than having them provided and paying substantial charges to the local authority. (Note, however, the present prohibition on cash grants in s 29 of the NAA 1948. This would have to be amended. See also **5.2**).

The *Guidance* mentions three types of purchasing arrangements.

– Block contracts, which buy access to facilities rather than provision for a defined number of clients. They specify the quality and quantity of services, rather than the outcome for individual users. They are the cheapest arrangements to negotiate, and are likely to be used where there is little competition. Large providers, including public limited companies, will be able to offer block contracts based on economies of scale. Such arrangements tend to limit user choice, and, sooner or later, to force other, often smaller, providers out of the market.

– Price by case, or 'Spot' contracts, where the price is quoted for each unit of provision, on each case dealt with. For providers, these arrangements carry the risk that they may not receive the number of referrals they have budgeted for, and may have to operate at a loss. Users may then suffer if providers try to contain costs by limiting the services. Local authorities may seek to negotiate contracts for services to be delivered as and when required at a fixed price. If no minimum take-up is specified, all the risk lies with the provider.

–   Cost and volume or 'call off' contracts. Here a quantity of service is purchased for an agreed sum, and any additional service required is purchased on a cost-by-case basis. This reduces the risks to the provider by guaranteeing a minimum income, but there must be enough capacity for the maximum number of referrals. If local authorities try to include their most costly clients in the fixed volume part of the contract, providers will be at risk once again.

The Audit Commission's monitoring of early progress in implementing the community care reforms gathered information mainly about purchasing arrangements for residential care. It found that local authorities were using a range of contract types, but that most relied initially on 'spot' contracts (*Taking Care*, 1993).

8.3   Relationship with health care contracts

Although the local authority will be the lead authority for community care, health authorities will also be purchasing services, such as community nursing for people needing care in their own homes. There is already a good deal of internal contracting between health authorities and NHS Trusts, but health authorities may also commission services from independent sector providers. These play a large part in caring for people with disabilities by providing specialist support such as occupational therapy, speech therapy and clinical psychology and also general care via community nurses and healthcare assistants.

In order to promote the 'seamless' web of services referred to in Chapter 2, care managers may act as agents for health services commissioners as well as social services departments to assess, purchase and monitor complex care packages. Ultimately, it is possible that single care managers may hold budgets devolved from both health and local authorities in order to purchase both health and social care services. Equally, local authorities may wish, in some instances, to act jointly with district health authorities in commissioning care services. 'Joint finance' schemes may already be set up under s 28A of the NHSA 1977.

8.4   Contractual terms and conditions

Community care contracts contain:

(a) basic contractual conditions, such as would be found in any commercial contract;

(b) detailed service specifications.

As a result, such contracts tend to be very long, very legalistic and not very user-friendly, especially for small providers unaccustomed to such documentation. The *Guidance* states that it is essential for the local authority to seek legal advice on a proposed contract at the outset of the negotiations. The same is true of providers, especially since local authorities will be in the dominant bargaining position. Since opportunities for negotiation will be limited, it will be important for providers to assess the terms which are most crucial for them and to negotiate tactically.

The *Guidance* states that local authorities must involve users, carers and other bodies in determining specifications. Consumer and carer involvement will normally be secured through representative bodies, but feedback from individual consumers on the operation of existing contracts will also be utilised as time goes by.

8.4.1 Conditions

Conditions should cover:

– duration of the contract (fixed or renewable);
– purchasing arrangements;
– variation procedures;
– procedure for resolving disputes;
– default arrangements;
– insurance;
– authorised officers;
– details of any sub-contracting;
– complaints procedures for consumers or carers;
– review procedure (for both specification and conditions).

(*Practice Guidance*, para 4.3).

The *Guidance* also insists that social services departments should use both race relations and equal opportunities legislation to ensure that opted-out services do not discriminate against women, people with disabilities or people from minority ethnic groups.

8.4.2 Service specifications

These should cover all aspects of the service being contracted for. They should include quality standards and provision for monitoring by the local authority. It is accepted that quality cannot be achieved without consulting users, and there should be opportunities for users and carers to express their views as part of the monitoring process (*Policy Guidance*, para 4.20).

8.5 Quality assurance

Some interesting questions have been raised recently regarding the legal nature of the 'market' in social care. Since April 1993, social services departments, quite understandably, have begun to use their purchasing power to promote higher standards of care, especially in the residential sector where most of the contractual activity is still concentrated. Stringent service specifications have put providers under pressure, particularly financial pressure, and, in two recent applications for judicial review, providers have sought to challenge local authority contracts on the grounds of unreasonableness. In both cases the underlying question was: are community care contracts like other commercial contracts, and so subject to individual bargaining power and pure market forces? Or is there a public interest factor which requires the local authority to restrain its superior bargaining power and make only 'reasonable' demands on its contracting partners? Both cases were fought over residential care contracts, but the arguments, and the decisions, are applicable across the whole area of community care services.

8.5.1   *R v Newcastle City Council ex parte Dixon* (1993) 17 BMLR 82

In this case the Newcastle Association of Care Homes sought a declaration that the city council's standard contract for the provision of social and nursing home care was ultra vires and unreasonable under the *Wednesbury* principle (ie that no reasonable local authority could have reached such a decision). The argument was that, in imposing service specifications which cut across, and in some instances were more onerous than the statutory requirements of the Registered Homes Act 1984, the local authority was acting unlawfully and/or unreasonably. The RHA 1984 lays down minimum quality standards for residential care, linked to a process of registration and de-registration. Registration is now a precondition for all providers of residential care services commissioned by local authorities under ss 21 and 26 of the NAA 1948 (see Chapter 10). All members of the Association were registered under the 1984 Act, and they wished to be included on the city council's list of approved homes. The council's practice was to spot purchase beds from homes on the list for clients assessed as needing residential care.

In a forthright judgment, Auld J held:

(i) There is no reason in law why local authorities should not impose on homeowners a tougher regime than that laid down by the RHA 1984. Homeowners are not obliged to contract with the local authority; if they do so the relationship is purely commercial.

(ii) The local authority has a statutory obligation to provide services and a fiduciary obligation not to waste taxpayers' money. It must balance these duties, and an insistence upon high contractual standards is an essential means of achieving such a balance. There is no public law duty of restraint in the contractual terms on which it seeks to rely; the contracts are of a wholly commercial nature.

8.5.2   *R v Cleveland County Council ex parte Cleveland Care Homes Association* (1993) 17 BMLR 122

The facts here were substantially as in *R v Newcastle City Council ex parte Dixon* (above), but the local authority had invited tenders from would-be providers.

The authority had adopted an intransigent position over possible negotiations and there was also some ill-feeling amongst the homeowners about inadequate consultation. Compliance with the disputed contractual terms would require considerable expenditure, and the council had not established a phasing-in period.

The homeowners argued that many of them would be forced out of business by the council's stance, and that this would defeat the object of promoting a mixed economy of care. In particular, if a local authority sets standards with which providers are unable to comply, the requirement to promote choice for users is nullified (LAC(92)27; see Chapter 9).

Potts J held:

(i)   There is no reason in law why local authorities should not impose a stricter contractual regime on homeowners than that provided by the RHA 1984.

(ii) However, the council's decision in this case was reviewable, because it was likely to defeat the purpose of the 1990 Act by making impossible demands of the independent sector. This was a public law issue.

(iii) On the facts, the council had acted unreasonably in refusing to negotiate the terms of the contract and in refusing also to phase in the new requirements.

8.5.3   Conclusions

These decisions are distinguishable on the facts. Cleveland County Council had perhaps unnecessarily taken a hard-line approach and had failed to adopt the consultation model put forward by the White Paper on community care. In *R v Newcastle City Council ex parte Dixon*, the issues were of less financial importance, and the local authority seemed more amenable. Nevertheless, there is a clear conflict. Are community care contracts 'public' contracts which affect the rights and duties of citizens and so may be challenged by public law means? If not, then remedies lie in private law only and are restricted to contracting parties.

The conflict raises some difficult questions. What happens, for example, when tight pricing by local authorities drives smaller providers out of business? (There is already some evidence of this.) Will there be a breach of a public law duty? Or will the basic private law principle that the seller fixes the price and the buyer can negotiate but not complain apply in all cases, leaving the 'market' to define itself?

Or again, could a user wishing to exercise choice in respect of residential accommodation challenge a local authority's decision not to make arrangements with a registered provider who is prepared to contract at the local authority's price, but cannot meet all the service specifications?

Jurisprudentially speaking, it would perhaps be helpful if English law, like some European systems, were to acknowledge the general concept of 'public law

contract' as a means of governing commercial relationships between public
and private bodies.

8.6 Rights of service users

Although the introduction of a mixed economy of care has been presented as
the best means of ensuring more choice and better quality services for
consumers, the structure of the system is such that the consumer has no direct
control over quality and often little real choice. There are several reasons for
this:

(i) All services, whether delivered at home or in a residential setting, are
commissioned by local authorities on behalf of service users. Under their
contracts, local authorities are liable to pay for those services. The service
user will be asked to underwrite the local authority's financial responsibility and may, indeed, pay the full economic cost of certain services, but
he or she is not the paymaster, and is not, therefore, in a position to
withhold payment from a provider whose services are unsatisfactory.

(ii) Many service users will not be in a financial position to purchase services
for themselves from the private sector. If, therefore, they decline to accept
what the local authority arranges for them, they will receive no outside
help at all.

(iii) Given that the contractual relationship lies between the local authority
and the service provider, a private law remedy will not generally be
available to the dissatisfied service user. He or she will be expected to
resort to the complaints procedure, which is directed at the local
authority, and will not immediately impact on the performance of the
contract itself. From the legal perspective, 'empowerment' of the
consumer is wholly absent from this model.

(iv) It is, therefore, of considerable importance that, in the absence of direct
negotiating power, service users at least have the opportunity to influence
the preparation of contractual specifications and are involved in the
monitoring process. The *Guidance* provides plenty of encouragement for
the development of such a role, but only local authorities are in a position
to generate the information and awareness amongst service users which
are essential prerequisites.

(v) There is evidence that people prefer to make their own care arrangements where funding is provided, and that this may be an effective use of
public resources. The Independent Living Fund, for example, makes
resources available to disabled people to pay for personal care which may
enable them to remain at home. The attendance allowance itself, a
mainstream social security benefit, is paid to claimants on the same
premise. Nevertheless, social services departments are not generally
empowered to make cash payments to service users. Late in 1995,

however, the Secretary of State for Health announced plans to introduce legislation in 1996 which will permit direct payments to people who are disabled, and a Bill was published soon afterwards (Community Care (Direct Payments) Bill).

Chapter 9

RESIDENTIAL CARE SERVICES

'The Government believes that entering residential or nursing home care should always be a positive choice' (*Caring for People*, 1989).

'Community care is about changing the balance of services and finding the most suitable placement for people from a wide range of options. It is not about imposing a community solution as the only option, in the way that institutional care has been the only option for many people in the past' (*Making a Reality of Community Care*, Audit Commission, 1986).

For many older people and their advisers, the changes in the organisation and delivery of residential care services has been the most important outcome of the implementation of Part III of the NHSCCA 1990. This is paradoxical, of course, because the thrust of the new legislation was towards keeping people out of residential establishments as far as possible, but in fact the bulk of the STG funding earmarked for community care is still spent on sustaining residential care arrangements. The demographic factors discussed in Chapter 1 help to explain this.

For clients who need residential care services, or anticipate that they may need them in the future, the new financial regime for residential care is causing considerable concern. As observed in Chapter 2, the community care changes have always contained a hidden agenda: the capping of social security spending on residential care. The object of the transfer of resources to local government has been to provide more cost-effective, as well as more appropriate services for elderly and vulnerable people, hence the new assessment of need and the financial means test. Both are now liable to evoke concerns about paying for residential care in the long term. The implications of the new statutory means test are extensively discussed in Chapter 15. This chapter will address how residential care arrangements have been made since 1 April 1993, and will start by putting the changes in the law into context.

9.1 The previous regime

9.1.1 Part III accommodation

Since the 1940s, local authorities have had a duty to provide residential accommodation for the elderly and infirm and others needing care. Section 1 of the NAA 1948 provides:

'the existing poor law shall cease to have effect, and shall be replaced by the provisions of ... Part III of this Act as to accommodation and other services to be provided by local authorities ...'

The responsibility for providing a safety net for the most vulnerable members of society was, therefore, a natural successor to the previous parish responsibilities under the 1832 Poor Law. It devolved to social services departments of local authorities under s 195 of the Local Government Act 1972. Before responsibility for homelessness passed to housing departments in the 1970s, s 21 also covered provision for homeless people; s 21(1)(b) gave power to provide temporary accommodation for people 'in urgent need thereof'. Under s 24, the whole range of the local authority's responsibilities was owed to people ordinarily resident in its area, although it nevertheless had a residual power to provide for those with no settled residence, and others in urgent need of residential accommodation.

Authorities could discharge their s 21 duty by providing accommodation in their own, managed, premises (s 21(4)); through arrangements made with another local authority; or by 'sponsoring' beds in the voluntary or private sectors (s 26(1)). The extent to which s 26 powers were used varied considerably between local authority areas, and was influenced by political factors. Inner London boroughs, and many metropolitan authorities regarded it as important to maintain a substantial stock of Part III homes. Other authorities were always prepared to sponsor beds and avoid the costs of running their own accommodation. By the 1970s, some authorities were transferring their Part III accommodation to the independent sector in order to release resources for other purposes. The Local Government Act 1988 allowed authorities to provide financial assistance to transferees in connection with the disposal of residential establishments.

Local authorities were required to fix a standard rate of charge for Part III residents, whether they were providing directly for them, or sponsoring them (s 22). A means test was operated, latterly based on Sch 3 to the Supplementary Benefits Act 1976. A minimum charge was payable, and residents could claim social security benefits (national assistance; then supplementary benefit; and, since 1988, income support) if their resources were insufficient to meet it (see Chapter 2).

9.1.2 Schedule 8 to the National Health Service Act 1977

This part of the NHSA 1977, originally enacted in 1946, described certain functions which were exercisable under s 21 of the Act by social services departments. They included making arrangements for the care of persons suffering from illness, for prevention of illness and for after-care, and departments were expected to arrange various services and, in particular, to provide and maintain residential accommodation. 'Illness' here included mental disorders within the meaning of the mental health legislation, latterly the MHA 1983.

It will be apparent that the Sch 8 powers overlap with the duty laid on the Secretary of State for Health under s 3 of the NHSA 1977 to make provision for nursing care and after-care. This duty has been discussed in Chapter 2.

9.1.3 The independent sector

Comment has already been made in Chapter 2 on the demographic and economic factors which have affected the rapid development of residential provision made by voluntary or commercial organisations over the last 15 years. The combined effect of such matters was to trigger a 500% increase in private residential provision between 1983 and 1993. Before implementation of Part III of the NHSCCA 1990 on 1 April 1993, the independent providers relied on two main client groups:

(i) people taking up beds 'sponsored' by local authorities under s 26 of the NAA 1948. The willingness of local authorities to use this option had some influence on the extent and range of independent provision;

(ii) people entering residential establishments by a direct route, making their own arrangements with providers. Some would fund their own placements from beginning to end, so that the arrangements would always be 'private'. Others, initially or at a later stage, would need financial help to maintain placements, and could claim income-related benefits from central government through the DSS. The ready availability of such funding was, of course, a considerable incentive in the growth of the independent sector (see Chapter 2). Even after benefit was claimed, however, accommodation arrangements were still made direct, without the involvement of the local authority, and funding was conditional only on financial need.

9.1.4 Residential care homes and nursing homes

The complex history and development of the NHS alongside social services provision has meant that residential establishments have, for many years, provided places for those needing either 'social care' or 'nursing care', but without funding necessarily following the event. For example, the NHS has not consistently funded nursing home placements, notwithstanding its statutory responsibilities to provide nursing care, and local authorities have made nursing home arrangements under Sch 8 to the NHSA 1977. Meanwhile, individuals have made their own arrangements, at their own expense, for both personal and nursing care, and the market has responded to their needs. The DSS funded placements in either sector. Until the 1970s, the health service and social services were both run locally, which meant that a seamless web of service provision could more easily be maintained. After that, the complexity of funding arrangements, plus political and economic pressures, meant that elderly clients facing important decisions about future care found it very difficult to understand how the system worked.

9.1.5 Quality standards

A legal distinction between residential care homes and nursing homes has been made only in legislation which purports to lay down quality standards for all residential care provided by the independent sector. The NAA 1948 originally contained requirements for the registration, conduct and inspection of residential care homes, and the Nursing Homes Registration Act 1927 did the same for nursing homes – long before the NHS was set up. The legislation has been updated over the years, and the two strands are now consolidated in the Registered Homes Act 1984. The quality standards themselves, and the inspection process, are discussed in some detail in Chapter 10.

As will be seen, the changes brought about by the NHSCCA 1990 have meant that compliance carries greater economic importance than before April 1993.

9.2   The new regime: local authority responsibilities

From April 1993, Part III of the NAA 1948 is substantially amended by Part III of the NHSCCA 1990, and the power in Sch 8 to the NHSA 1977 to make residential arrangements in respect of illness and the after-care of illness has been removed. As has been seen, the policy of the legislation is to encourage local authorities to act as facilitators and purchasers of services rather than providers, and the new funding arrangements provide such 'encouragement' (see Chapter 2).

The purchasing power now extends to:

– residential care homes;
– nursing homes and mental nursing homes;
– homes which have a dual purpose (see Chapter 9).

The duty contained in s 21 of the NAA 1948 to 'make arrangements' as the Secretary of State directs remains. However, the description of the client group is amended to: 'persons who by reason of age, illness, disability or other circumstances are in need of care and attention which is not otherwise available to them' (s 21(1)). The explicit inclusion of 'illness' rather than infirmity in this description is the key to local authorities' new duties to make arrangements for nursing home care. Section 21(4) which provides for local authorities to exercise their functions by making residential care arrangements in their own premises survives intact, and the Government previously indicated that this function must be preserved for some users. The House of Lords has now undermined this position by its decision in *R v Wandsworth LBC ex parte Beckwith* (1995) *The Times*, 15 December. The overriding requirement to *purchase* services means that the focus of attention is now s 26 of the NAA 1948, which is considerably amended, and which imposes conditions on the exercise of the purchasing power.

9.2.1   Ordinary residence

As already observed, the NAA 1948 gave local authorities powers and duties to provide residential accommodation (and certain other welfare services) for people 'ordinarily resident' in their areas (s 24). The NHSCCA 1990 has not amended this provision. Ordinary residence is not defined by the Act, and the *Guidance* suggests that the concept should be given its natural meaning (Circular LAC(93)7). The courts have thrown some light on what this might be (see, for example, *Shah v London Borough of Barnet* [1983] 1 All ER 226), suggesting that ordinary residence depends on an act of volition based on an individual's appreciation of the 'regular order of his life'. It is apparent that most problems will arise in respect of people with learning disabilities who may lack the capacity to decide where to live, and may therefore be designated as having no settled residence. Section 24(3) of the NAA 1948 gives power to provide accommodation for people with no settled residence only where they are in 'urgent need'.

Section 24(6) of the NAA 1948 provides that a patient in an NHS hospital or NHS Trust hospital shall be deemed to be ordinarily resident in the area in which he was ordinarily resident before admission. The *Guidance* suggests that a person who makes his or her own residential care arrangements, will be considered to be ordinarily resident in the local authority area where the home is situated. Where, however, a local authority arranges a placement for an elderly person resident in its area, and purchases accommodation in the area of another local authority, ordinary residence will not alter and the purchasing authority will usually retain responsibility for the resident in the event, for example, of a new placement having to be made.

9.2.2 The extent of the local authority's enhanced powers

(i) A local authority may not make arrangements for an individual in any establishment providing nursing care without the consent of the health authority. The implications of this provision for hospital discharge procedures are described in Chapter 7. The Residential Accommodation (Determination of District Health Authority) Regulations 1992 identify the 'relevant' health authority in each case. In an emergency, the local authority may place a person in a temporary nursing home placement without reference to the health authority, but the necessary consent must be sought as soon as possible after that (s 26(1B), (1C) and (1D) of the NAA 1948).

(ii) As a general rule, arrangements may only be made with homes which are registered under Parts I or II of the RHA 1984, or are specifically exempt from registration. Since 1 April 1993, registration has been extended to 'small homes', which provide residential accommodation with board and personal care for fewer than four persons (relatives excepted) (Registered Homes (Amendment) Act 1991, amending s 1 of the RHA 1984). For further discussion see Chapter 10. As noted in Chapter 8, however, local authorities are likely to treat the registration standards as minimum requirements only (s 26(1A) and (1B) of the NAA 1948). In addition, authorities are expressly prohibited from making arrangements with providers who have been convicted of any offences created by the RHA 1984, or by regulations made under it (s 26(1E) of the NAA 1948). The range of such offences is broad; not all reflect directly on the 'fitness' of the provider to have care of elderly people (see, for example, s 5(5) of the RHA 1984).

Restricting local authority purchasing power to registered establishments was new; the NAA 1948 originally permitted residential accommodation arrangements to be made without such restriction. The effect was to render ultra vires placements made by the local authority in establishments such as Abbeyfield Homes, which do not provide 'board or personal care' within the definition in s 1 of the RHA 1984 and so do not fall within the scope of the registration system. Since such establishments are regarded as exemplifying best practice in community care, a small amendment was made to the drafting of the new s 26(1A) of the NAA 1948 by the Community Care (Residential Accommodation) Act 1992. This makes clear that the requirement to deal with registered premises applies only where the local authority is specifically making arrangements for 'board and personal care'. Arrangements may, therefore, be made without statutory restriction in establishments where a more independent regime is adopted, but they will of course be subject to the local authority's own service specifications.

(iii) Residential care homes must be inspected by the local authority's inspection unit. This is a new requirement, and goes beyond the inspection requirements laid down in the RHA 1984 (see Chapter 10).

(iv) Local authorities are also prevented from arranging accommodation under s 21 or s 26 of the NAA 1948 for any person who was ordinarily resident in relevant premises before 1 April 1993. 'Relevant premises' are residential care homes or nursing homes registered under the RHA 1984, or those exempt from registration, or 'such other premises' as are prescribed by regulations (s 26A of the NAA 1948).

The regulations referred to are the Residential Accommodation (Relevant Premises, Ordinary Residence and Exemptions) Regulations 1993.

Most people covered by this exclusion have 'preserved rights' to income support, and so can claim benefit to meet all, or most of the costs of a care bed. Nevertheless, advisers are increasingly coming across financial problems associated with it. (For further discussion, see Chapter 16.)

9.2.3   The gatekeeping role of the local authority

An elderly person who is having difficulty in managing at home, but who has insufficient resources to fund a care package for himself or herself must now ask the local authority to carry out an assessment of need. The authority must then decide whether it will provide services to meet the assessed needs and, assuming that the criteria in s 21 of the NAA 1948 are met, it will have a duty to make residential care arrangements, subject to the elderly person's wishes.

If, however, those assessed needs could be met more simply and more cheaply by providing services at home, the local authority will not be obliged to make arrangements for a residential placement, which means that there will be no State support with home fees. The argument is that residential care should not be used inappropriately at the public expense. The problem is that there is not enough provision in the community to remedy the social isolation and lack of simple day-to-day assistance which drives some older people to seek residential care. (For further discussion on assessment see Chapter 5.)

9.2.4 Individual choice of home

Assessments will specify whether residential care home or nursing home accommodation is required and whether an individual needs a place in a specialist unit, offering care to, for example, elderly people with dementia. The local authority will be expected to provide a range of options within this specification. Most authorities will publish lists of providers which they are prepared to recommend to users. In some instances, complaints have been made against local authorities on the basis that the choice offered is too narrow. If homes do not fulfil the criteria in ss 26 and 26(A) of the NAA 1948, they cannot be offered to users, but local authorities themselves may also create ineligibility by adopting overly stringent service specifications for their providers (see Chapter 8). Either way, choice will be restricted.

An underlying factor is cost. Because of the pressures on their budgets, local authorities will expect prices to be keen, and may simply ignore providers who cannot compete on price. One danger here is that large public limited company providers can offer residential accommodation at a lower unit cost than smaller more 'homelike' establishments, and already the growth of large residential units is being noted. Such a development clearly does not equate with community care policies and is driven wholly by market forces. Local authority lists will be similarly price driven.

Early research on the effects of the community care changes indicated that prices throughout the residential sector, but for nursing home care in particular, were being held down to former DSS rates. Bearing in mind that such rates did not usually match full bed fees, it is clear that prices have fallen, relatively speaking, since before April 1993 (*Taking Care*, Audit Commission, 1993). There is further evidence that some local authorities are placing in residential care homes people who would have had nursing home care before April 1993.

The Secretary of State has issued directions which are intended to ensure that people entering residential care homes or nursing homes have a genuine choice as to where they should live (National Assistance Act 1948 (Choice of

Accommodation) Directions 1992; Circular LAC(92)27; Circular LAC(93)18). The earlier Circular states that if a preference is expressed, the local authority must give effect to it provided that:

–   the accommodation chosen is suitable in relation to the individual's assessed needs;
–   to do so would not cost the authority more than it would usually expect to pay for accommodation for someone with the individual's assessed needs;
–   the accommodation is available;
–   the person in charge of the accommodation is prepared to accept the placement subject to the local authority's usual terms and conditions.

Cost factors underlie two of these four provisos. In particular, the local authority may argue against a preferred placement because it is too expensive by reference to other possible placements. The emphasis in the Direction is, however, on provision for equivalent needs, not cheaper and less appropriate provision. The local authority may not put a ceiling on what it is prepared to pay for residential placements, and must be prepared to meet appropriate fees of establishments which provide for certain types of need and deliver a service which is not available elsewhere. In *R v Avon County Council ex parte M* [1994] 2 FLR 1006, it was held that the local authority was obliged to provide residential accommodation which was appropriate to the assessed needs of the individual. In this case, that meant a placement outside the county which would cost £3,000 per year more than the local placement proposed by the authority.

The *Guidance* which accompanies the Direction on Choice makes it clear that local authorities may not restrict choice to their approved lists of providers. Suitability cannot reasonably be related to inclusion on a list, which is simply a convenient tool for placement when no preference is expressed.

9.2.5   Paying for choice

Paragraph 4 of the Direction deals with topping-up arrangements. Where a third party is able and willing to make a sufficient contribution towards the cost of the preferred placement, the local authority must, on principle, accede to the preference. The amount of the third party contribution will have to be the difference between the actual fee for the accommodation chosen and the amount that the local authority would usually expect to pay for someone with the individual's assessed needs. Bearing in mind that the contractual obligations to the provider will rest on the local authority (see Chapter 8), it will be entitled to satisfy itself that the offer of financial help is a serious one, and that there are resources to back it.

Third parties are likely, therefore, to be subjected to financial checks and may be asked to enter into a top-up contract with the local authority. They will be told that they must cover fee increases, which will not necessarily be apportioned equally between themselves and the local authority. In addition, they will be advised that, if fees are not met in the future, the local authority will normally move the resident to cheaper accommodation.

Third party contributions will be treated as part of a resident's income for charging purposes, and the local authority will be able to recover them through the financial assessment procedures (see Chapter 15). It should be noted, however, that local authorities need not engage in topping-up arrangements with 'liable relatives' (spouses: see Chapter 15) because they have a statutory duty to contribute to the cost of accommodation under s 42 of the NAA 1948, and an agreement to top-up would not pre-empt this. Elderly spouses should be advised that if the local authority accepts their offer to top up the fees of spouses in residential accommodation, the local authority will nevertheless retain the option of enforcing the liable relative obligation.

9.3 Residential care contracts

The contractual role of the local authority, as commissioner of services, has already been discussed in Chapter 8. Residential accommodation arrangements under s 21 of the NAA 1948 will be made between the local authority and the provider on behalf of a third party, the resident, whose identity may or may not be known, depending on the type of contract being used (see p 87).

9.3.1 Fees

The local authority will always contract to pay the accommodation fees in full and will then expect to recoup contributions from residents. The statutory duty to charge residents for their accommodation is laid down by s 22 of the NAA 1948 which also authorises means testing. The duty to impose and recover charges is, legally, quite independent of the s 21 duty and this important point is reinforced by the contractual structure which makes the local authority liable to pay providers the contracted price for beds, whether or not contributions are recovered from individual residents (s 26(2) of the NAA 1948). Providers have, therefore, a degree of security, despite the fact that the contracted fees may not be the best obtainable in the open market place.

Section 26(3A) of the NAA 1948 creates a different payment option. The local authority may agree with providers and with residents that contributions by the latter will be paid direct to the providers and not collected by the local authority. The advantage of such an arrangement (illustrated in Figure 5 below) is that it gives residents status vis-à-vis providers rather than leaving them as the objects of contractual arrangements made between third parties. Different contractual arrangements are possible under s 26(3A) but the net effect is to involve residents directly as 'part-purchasers' of their own care services, and this fits in with the user-led approach to community care emphasised in the White Paper. Legally, a resident will become 'liable' to pay his or her assessed contribution direct to the provider. The local authority, in turn, will make net payments to the provider. If a resident fails to meet payments, however, the local authority's obligation to the provider to cover the full cost of the bed is resumed and the local authority, not the provider, will then take steps to enforce the contribution. When this model is used there may be a single contract between local authority, provider and resident, or two linked contracts between local authority/provider and provider/resident. Many local authorities favour the latter approach.

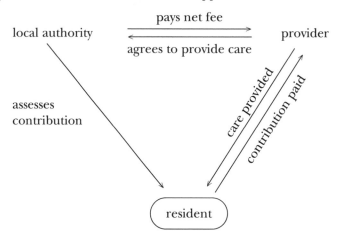

Figure 5. Contractual arrangements between local authorities, providers and residents made under s 26(3A) of the NAA 1948.

9.3.2   Standard terms and conditions

Apart from the standard form requirements discussed in Chapter 8 there are several clauses which the local authority will generally wish to include in contracts with providers of residential care:

(i)   a stipulation that the local authority care manager may enter and inspect the premises, at reasonable times, with or without notice. This is derived from s 26(5) of the NAA 1948 which gives a statutory power of inspection. The power is separate from the rights of inspection laid down in the Registered Homes Act 1984, and the implication is that providers will be subject to a good deal of inspection;

(ii) a stipulation that the contract will be terminated forthwith if the proprietor is convicted of any offence under the Registered Homes Act 1984 or regulations made under it. This is in line with s 26(1E) of the NAA 1948, previously discussed;

(iii) where the payment procedure authorised by s 26(3A) of the NAA 1948 is to be adopted, a stipulation that the provider must give the local authority (immediate) notice if the resident fails to pay an assessed contribution;

(iv) full details of what services are covered by the contract price and what, if any, will be regarded as 'extras' (see **9.5**);

(v) a possible stipulation that proprietors of homes or members of staff should not normally act as social security appointees for residents. In practice, where residents do not have relatives or friends who can take on this role, care managers may have to do so. There is, however, the potential for conflict of interest or for financial abuse and the local authority will certainly wish to be satisfied that the provider's financial procedures offer adequate safeguards for residents.

9.4 Private residential care arrangements

Nothing in the new legislation prevents elderly people from making their own private arrangements for residential care where they are in a position to fund it from their own resources. Two points, however, are worth emphasising.

(i) Just as the statutory responsibility of the local authority to make residential accommodation arrangements under s 21 of the NAA 1948 is independent of the duty to charge residents for their accommodation, so it is also independent of whether or not residents will or may need to rely on State financial support. The local authority may therefore be asked to arrange a placement for a person who will be able to fund it in full, perhaps indefinitely, provided that there is a need for such care. Chapter 5 includes a discussion on when s 47 assessments may be indicated for elderly clients with moderate means (see p 65). The local authority's purchasing power will be an influencing factor in the decision to seek assessment with a view to a residential placement being arranged. There is now anecdotal evidence that local authorities are purchasing residential care beds significantly more cheaply than individuals entering the same establishments under private arrangements. On the other hand, the limitations placed on individual choice in such circumstances, as discussed earlier in this chapter, may be a disincentive.

(ii) If private arrangements are made, it will be essential that elderly clients have the protection of a contract with the provider. Legal advisers should always insist on a contract and it will be helpful to make all clients aware of the importance of seeking legal advice before they make residential care arrangements. Paragraph **9.6** contains some detailed suggestions as to the issues which need to be addressed when negotiating residential care contracts on behalf of private clients.

9.5 Healthcare services for residents

Elderly people living in residential care homes and nursing homes will rely on NHS provision for most of their medical or health care needs, just as if they were still in their own homes. The *Guidance* issued to local authorities emphasises that contracts for independent sector residential care should not include provision of any service which it is the responsibility of the NHS to provide (Circular LAC(92)24).

The health authority in whose area the elderly person is usually resident must purchase appropriate community health services. In this context, basic NHS provision includes GP visits, district nursing services, physiotherapy, speech therapy and incontinence services and aids.

For those in residential care homes there seems to be a reasonably clear distinction between community health services and personal care. For nursing home residents, however, the demarcation is far from clear. Since nursing homes are supposed to deliver 'nursing' care, the *Guidance* states that local authorities must purchase services to meet the general needs of residents in this respect. Health authorities/GPs will be responsible for purchasing, 'within the resources available', specific services such as physiotherapy, plus 'specialist' nursing advice. Quite apart from the fact that it will be difficult to distinguish between general or specialist nursing advice, the *Guidance* also seems to indicate that health authorities have some discretion over what services they will purchase. This means that local authorities may end up by providing services which would more appropriately be labelled 'health', and will have to pass on the costs to residents wherever they can. Elderly people who purchase their own residential or nursing care should be advised to make enquiries as to the community health provision they can expect.

9.5.1   Incontinence services

Incontinence services which are not provided by the NHS can be a substantial addition to weekly home fees. Older people in residential care homes may find that incontinence supplies are charged for as 'extras'. This should always be questioned, for health authorities must publish criteria which should be even-handed between residents and users who live in their own homes. As far as nursing home residents are concerned, HSG(95)8 states that incontinence supplies should be included in the basic price of the bed and not provided by the NHS. Advice about incontinence is the responsibility of the community health services.

9.6   Practice points

(i) The local authority contracts should specify, in detail, all services covered by the contract price. It will be important for residents to know exactly what is already paid for and what are 'extras'. There is evidence that residents are being expected to use their personal expenses allowances to pay for items such as light refreshments, or even incontinence services. Some local authorities do not allow residents to keep their own personal allowance, but purport to distribute it for them. These practices undermine the policy already noted that the personal expenses allowance should be available to residents to spend as they wish.

(ii) Clients making private residential care arrangements must be advised of the importance of having a contract with the home, specifying details of services, quality standards and price. Advisers should seek to clarify arrangements for price increases. It is foreseeable that providers will try to make their margins on private arrangements if local authorities are driving a hard bargain on price.

Particular attention should be paid to:

–   how often fees are to be reviewed;
–   what services are included in fees (for example, personal laundry, hairdressing, physiotherapy, chiropody, outings, incontinence services);
–   the minimum period of notice to vacate the home;
–   the effect on fees of a resident's admission to hospital.

(iii) Sometimes it will be necessary to clarify whether residential care arrangements are temporary or permanent. When a client is in respite care the value of his or her home is not assessable under the Assessment of Resources Regulations 1992 (see Chapter 15). Once the arrangement becomes permanent there should be a re-assessment of resources, and appropriate information should be given to the resident.

(iv) Advisers should note the implications of Circular LAC(93)7, on ordinary residence.

If, for example, an elderly client who has previously lived in Leeds makes her own arrangements to enter a nursing home in Scarborough, but at some later stage needs financial assistance from the local authority, North Yorkshire County Council, not Leeds City Council, will be responsible for assessment and future service provision.

It will be sensible, therefore, to advise the client to give notice to North Yorkshire of her presence, and if local authority funding is likely to be needed, to investigate North Yorkshire's policy and practice regarding residential placements.

Chapter 10

RESIDENTIAL CARE – QUALITY ASSURANCE

'Living in a Residential Establishment should be a positive experience ensuring a better quality of life than the resident could enjoy in any other setting' (*Residential Care: A Positive Choice*, HMSO, 1988).

The implementation of the new community care system has once again highlighted public concern about the quality of care provided for older people in residential establishments. Hardly a month goes by without publication of individual horror stories involving neglect or abuse of vulnerable older residents, or of surveys which purport to identify poor standards of care. There is now considerable public awareness that the Government's willingness throughout the 1980s to fund beds via the social security system (see Chapter 2) probably created a market in which some providers of services were more interested in profit than in caring.

Yet, legislation has been in place for some time laying down minimum quality standards and creating a registration and inspection process which should at least guarantee decent living conditions and protection from harm. This chapter will review the quality assurance standards now set out in the Registered Homes Act 1984 and subordinate legislation, and will consider the gloss added by Part III of the NHSCCA 1990. It will then address, very briefly, best practice and the checks and balances in the new social care market which are capable of promoting best practice.

10.1   The Registered Homes Act 1984

The Registered Homes Act 1984 consolidated various pieces of earlier legislation, dating back to 1948. There was, in particular, a flurry of legislative activity during the 1980s, which was mainly a response to the rapid expansion in private sector care, fuelled by demographic changes and by the availability of public funds. Between 1976 and 1986, for example, there was a growth of about 260% in the number of places in private residential care homes, and between 1982 and 1986, numbers of private nursing home beds increased by 132% (Parker, 1990). The legislative intention was to raise standards of care generally and evenly, and to ensure 'that no homes are inadequately run by people who are inadequately experienced, trained or equipped' (Hansard, 24.3.83, col 354).

The Act seeks to achieve its objectives by means of an accreditation or registration process; minimum quality standards are prescribed and sanctions such as deregistration or even criminal prosecution built in. Codes of Practice

(Home Life: A Code of Practice for Residential Care, 1984; Registration and Inspection of Nursing Homes; a Handbook for Health Authorities, NAH, 1985) are added to promote better or best practice, but are not legally binding.

10.2   Quality standards

The Residential Care Homes Regulations 1984 and the Nursing Homes and Mental Nursing Homes Regulations 1984 list minimum standards for residential establishments in terms of activities to be performed, records to be kept and facilities and services to be provided. In each set of regulations, 'adequate' facilities and services are specified. For residential care homes, the concept of adequacy is left undefined, but for nursing homes it means 'sufficient and suitable'. Either way there is clearly scope for variation in interpretation of the standards laid down. In addition, it is quite clear that registration authorities may impose their own standards, in excess of the minimum requirement. For example, some local authorities will restrict the size of home that they will register, although the regulations make no reference to size.

The Residential Care Homes Regulations 1984 emphasise that first consideration must be given to the need to safeguard and promote the welfare of the resident when making any decision affecting his or her care, and to ascertaining and giving due weight to his or her wishes and feelings, so far as is practicable. Significantly, neither set of nursing home regulations contains such a principle.

Regulation 10 provides a good illustration of the nature, and the limitations, of the present regulatory system. It describes the facilities and services to be provided, which include:

–   by day and, where necessary, by night enough suitably qualified and competent staff in numbers which are adequate for the well-being of residents;
–   'reasonable' day and night-time accommodation and space;
–   adequate and suitable furniture, bedding, curtains, floor covering and other equipment;
–   'sufficient' washing facilities;
–   adaptations and facilities necessary for physically handicapped residents;
–   suitable, varied and properly cooked wholesome and nutritious food;
–   suitable arrangements for the recording, safekeeping, handling and disposal of drugs;
–   suitable arrangements for the training, occupation and recreation of residents;
–   arrangements for residents to receive medical and dental services.

Regulation 11 requires that suitable facilities for private visits to residents be provided. Regulation 10(1) emphasises that these requirements must be interpreted relative to the size of the home and the number, age, sex and condition of residents.

It will be seen that reg 10 focuses on the maintenance of physical standards, and the safety of residents, which is characteristic of the legislation as a whole. The Codes of Practice referred to in **10.1** show a similar emphasis on best practice so far as it relates to the maintenance of acceptable physical standards of care. More recently, however, the Social Services Inspectorate has, through *Guidance*, addressed the importance of basic values which contribute to the quality of life of residents ('Homes are for Living In', 1992). These are:

– privacy: the right of individuals to be left alone or undisturbed and free from intrusion;
– dignity: recognition of the intrinsic value of people regardless of circumstances by respecting their uniqueness and their personal needs;
– independence: the opportunity to act and think without reference to another person, including willingness to incur a degree of calculated risk;
– choice: the opportunity to select independently from a range of options;
– rights: the maintenance of all entitlements which are associated with citizenship;
– fulfilment: the realisation of personal aspirations and abilities in all aspects of daily life.

In practice, the maintenance of such values may not infrequently cut across physical quality standards, particularly insofar as the latter are concerned with safety and the elimination of risks. There is now some evidence that stringent application of regulatory standards by registration authorities can create tensions with care providers who are trying to achieve care in a 'homely' setting.

10.3 The scope of the Registered Homes Act 1984

The registration scheme applies to independent residential care homes and nursing homes, but not to Part III accommodation owned and/or managed by the local authority. The Act creates two parallel accreditation systems which are almost, but not quite, mirror images of one another. Part I is concerned with the registration and conduct of residential care homes, which are defined as establishments providing residential accommodation with both board and personal care for 'persons in need of personal care by reason of old age, disablement, past or present dependence on alcohol or drugs, or past or present mental disorder'. Part II is concerned with nursing homes and mental nursing homes. Section 21 refers to premises used 'for the reception of, and the provision of nursing for, persons suffering from any sickness, injury or infirmity'. Section 22 refers to the provision of nursing or other medical treatment for mentally disordered patients.

It becomes immediately apparent that the demarcation envisaged by the Act between residential care homes and nursing homes is not at all clear cut.

Indeed, the distinction made between 'personal care' and 'nursing care' reflects a central dilemma for health authorities and local authorities – ie in drawing the boundary lines between health and social care. Section 20(1) defines personal care as 'care which includes assistance with bodily functions where such assistance is required'. This echoes the conditions for legal entitlement to the attendance allowance or the disability living allowance (care component) (see Chapter 19). Bodily functions include eating, drinking, walking, hearing, seeing, washing and using the toilet. In *Harrison v Cornwall County Council* 90 LGR 81, however, the Court of Appeal held that the fact that residents in a care home neither require nor receive assistance with bodily functions does not prevent them from being persons who require or who are provided with personal care. 'Nursing' is not defined at all in the Act.

The *Guidance* suggests that personal care delivered in residential care homes should be regarded as an extension of the sort of care that would be provided in a private home by a caring relative. This might include 'household nursing' tasks like changing simple dressings, administering medication and managing incontinence. However, the concept of nursing care used in the Act implies a degree of professionalism and also the use of technical and potentially invasive procedures, such as the administration of injections, the management of bed sores, the dressing of serious wounds, and rehabilitation after surgery. Although this distinction is patently vague and unsatisfactory it has important financial consequences, since nursing home fees are considerably higher than fees in residential care homes.

10.4   Registration of residential care homes

All establishments falling within the scope of Part I of the RHA 1984 must be registered by the local authority social services department (s 20(1)). The Act speaks throughout of the registration of persons rather than of premises. So, for example, a person who carries on a residential care home without being registered in respect of it commits an offence under s 2. Consequently, if a home is sold as a going concern, the registration does not run with it, and the new owner will have to seek registration on his own account. An outgoing owner does not, however, have to give notice to the registration authority that he is about to cease running the home. The social services department must, therefore, use its power to enter and inspect under s 17 where it has reasonable cause to suspect that an unregistered establishment is operating in its area.

Section 12 contains power for the registration authority to cancel a registration. A conviction for carrying on an unregistered establishment does not permit automatic cancellation but it may go some way towards demonstrating that an owner is not a 'fit' person to manage the home (see **10.6**). Part III of the NHSCCA 1990 has now added considerable weight to the power to prosecute under the Act by preventing the local authority from purchasing residential care from a provider with any conviction under the RHA 1984 (s 26(1E) of the NAA 1948).

Where a home is managed by one person and that person is not 'in control' of it (whether as owner or otherwise), both the manager and the owner/person in control are to be treated as carrying on the home, and both are, therefore, required to be registered. A person can manage more than one home. The term 'owner' refers to ownership of the business which controls the operation of the home, and not necessarily to ownership of the building. There can also be more than one owner (s 3).

10.5   Registration of nursing homes

Health authorities are at present the registration authorities for nursing homes and mental nursing homes. Section 23 of the RHA 1984 provides that any person (corporation) who carries on an establishment described in s 21 or s 22 without registration is guilty of an offence. Once again, the registration is personal and does not run with the home. There is, however, no equivalent of s 3 in this part of the Act. In other words, the person registered in respect of a nursing home or mental nursing home need not also be the person in charge (manager), and the person in charge need not be registered. The registration authority will, however, be concerned to ensure that both the person registered and the person in charge are 'fit' people and, in particular, registration may be refused if the person in charge is not either a registered medical practitioner or a qualified nurse (s 25(1)).

10.6   Refusal of registration

Registration may be refused under s 9 or s 25 where the registration authority has concerns about the 'fitness' of those who run a home, the fitness of the premises themselves or the way in which the establishment is to be run. In addition, registration of a nursing home may be refused if the home is not in the charge of a registered medical practitioner or a qualified nurse, or if it has insufficient nursing staff. For registered care homes, the registration authority will be concerned with the fitness for registration of the applicant and of any other person concerned or intended to be concerned in carrying on the home (s 9(1)). In this context, such a person could include someone who is concerned with the financial administration arrangements rather than with the day-to-day care of residents. For nursing homes, however, s 25 extends the concept of unfitness beyond owners and managers to 'any person employed' in the home.

The Act contains no definition of 'fitness' or 'fit person'. Decisions of the Registered Homes Tribunal suggests that fitness speaks for itself. A fit person is one who is upright and honourable, who inspires confidence, and who acts in a principled way. A person will therefore be unfit if he or she is untrustworthy, dishonest or exploitative. In practice, however, questions of possible unfitness range from marriage breakdowns to previous criminal convictions; from failure to keep records and comply with fire regulations to lack of managerial skills and setting up an authoritarian regime.

The Act permits conditional registration (s 5(3)) but it has been held that the imposition of conditions is a derogation from the primary duty of the registration authority to make the registration unless one of the grounds for refusal in s 9 applies. The courts have, therefore, construed s 5(3) narrowly, saying that conditions may only be imposed as to matters mentioned there – namely the age, gender or category of residents who may be cared for in the home (*Warwickshire County Council v McSweeney*, unreported, 1988).

It has also been held that, in imposing any conditions, a local authority must act fairly and reasonably, and that policies which postulate conditional registration (for example regarding maximum numbers of residents) should similarly be fair, reasonable and also transparent (*Isle of Wight County Council v Humphreys* (1991) 90 LGR 186).

Section 5(4) provides that a registration authority may on an application from a registered proprietor or on its own instigation vary a condition of registration or impose an additional condition or conditions. If a registered proprietor makes an unsuccessful application under s 5(4) there is no right of appeal to the Registered Homes Tribunal because s 15(1) provides a right of appeal only against a *decision* of a registration authority (*Coombs v Hertfordshire County Council* (1991) 89 LGR 774).

10.7 Small homes

The Registered Homes Act 1984 originally excluded from the requirement to register, homes which provided board and personal care for fewer than four people. The position changed in April 1993 with the implementation of the Registered Homes (Amendment) Act 1991, when a modified form of regulatory control was established for such homes.

It is now an offence to operate an unregistered small home unless it is exempt from the requirement to register. The Secretary of State may prescribe such exemption – for example, in respect of respite care. In particular, registration is specifically not required in respect of a home which provides care for fewer than four people all of whom are proprietors or employees of the business or their relatives. This means that individuals who look after elderly relatives are not required to register. The Act does not, however, prevent them from registering, and since financial benefits may accrue from registration (for instance, residents may become eligible for increased income support payments) there is some need for clarification on this point.

In general, registration may only be refused in respect of a small home if a person involved in running the home is not a 'fit' person. There is no equivalent special treatment for any type of nursing home care. All nursing establishments, however small, are registrable under the mainstream provisions of the Registered Homes Act 1984.

10.8 Dual registration

The 1984 Act envisages the possibility of dual registration, and many establishments seek this, ostensibly in order to avoid residents having to be transferred from one home to another as their physical condition deteriorates. In the present market, however, there may be powerful economic reasons for dual registration.

An establishment seeking dual registration will have to be accredited and subsequently monitored by both registration authorities, and double registration fees will have to be paid. These requirements create an administrative burden for the establishment and there is a need for co-operation over procedures, particularly inspections. The net effect of the dual registration provisions is that a residential care home which provides nursing care for any resident must additionally be registered as a nursing home and must have either a doctor or a nurse as the 'person in charge'. Nursing homes which provide personal care for four or more patients must also be registered as care homes; where personal care is provided for fewer than four patients, however, there is an option of additional registration either as a care home or as a 'small' home. Full registration here means that higher fee levels will apply.

A recent survey conducted by the Royal College of Nursing (*A Scandal Waiting to Happen?*, 1992) revealed that there is an overwhelming impression among nurses of a false divide between residential and nursing homes. Differential rates of income support before April 1993 may have had something to do with this, because payment followed the placement whether or not it was appropriate for the needs of the individual claimant. The new assessment procedure, coupled with the change in the way State subsidies are paid, should mean that people are more appropriately placed in future, but there is still strong evidence that all people entering residential care nowadays are increasingly old, increasingly dependent and increasingly frail. In the survey, dual registration was highlighted as a way of providing residential care that can meet people's changing needs.

Comments made were along the following lines:

> 'Dual registration enables a resident to move from one category of care to another without moving into another establishment';

or again:

'If all homes were dual registered it would solve many problems. There would be no necessity to seek hospital or nursing home admission if the patient's condition deteriorated.'

Respondents were clearly aware of the emphasis in the Wagner Report on the importance of providing continuity of care in one setting (*Residential Care: A Positive Choice*, HMSO, 1988). The following comment was typical:

'The Government White Paper states that its aim is to provide resources to keep patients in the community in their own homes for as long as possible. Many people have lived in residential homes for many years – this is their home. Therefore resources are needed to provide nursing care in residential homes.'

10.9   Cancellation of registration

Sections 10 and 28 of the RHA 1984 allow registration authorities to cancel registration on any ground which would enable them to refuse an initial application for registration; or because the annual fee (per bed) has not been paid; or on the basis of a conviction of a criminal offence under the Act or failure to comply with a condition of registration. The registration authority itself makes any decision as to cancellation, and must give notice of its intention, with the underlying reasons, to the registered person (s 12(4) and (5)). That person may make representation to the authority (s 13) and, ultimately, there is a right of appeal to an independent Registered Homes Tribunal (s 15).

There is also, however, an urgent procedure for cancellation of registration, which requires an application by the registration authority to the magistrates' court for a cancellation order (ss 11 and 30). The application must be based on one of the ordinary grounds for cancellation described above and may be made ex parte to a single magistrate. An order may only be made, however, where it appears that there will be a serious risk to the life, health or well-being of the residents in the home concerned if it is not made. Once again, the Act contains no definition of 'serious risk' but it is clear from the case-law that the urgent procedures should be used only in exceptional circumstances where, for example, there is evidence of physical, sexual or financial abuse of residents.

The same urgent procedure may be used to achieve a variation in any condition attached to the original registration or to impose additional conditions. Appeal against any decision lies to the Registered Homes Tribunal.

Cancellation of a registration by either the normal or the urgent procedure will not inevitably result in the closure of a home. Neither registration authority has power to enforce closure or to take over the management of the home, although their officers have a right of access under their inspection powers (see **10.10**). Continued operation of a home which no longer carries registration does, however, render the management open to prosecution. In the final analysis, however, if further action is needed to protect residents the registration authority may seek an injunction to close the home or else invoke the magistrates' powers under s 47 of the NAA 1948 to order removal of the residents, in their own interests, to other establishments. In doing so, the co-operation of the community physician will be required. Research suggests that such disruption has a very serious effect on frail, perhaps confused, elderly people; for many it will be a death sentence.

10.10   The inspection process

Section 17 of the RHA 1984 gives social services departments power, at any time, to enter and inspect premises which are used or reasonably believed to be used for the purposes of a residential care home. Advance notice is not required. There is a similar provision in s 35 which refers to mental nursing homes, and a further power to inspect ordinary nursing homes is given by reg 10 of the Nursing Homes and Mental Nursing Homes Regulations 1984. Establishments carrying dual registration are subject to inspection by both registration authorities, and joint inspection is desirable to prevent undue disruption and to maintain consistency in approach.

One purpose of inspection is clearly to investigate unauthorised establishments in order to protect the interests of residents. Many small seaside boarding houses fall within the definition of a residential care home contained in s 1 of the Act, and should be subjected to the standards laid down by the Act. In addition, inspection provides a means of enforcing the regulatory standards in premises which are already registered. The minimum requirement is that residential care homes should be inspected at least once a year, and nursing homes at least twice a year.

The White Paper on community care emphasised that securing and safeguarding the quality of services for elderly people must be a central objective for all agencies involved in the delivery of community care. To this end, it proposed that local authorities should set up independent inspection units under the director of social services, with responsibility for inspecting and reporting on both local authority Part III homes and registrable independent residential care homes. This was implemented by s 48 of the NHSCCA 1990. The inclusion of a requirement that local authority managed homes should be subject to inspection and quality assurance was a major step forward, but it meant that the new inspection units have to be seen as being at 'arm's length' from day-to-day supervision and management of homes by the social services department (LAC(90)13 and LAC(94)16). Technically, responsibility for inspecting independent sector homes is still vested in the social services department under s 17 of the RHA 1984, and the department must therefore delegate this responsibility to the new inspection units.

10.10.1 Inspection units

All local authorities were required to have new inspection units in place by April 1991, and the Social Services Inspectorate has been responsible for monitoring the implementation process. It was intended that the units should undertake inspection of all local authority residential care homes and the registration and inspection of registered private and voluntary residential care homes. It is also intended that they will increasingly develop and monitor quality assurance programmes.

As part of this process, the inspection unit may advise on staff training or on equipment or alterations which would help a home to provide better care or may work with managers on reviewing their attitudes to service delivery.

Where inspection reveals unacceptable practices or abuse of elderly residents, the inspection unit may serve notice that, if changes are not carried out, steps will be taken to deregister and so, effectively, to close the home. When it comes to initial registration or cancellation of registration, however, social services departments have no power to delegate their function to the inspection units. This separation of inspection/quality assurance functions from enforcement responsibilities seems questionable.

10.10.2 Inspecting nursing homes

Also questionable is the fact that the community care legislation has not specifically affected the registration and inspection responsibilities of health authorities in relation to nursing homes and mental nursing homes. Policy *Guidance* states that 'effective collaboration between local authorities and health authorities in the management of their quality control systems will be vital', but bearing in mind that social services departments are now responsible for purchasing the majority of nursing home beds, and will be seeking to impose service specifications by contractual means, this failure to impose joint working between local authorities and health authorities is regrettable. In some local areas, co-operation has gone beyond the requirements of the legislation, and joint inspection units combining health and local authority inspectors have been set up.

10.10.3 Lay assessors

From October 1994, the DoH has required the involvement of lay assessors in the inspection process (LAC(94)16).

Assessors should now take part in all full inspections of adult residential homes which care for people with high levels of dependency and disability and full inspections of all other independent homes for adults at least once every three years. In addition, they must take part in annual inspections of Part III accommodation.

Assessors are expected to add the views of users, families and the wider community to the inspection process. They are expected to be people with no direct or professional responsibility for the purchasing or provision of services, and may include former or present users, their relatives and friends.

10.11   Inspection and quality assurance

As an evaluative process, inspection clearly offers a vehicle for enhancing quality and promoting best practice beyond the modest legal requirements of the Regulations. On the other hand, the still fragmented inspection process and even the continued absence of universally accepted standards all create obstacles. There is, for example, a real dilemma for the inspection units in determining how far to go in addressing bad practice which is not, technically, a breach of regulations.

At this point, the question of individual rights becomes important. Whilst the RHA 1984 was concerned to provide appropriate standards for those in residential care, the accreditation model itself ignored individual rights. The Act, for example, makes no reference to consultation with residents (*R v Devon County Council ex parte Baker* [1995] 1 All ER 73) and provides no *locus standi* for individual residents to bring complaints before the Registered Homes Tribunal. Although individuals now have the option of invoking general complaints procedures (see Chapter 13) the legislation still does not require homes to have written contracts with individual residents.

It may be, however, that the best agent for promoting quality assurance will be private law, via the contracts made between local authorities and providers of residential care. It is now established that local authorities may insist on the inclusion of service specifications which exceed the regulatory standards, and that they may use their purchasing power, with or without the assistance of the courts, to ensure that the specifications are met (see Chapter 8).

Chapter 11

CARERS

'Care in the community . . . usually means care by the family, and especially female relatives, not the community' (*A Crisis in Care?*, FPSC, 1994).

'When my wife was in hospital, it took four nurses to lift and turn her; now she's at home I have to do it all on my own. Is that what they call Community Care?' (60-year-old carer, quoted in Pitkeathley, *It's My Duty, Isn't It?*, 1989).

The family is overwhelmingly the main source of care for older people. In the European Union as a whole, about two-thirds of all 'care' is given informally within the family. The main burden is often borne by one family member, and that person tends to be a woman (between 60% and 80% of family carers are women). In the UK, there are more than 6 million informal carers, 75% of whom look after elderly people. Most carers are spouses, or adult children.

Many people, of course, gain satisfaction from caring, but a substantial body of research draws attention to the strains and pressures associated with the caring role. There are emotional costs: the pain of witnessing the decline of a loved older relative; the loss of independence involved; the strain on carers' other family relationships. There are also physical costs: many carers are in poor health and there is evidence of physical strain, back pain, and psychosomatic illness. Caring for someone with a mental disorder is particularly stressful. In fact, 50% of all carers of people with dementia spend more than 80 hours per week in caring; 97% of such carers suffer some form of emotional difficulty and 36% have physical problems, such as back pain, associated with caring (*Deprivation and Dementia*, Alzheimer's Disease Society, 1993).

There is also some evidence that families are becoming less willing to care for elderly relatives suffering from conditions such as Alzheimer's disease. Bearing in mind that the numbers suffering from mental disorders of this type are projected to rise by 30% between 1990 and 2020, any substantial reluctance to provide care will create a major challenge for social policy over the next few years.

Caring also carries financial costs: loss of earnings, associated with additional expenditure. Carers' personal incomes are lower than those of non-carers. Furthermore, households composed of care-givers and recipients of care have substantially lower incomes than similar sized households where there is no caring relationship. Carers find it difficult to save, and are often under pressure to spend existing capital (*The Costs of Informal Care* Glendinning, 1992). There is evidence too, that many carers meet from their own resources expenses which arise directly from the needs of the person cared for, such as extra heating, laundry, clothing, bedding and toiletries. The main source of Government financial support specifically directed at carers is the invalid care allowance, which is insufficient to live on (£36.60 per week in 1996/97), and is restricted in its scope. Consequently, many carers have to top up with means-tested benefits. There is also some protection for the pension entitlements of carers who give up their employment.

Regardless of the known facts about caring, implementation of the NHSCCA 1990 has done nothing, legally, to empower carers, nor have there been any associated financial benefits. Indeed, first impressions of the new system are that day-to-day domiciliary services are taking the brunt of social services expenditure cuts and that people who do receive informal care from family or friends are less likely to obtain services than those who are entirely alone (*Mapping the Change: No Time to Lose*, Age Concern, 1993).

This chapter will look at assessment and service provision from the carers' perspective.

11.1   Assessment

The *Policy Guidance* on community care acknowledges the role of carers and the importance of partnership between carer, user and statutory authority:

> 'The assessment will need to take account of the support that is available from ... carers. They should feel that the overall provision of care is a shared responsibility between them and the statutory authorities and that the relationship between them is one of mutual support. The preferences of carers should be taken into account and their willingness to continue caring should not be assumed' (para 3.28).

Notwithstanding the *Guidance*, the NHSCCA 1990 itself makes no direct reference to carers. By implication, s 47 of the Act permits carers to request assessments of need for those for whom they care, but it falls far short of s 4 of the DP(SCR)A 1986, which explicitly requires a local authority to assess a disabled person when requested to do so by a carer. The *Policy Guidance* states that carers are entitled to be involved in the assessment process itself, with the agreement of those being cared for (para 3.16). Carers should also expect to be informed of the outcome of the assessment. Section 8 of the DP(SCR)A 1986 goes further in requiring the local authority, when assessing the needs of a disabled person, to have regard to the ability of a carer to continue providing care on a regular basis. It creates, however, no obligation to follow that up by providing services or support.

Most critically, however, s 47 of the NHSCCA 1990 requires social services departments to assess the needs only of someone who may need community care services, and to determine provision in respect of the needs of that person alone. Accordingly, carers have no entitlement to an assessment under the NHSCCA 1990 unless they need services themselves, perhaps because they are disabled – which is not infrequently the case when elderly spouses are also carers. This restriction applies even to an assessment for respite care which is primarily in the interests of the carer, but is nevertheless regarded as a service provided for the recipient of care.

The *Guidance* recognises that carers may themselves be in need of community care services, and that they may ask to be assessed in their own right (para 3.29). It is clear, however, that this option has not been available for every carer. In 1994, following a year-long study of 100 carers of people with dementia, the Alzheimer's Disease Society found that: 59 care givers had received no assessment whatsoever; 13 had been separately assessed; 61 had not been offered a regular review of their needs (*Deprivation and Dementia*, 1994). A study by the Carers National Association reported similar findings in June 1995. Most respondents saw few, or no benefits at all in the new community care regime (*Better Tomorrows*, 1995).

In the event of assessment being offered to a carer, the Guidance gives no assistance on whose needs will be paramount – the primary user, or the secondary user/carer – or on how conflicts might be resolved. This issue is increasingly being linked with the withdrawal of services by local authorities in circumstances where informal care arrangements exist.

The Consultation Paper on community care charters states that carers have 'an entitlement to expect' that:

–   their views and ideas will be listened to;
–   they will be involved in assessments and the inspection of care homes and other services;
–   their ability and willingness to care will be taken into account;
–   they will be offered a separate assessment if they want one;
–   they will be entitled to a written copy of the care plan.

Notwithstanding the rhetoric, however, the lack of an explicit right to assessment 'qua' carer has caused concern for some time. In 1990, for example, a House of Lords amendment to the original NHSCC Bill, creating a duty to assess carers, was rejected. At the time of writing, however, a fresh initiative is under way: the Carers (Recognition and Services) Act (which originated as a private Member's Bill with all-party support) has reached the statute book, and will be implemented in April 1996. Its advent is timely, given the evidence of increasingly early discharge from hospital of elderly people needing a high level of care (see Chapter 2).

11.2   Carers (Recognition and Services) Act 1995

The Act provides that where a local authority assesses the needs of an elderly person under s 47(1)(a) of the NHSCCA 1990, and the carer provides or intends to provide a 'substantial amount of care on a regular basis' for that person, the carer may ask the local authority to assess his or her ability to provide and to continue to provide care for the elderly person before determining care for the elderly person (s 1(1)).

Having done so, the local authority must then take into account the result of that assessment in making its decision as to services for the elderly person. In this context, 'carer' excludes someone who is employed to care, or who acts as a volunteer for a voluntary organisation (s 1(3)).

Legal advisers should note that the Act creates a 'piggyback' right. A carer is entitled to a separate assessment only where the person cared for has had, or is having an assessment of need under s 47 of the NHSCCA 1990. Sometimes elderly clients who are comfortably off may not wish to be assessed by the local authority and will be content to rely on a caring relationship, supplemented perhaps by services which they purchase themselves. The perspective of the carer may be different and conflicts of interest may therefore arise.

There is likely to be some debate as to when care is 'substantial' and provided on a 'regular basis'. Entitlement to the invalid care allowance is based on caring 'regularly and substantially' for a disabled person, and this requirement is met by giving care for 35 hours per week or more. If, in any week, care falls below 35 hours it is not regular and substantial, and benefit is not payable (SSCBA 1992, s 70; ICA Regulations 1970, reg 4). The Government has made it clear, however, that it is up to local authorities to determine the meaning of 'regular' and 'substantial'. Clearly, the test will be subjective; what is 'substantial' for a frail older person may not be so for a middle-aged person in excellent health.

Finally, it is clear that, while the Act creates a right to assessment for carers, it creates no rights to services. The local authority must determine whether the assessed needs of the elderly person call for some provision. The implication is, however, that any services provided by the local authority will reflect the carer's ability to cope, as well as the needs of the elderly person. 'Assessment' must look at the circumstances of the whole family or the whole situation in which a person will be cared for. '... Although the elderly person did not mention respite care, the carer is crying out for it, and among the services that we will provide, albeit to the cared-for person, respite care will be there regularly' (Hansard HC vol 258, col 432 and vol 564, col 630). The aim will therefore be to bring together the needs identified by the two assessments into one care plan. Services which would assist carers to go on providing care might include:

–   provision of day centres (NAA 1948, s 29);
–   night sitter services (NHSA 1977, Sch 8);
–   home help and laundry facilities (NHSA 1977, s 21 and Sch 8);
–   recreational facilities (HSPHA 1968, s 45); and
–   above all, respite care (NAA 1948, s 21).

Nevertheless, the question remains: what will be the position, for example, when a carer wants/needs a day centre placement for an elderly relative when the latter prefers to remain at home? Such tensions are, of course, an inescapable part of the caring process, but the Act offers no obvious resolution.

11.3   Respite care

The service most likely to enhance a carer's ability to continue caring may be respite care. The local authority may arrange such care under s 21 of the NAA 1948. It is also worth noting that the new *Guidance* on NHS responsibilities for meeting continuing health care needs (discussed at pp 30 and 75) emphasises that respite health care is an integral part of NHS provision for elderly and incapacitated people. Reference is made to a duty to address the needs of people who are receiving 'palliative' care at home, where they, or their carers, need a period of respite care (Annex A, para F). There are strong arguments in favour of targeting resources towards respite care in order to postpone or avert the need for full-time residential care. Hopefully, new schemes jointly funded by health authorities and social services departments (NHSA 1977, s 28) will begin to fill the present yawning gap in respite care provision.

The Carers (Recognition and Services) Act 1995 impliedly designates respite care as a service for carers, rather than for people in need of care. At present, however, provision is based not on the caring role, but on assessment of the person in need of care and, possibly, of the carer. If the service 'user' does not need respite care but the carer does, the local authority has to resolve that conflict. Clearly, if the carer is not assessed at all the conflict will not necessarily be made explicit, unless there is stringent consultation with the carer during the primary assessment.

A recent High Court ruling on judicial review may presage a spate of applications by carers. In *R v North Yorkshire County Council ex parte Hargreaves* (Lexis transcript QBD, 30 September 1994), Dyson J upheld a carer's application to review the local authority's decision to alter a long-standing respite care arrangement on the basis of a new assessment of the user's needs. The decision was quashed because the latter's preferences had not been taken into account by the local authority, in breach of paras 3.16 and 3.25 of the Policy *Guidance.* The decision emphasises the importance of the *Guidance* itself; the judge ruled that decisions made in breach of it will be unlawful. It also emphasises that a carer is entitled to seek a review of service provision based on the assessed needs of someone else.

From April 1996, carers may wish to press their own claims to respite care services. Conflict between the wishes and needs of the carer and the person cared for is entirely foreseeable, and once again legal advisers must ask themselves: 'who is my client?'.

11.4   Charging carers for services

11.4.1   Home-care services

As noted in Chapter 17, local authorities have power to levy reasonable charges for non-residential care services (HASSASSAA 1983, s 17). Most, but not all of these services are also 'community care services' (see Chapter 4).

As already observed, the Carers (Recognition and Services) Act 1995 does not distinguish 'carers' services' from services for primary users. Bearing in mind that local authorities are now increasingly operating means tests for home-care services the decision as to 'who' has the benefit of a particular service may carry financial implications. This issue might become a further complicating factor in the relationship between carer and primary user. It remains to be seen what strategy local authorities will adopt. It may indeed be argued that, in principle, no charges at all should be made to carers because their efforts are mitigating the financial obligations of the State (but see **11.4.2**).

11.4.2   Respite care

Short breaks in residential care (up to eight weeks) may attract a charge. The local authority has discretion, however, not to apply the statutory means test, but to charge a flat fee, irrespective of means. The fee will often be lower than the standard bed fee for a permanent resident (ss 22(5A) and 26(4) of the NAA 1948). The legislation makes it clear that the person to be charged is the resident, not the carer. Nevertheless, some local authorities regularly assess the resources of the carer in determining a charge for respite care ('Charging Consumers for Social Services', National Consumer Council, 1995).

11.5   Complaints by carers

Section 50 of the NHSCCA 1990 permits carers to make complaints on behalf of service users. In addition, the Complaints Procedure Directions 1990 provide that a carer making a complaint has the same rights as the service user to make representations, to receive information and to have notification of the recommendations made. These provisions will be of assistance to carers in situations where service users are too frail or too confused to take the initiative themselves.

11.6   Future indicators

Research conducted all over Europe shows that changes in family lifestyles over the past generation, coupled with economic forces, may have brought about a further, cultural change as regards attitudes towards care. Families may now be less willing to offer care than in the past, especially (as noted) where the person needing care has dementia. In addition, there is hard evidence that older people's preferences are changing. In 1992, a British Gallup Poll Survey found that nearly three out of five people over 65 thought that the responsibility for long-term care should shift to the State. There now seems an expressed reluctance to place a major burden on informal carers and a desire to see community-based, professional care. There are also indications that the older generation no longer feels that adult children should take responsibility for their parents to the extent of becoming 'front line carers'.

All this suggests that the underlying assumptions on which community care strategies are undoubtedly based – that families 'will' care – may be misplaced. As yet, UK law recognises no obligation to care for older family members (unlike Germany, for example). That may change; introducing legal responsibility for financial maintenance is no doubt under consideration. Whatever emerges, there may be a mismatch between individual perceptions of where the family/State interface should be, and the State's likely allocation or re-allocation of family responsibility.

Chapter 12

HOUSING AND COMMUNITY CARE

'The Government's policy remains that care should be provided to people as far as possible in their existing housing where this is their preference and it is practicable and cost effective to do so. Appropriate health and social care services, where necessary in conjunction with suitably designed or adapted housing, will be key components in enabling people to live independently. For those people who cannot remain in their own homes, even with support, there will be a continuing need for other forms of housing, or residential care or nursing homes' ('Housing and Community Care', DoE 10/92; DoH LAC(92)12).

12.1   Introduction

It may not be overstating the case to say that housing is the keystone for community care. First, a literal interpretation of 'care in the community' is care 'at home' as opposed to care 'in a home'. (For further discussion, however, of the failure of community care policies to address the distinction between these two meanings, see Chapter 2.) Secondly, it has long been recognised that older people have specific housing needs and accommodation which meets those needs may be an important determining factor in maintaining an independent lifestyle.

A recent research report commissioned by the Department of Environment (McCafferty, 1994, para 1.5) identified five basic housing and housing with care options for older people:

–   staying put with no additional support;
–   staying put with necessary repairs only;
–   staying put with repairs and adaptations only or with domiciliary care as well;
–   moving to smaller, ordinary or mainstream housing;
–   moving to specialised housing such as sheltered housing.

There is a sixth option whereby the older person moves in with family members, perhaps in a self-contained granny flat.

To put the legal framework of these various options in context, we will first briefly review the features which characterise the housing circumstances of the elderly and then examine the policy background.

12.2   Profile of the housing circumstances of the elderly population

The heterogeneous nature of the elderly as a group is no less apparent in relation to their housing circumstances than in relation to other areas of their lives. In particular, the distinction between the 'young' old (65 to 74-year-olds) and the 'old' old (over 75 years) is increasingly recognised as significant. For example, in relation to tenure, the present cohort of the very elderly (75 years +) is less likely to be owner-occupiers than the cohort immediately below them, who have levels of owner-occupation roughly comparable to the rest of the population (*Living Independently*, DoE, 1994, para 4.27). Correspondingly, the over-75s are more likely to rent their accommodation than the younger elderly. At the same time, it must be remembered that housing tenure for elderly individuals may reflect their structural position in society at earlier stages of the life-cycle. It is not surprising therefore that elderly owner-occupiers are more likely to be in receipt of occupational pensions or unearned income than other elderly people. Nevertheless, there is a significant minority of elderly owner-occupiers who do fall into the 'house rich, income poor' bracket with consequences in relation to the repair and maintenance of their properties (see below). It is also well known that houses in the private rented sector are in worse condition than any other sector and that this disproportionately affects single elderly tenants, who are mainly women.

	Well-off: 20%	*Not rich, not poor: 40%*	*Poor: 40%*
Income	*High*	*Middle to low*	*Low*
Savings/ investment	Substantial	Limited	Limited
Tenure	Owner-occupiers	Mainly owner-occupiers	Local authority tenants or private tenants
State benefits	None	Partially dependent	Highly dependent
Occupational pensions	High levels	Small amounts	Low

Source: Bull and Poole, *Not Rich: Not Poor – A Study of Housing Options for Elderly People on Middle Incomes*, London: SHAC/Anchor Housing Trust (1989).

12.3   Housing policies and the elderly

From the mid-1960s through to the mid-1980s, the development of sheltered housing for rent was really the only policy response to the housing problems of older people. This development was pioneered by local authorities and then, in the 1970s, housing associations became involved, with Anchor and Hanover becoming major sheltered housing providers. In the 1980s, the private sector spotted a gap in the market and sheltered housing for sale became available. It is estimated that by the end of the 1980s there were approximately 90,000 private retirement units. The 1980s also saw the public sector facing constraints on capital funding and this, together with research showing that most elderly people wish to stay in their own homes, provided the impetus for a shift in policy and the development of 'Staying Put' initiatives. These have taken the form of setting up home improvement agencies which provide practical help and support for householders seeking to maintain their homes. In 1986, a national co-ordinating body, Care and Repair Ltd, was set up and by 1992 agencies were operating in one third of local authorities. Although 'Staying Put' schemes were promoted by local authorities, and housing associations in collaboration with building societies, central government assisted by providing core funding for the agencies (£3.9 million in 1993). The introduction of the Disabled Facilities Grant in the Local Government and Housing Act of 1989 (see later) also confirmed Government support for 'Staying Put'.

These policy developments and initiatives form a separate parallel stream to the development of community care policies in the 1980s, which tended to concentrate on the interface between social and health care (see Chapter 2). For example, the 1988 Griffiths report (*Community Care: Agenda for Action*) took a limited view of the role of housing authorities in relation to community care, describing it as 'the provision of "bricks and mortar"' (at p 8). The White Paper (*Caring for People, Community Care in the Next Decade and Beyond*, Cm 849, 1989) placed a greater emphasis on housing, stating that 'The Government believes that housing is a vital component of community care and it is often the key to independent living' (at p 25). Despite this exhortation, it has taken considerable time for the role of housing in community care implementation to be fully recognised. Indeed, this lack of integration and marginalisation of housing is evident in the NHSCCA 1990.

12.3.1 Housing and the National Health Service and Community Care Act 1990

Despite the White Paper's recognition of the role of housing, housing services do not fall within the legal definition of community care services set out in s 46(3). The framework of duties imposed by the Act further illustrates the marginalisation of housing, reflecting as it does the structural distinctions in local government between unitary and non-unitary authorities. Unitary authorities, historically London Boroughs and Metropolitan Districts, are single-tier authorities where housing and social services are administered by the same authority. Outside these areas, social services have been a function of county councils and housing a function of district councils. It is worth noting, however, that this system of local government organisation is currently in flux, with a shift towards the creation of new unitary authorities out of the old county and district councils.

Under s 46(2)(c), social services departments in county councils are placed under a duty to consult the district housing authority when drawing up their community care plan where the plan 'may affect or be affected by the provision or availability of housing'. There is no equivalent duty placed on social services within unitary authorities, presumably on the assumption that there will be consultation between the two departments anyway. In contrast, all local authorities come under the duty in s 46(2)(e) to consult voluntary housing agencies active in their area in relation to the community care plan.

Co-operation between county and district councils is also formally demanded in relation to the assessment process, again with no equivalent legal requirement placed on unitary authorities. Section 47(3) requires county social services to notify district housing departments if during an assessment there appears to be a housing need and invite them to assist in the assessment. In making their decision as to service provision, social services departments are directed to take into account any services which are likely to be made available by the housing authority. The requirements placed on the housing authority by s 47(3) are fairly dilute: they do not come under a duty to accept the invitation to assess and even if they choose to do so, they are simply asked to assist 'to such extent as is reasonable in the circumstances'. This allows considerable scope for disagreement between social services departments and housing authorities. The forum for resolving such disagreements is unlikely to be the courts, given the House of Lords decision in *R v Northavon District Council ex parte Smith* [1994] 2 AC 402 on the equivalent provisions in the Children Act 1989, and the declaration by Lord Templeman that 'Judicial review is not the way to obtain co-operation' (p 410G).

Detailed Guidance has been issued jointly by the Department of Health and the Department of the Environment in the Circular, *Housing and Community Care* (DoH LAC(92) 12, DoE 10/92). The Circular recommended that joint arrangements be developed to deal with assessments and that social services departments and housing authorities 'should consider the need to nominate particular officers to be responsible for liaising and agreeing possible housing options' (para 10). In relation to resources, it was stated that '[c]ommunity care in itself creates no new category of entitlement to housing, and housing needs which are identified by community care planning and individual assessments should be considered alongside existing processes and local priorities' (para 16). The Circular stressed the need for 'discussion, understanding and agreement in the planning of services, rather than unilateral decision-making' (para 19). The Annex to the Circular fleshes this out by listing some seven aspects of the joint planning process requiring inter-agency collaboration, including agreements on the appropriate balance of housing and social care input to very sheltered housing schemes and their continued funding, and establishing a record of special needs and adapted housing to enable properties to be matched with individuals (para 13, Annex).

Research has confirmed that there has been considerable success in getting housing involved in the joint planning process but that on the ground a 'seamless' service is some way off with front-line workers disputing the boundaries between housing and social services responsibilities. This may not be surprising, given the institutional and cultural differences between housing and social services. In particular, housing managers felt that they were being left to support vulnerable tenants and step into gaps left by social services. The response of some housing departments has been to create specialist posts with more of a social welfare role, such as tenancy support workers, resettlement workers, family welfare officers, housing alarm officers and concierges. These support services are then funded by an additional charge on the rent, which in turn is claimed as part of housing benefit by low-income tenants (Joseph Rowntree Foundation, Findings, Housing Research 135, January 1995).

The absence of clear duties placed on housing authorities by the community care legislation, together with pressures relating to resources, means that it is not surprising that there are inter-agency pressures to shift responsibility. Underlying this is a problem of definition, similar to the problem in defining the boundaries between health and social care, and like that problem perhaps not susceptible to clear and logical line-drawing. At the same time, it must be noted that housing authorities do have independent legal duties which may be relevant in the context of community care. For example, in relation to strategic planning, s 3 of the Chronically Sick and Disabled Persons Act 1970 places housing authorities under a duty to consider the special needs of disabled people when they are considering the provision of future housing in their district. The homelessness legislation may also be relevant in assessing and meeting the needs of those elderly individuals who require accommodation.

12.3.2 Homelessness

Elderly people may be threatened with homelessness as a result of various events, such as repossession by a landlord or lender, or as a consequence of relationship breakdown where they are sharing accommodation with relatives. Part III of the Housing Act 1985 places duties on housing authorities to secure accommodation for individuals who are unintentionally homeless, have a 'local connection' with the authority to whom they apply and are in priority need.

The definition of 'priority need' in s 59(1) of the 1985 Act includes people who are 'vulnerable as a result of old age, mental illness, or physical disability or other special reason, or with whom such a person resides or might reasonably be expected to reside'. The DoE Code of Guidance exhorts housing authorities to take a 'flexible and pragmatic approach' to assessing the needs of the elderly, but suggests that chronological age alone will not satisfy the test of vulnerability: 'Authorities should look not just at whether people are old, but at the extent to which their age has made it hard to fend for themselves' (*Homelessness – Code of Guidance for Local Authorities*, revised 3rd edn, 1994, para 6.9).

The specific housing needs of the elderly for accommodation which is warm, dry and accessible may be relevant in determining whether an elderly person is indeed homeless as s 58(2A) extends the definition of 'homelessness' to cases where it is no longer reasonable for an individual to continue to occupy their existing home. However, conditions may have to be fairly bad in objective terms before the courts will intervene to overturn a finding of 'reasonableness' by a housing authority, particularly as their assessment of reasonableness is influenced by local housing conditions including the availability of stock.

Even if the applicant fulfils all the statutory criteria, there is a further hurdle to overcome: the test of cognitive ability set out by the House of Lords in *R v London Borough of Tower Hamlets ex parte Ferdous Begum* [1993] AC 509. The test demands 'capacity to understand and respond to an offer [of accommodation] and if they accept it to undertake the responsibilities that will be involved' (per Lord Griffiths at p 520A).

The next section examines in more detail the housing options available to the elderly, looking first at the various grants which might enable elderly people to remain in their present home before reviewing other housing options.

12.4   Housing options for the elderly

12.4.1   Staying put with necessary repairs

Where the main housing problem facing the elderly person is the fabric and condition of their home, responsibility for any repairs will vary according to their tenure, and is likely to cause particular problems for elderly owner-occupiers, who may not have sufficient funds to pay for the work. Part VIII of the Local Government and Housing Act 1989 introduced a new framework of home improvement grants. In the particular context of repairs, depending on the extent of the work, there may be two routes for obtaining public funds from the local housing authority:

- via a renovation grant; or
- minor works assistance.

Renovation grants
These are available for major works and, if the condition of the home is very poor, then a mandatory grant may be available (s 112 of the LGHA 1989). The majority of awards are discretionary (s 115 of the LGHA 1989) and therefore are dependent on the availability of local authority funds. Renovation grants are means tested, although those on income support will automatically be below the income and capital thresholds. Although 100% grants are available, the ceiling is £20,000 (House Renovation Grants (Reduction of Grant) Regulations 1994, SI 1994/2711). Detailed information on renovation grants can be found in DoE Circular 12/90. There have been numerous administrative problems with the renovation grants system and complaints can be taken to the local government ombudsman.

Minor works assistance

Under s 131, housing authorities have a discretion to assist with minor works (see also DoE Circular 4/90). Although there are four types of assistance, the most relevant to elderly applicants who are seeking financial help with repair costs is 'Staying Put' assistance, available to householders who are aged 60 or over. To qualify for minor works assistance, the elderly applicant or their partner must be in receipt of income support, housing benefit, or council tax benefit. The maximum grant is £1,080 on any one claim but up to £3,240 can be claimed over a 3-year period.

12.4.2   Staying put with adaptations

In the DoE Circular 10/90 *Housing and Community Care*, it was said that 'the adaptation, where necessary, of existing dwellings occupied by elderly and disabled people is often a pre-requisite for the success of community care'. There are a number of different channels for obtaining public assistance with such adaptations. In addition to disabled facilities grants and minor works assistance under the LGHA 1989, housing authorities can carry out adaptations in relation to their own stock under Part II of the Housing Act 1985, while social services have a duty under s 2 of the CSDPA 1970 to arrange and carry out adaptations. This system of multiple and overlapping powers makes for complexity, with the consequence that it makes it difficult to know who should be funding what.

Disabled facilities grants (DFGs)

This is structured in a way similar to the renovation grants system in distinguishing between mandatory grants, directed towards meeting basic housing needs, defined primarily in terms of accessibility, and discretionary grants for a wide range of other works (s 114(3), (4) of the LGHA 1989). To qualify for a DFG, the occupier must be 'disabled', that is either registered or registrable as disabled under s 29(1) of the NAA 1948 (s 114(6) of the LGHA 1989). The same means test applies as in relation to renovation grants. DFGs can be claimed by council tenants, housing association tenants, and private tenants as well as owner-occupiers. The housing authority has to be satisfied that the works are 'necessary and appropriate to meet the needs of the disabled occupant' and that 'it is reasonable and practicable to carry out the relevant works, having regard to the age and condition of the building' (s 114(1)(a), (b) of the LGHA 1989). In relation to the assessment of necessity and appropriateness, the housing authority is under a duty to consult social services, and, in practice, such assessments are carried out by occupational therapists. Circular 10/90 sets out a series of factors which are relevant to the assessment criteria (paras 36–48).

The overlapping duties of housing and social services in relation to adaptations have given rise to difficulties. Paragraph 19 of the Circular suggested that minor non-structural adaptations should be funded by social services while major structural adaptations should be the responsibility of the housing authority as grant aidable under the DFG, but the Circular did not provide detailed lists of examples under the two headings. This was deliberate: in Circular 5/91 the DoE explained that rather than being too prescriptive, it was aiming to provide a 'broad policy framework within which local welfare and housing authorities [could] work up detailed practical arrangements appropriate to local circumstances' and exhorted the agencies to build on the conventions for the division of responsibilities which had grown up in relation to the CSDPA 1970, as well as learning from good practice in neighbouring areas.

The existence of the overlapping duties can work to the benefit of the elderly person in some circumstances. For example, the Circular makes it quite clear that the final decision to approve a DFG rests with the housing authority and there may be circumstances, albeit rare, where the housing authority decides not to follow the recommendation of social services (DoE 10/90, para 23). In those circumstances, social services will have a continuing duty to make arrangements under s 2 of the CSDPA 1970 (see DoE 10/90, paras 15, 16). The Circular goes on to identify a second instance where social services may find themselves under a continuing duty. This is where the disabled person approaches them for financial assistance with the costs of the adaptation under s 2(e) of the CSDPA 1970. A further problem arises because the Circular implies that in deciding whether to 'top up', social services will operate a different means test to the statutory means test applied by the housing authority: '[w]elfare authorities should not try to make their own separate assessment of what a grant applicant is expected to pay; but they might consider whether, in their opinion, the meeting of these costs would cause hardship' (DoE 10/90, para 17). The consequence has been that the availability of 'top-up' grants has varied from authority to authority, with some social services giving no assistance and others having substantial 'top-up' budgets (Joseph Rowntree Foundation, Findings, Housing Research 123, September 1994).

This research also uncovered similar inequalities in relation to the availability of DFGs across the country, with some housing authorities giving a hundred times more grants per thousand dwellings than others. There have also been delays in relation to initial assessments caused mainly by a shortage of occupational therapists. Many complaints about the DFG system have been investigated by the local government ombudsmen, mainly in relation to delay.

Minor works assistance
Some housing authorities use this as a quicker and simpler alternative to the DFG system for providing adaptations. However, the two types of assistance are not interchangeable. For example, minor works assistance is not available to council house tenants, whereas DFGs are. While minor works assistance is a completely discretionary scheme, DFGs may be mandatory or discretionary, depending on the type of work. Threshold eligibility for a DFG depends on an assessment of disability, whereas 'Staying Put' and 'Elderly resident' minor works assistance simply set the condition that the beneficiary be aged 60 or

over. Finally, not only is minor works assistance available within much lower financial limits than DFGs, it is confined to welfare claimants only.

The difference between the two types of minor works assistance mentioned above can be summarised as follows. 'Staying Put' grants cover not only repairs (see above) but also adaptations to enable an elderly householder to continue to live independently in his or her home, whereas 'Elderly resident' adaptations are intended to enable the elderly person to be cared for in the home of another person.

The relationship between adaptations and domiciliary care
The official guidance explicitly recognises that in some cases a balance will need to be struck and that in assessing that balance the social services and housing authorities should be aiming to secure 'the most appropriate and cost-effective' care package (DoE 10/92, para 16). The need for balanced decision-making is also addressed in the Circular on disabled facilities grants in relation to the assessment of the necessity and appropriateness of the works. In that context, the individual aspirations of the elderly person, together with the wishes of relatives were acknowledged as relevant factors in the decision-making process (DoE 10/90, paras 42, 43).

12.4.3   Moving to smaller mainstream accommodation

This may be an option considered by older people for a variety of reasons. For some it may be in order to live closer to their relatives, for others it may be tied up with the condition of their existing home, and for some it may be a desire to release housing equity. Setting aside the particular problems of a stagnating housing market, difficulties may be experienced by two particular groups.

First, owner-occupiers who wish to transfer to council housing in their own area may face a long waiting list due to the decline in housing stock. Housing authorities have a general discretion in the allocation of their housing (s 21 of the Housing Act 1985) and s 22 of the Housing Act 1985 merely requires 'reasonable preference' to be given to the various groups listed. Elderly owner-occupiers may fall within s 22 if they are living in unsatisfactory housing. Inflexible allocation policies which fetter the discretion of the authority are liable to be struck down by judicial review, and a policy never to allocate to an elderly owner-occupier would certainly be susceptible to such a challenge (see *R v Canterbury City Council ex parte Gillespie* (1986) 19 HLR 7).

If the elderly person is already a council tenant, then while they may find it relatively easy to move within their own area that might not be the case if they were seeking to transfer between housing authorities. Some authorities give special priority to existing tenants seeking to transfer to smaller homes, and may even offer financial incentives. There is a Government-sponsored mobility scheme (co-ordinated by an organisation called Homes) which might help where the elderly person is seeking to move out of the area. Unfortunately, councils tend to set tight limits on the number of lettings made available under this scheme. A further alternative is to seek an exchange with a tenant of the same or another housing authority, through the Mutual Home Exchange Scheme known as Homeswap (s 92 of the Housing Act 1985).

12.4.4   Moving to specialist housing

As outlined above, specialist housing for the elderly is now available for purchase as well as to rent. There is a diversity of provision, ranging from 'pure' housing, through the traditional form of sheltered housing with warden and/or an alarm system, to what is called 'very sheltered' housing, with additional support provided either by social services or the landlord. At this end of the continuum, the boundary between care 'at home' and care 'in a home' may have dissolved, as some of these 'very sheltered' schemes are registered as residential care homes under the Registered Homes Act 1984.

Despite the increase in the number of units provided by the private sector, most complexes are still owned and managed by councils or housing associations. There is no specific legislation regulating this type of housing, and advisers need to be familiar with the general law of property, landlord and tenant law and public law.

Renting specialist accommodation

Schemes in this sector tend to be classified under headings derived from the influential Ministry of Health and Local Government Circular 82/69 which laid down standards for the design of sheltered housing. The Circular was cancelled in 1980, but the terminology was retained and indeed subsequent developments have even been fitted within the original framework. Essentially, the classification turns on gradations in the levels of the independence of the residents:

–   Category 1 accommodation – which contains specially designed housing for the relatively active elderly. Communal facilities and a warden are optional;

–   Category 1.5 accommodation – which is specially designed housing with warden support but no communal facilities;

–   Category 2 accommodation – which is designed for the less active elderly. It has both communal facilities, such as common rooms, laundry rooms and guest rooms, and warden support, plus alarms for contacting the warden;

–   Category 2.5 accommodation – which is sometimes known as 'very sheltered' or 'extra care' schemes. This type of accommodation is designed for frail elderly people and provides enhanced care and facilities compared to Category 2.

In addition, there is 'supportive housing', associated chiefly with the Abbeyfield Society, where residents have their own room but may share communal facilities and meals.

The geographical spread of the different types of specialist housing is uneven, dividing along a north/south boundary (*Living Independently*, DoE, 1994, paras 2.8, 2.11). Category 2 is the most common form of specialist housing in England, and although the proportion of very sheltered accommodation is still very small in comparison, it is growing rapidly.

Moving into rented accommodation

Traditionally, there has been strong demand for sheltered housing reflected in long waiting lists. More recently, some providers have reported an increasing number of difficult-to-let units, explained by factors such as the nature and location of the stock as well as the success of 'Staying Put' policies in keeping people of low–medium dependency in their own homes (*Living Independently*, DoE, 1994, para 9.22). That study analysed the prior tenure of entrants to public sector specialist housing and found that in the sample surveyed over half of recent entrants had moved from council properties, a fifth had been owner-occupiers and a fifth private renters (para 5.28). Given that elderly people account for a mere 5% of those in private rented accommodation, the study suggests that local housing authorities are 're-housing elderly tenants rather than encouraging landlords to carry out repairs' (para 5.28). The remaining sixth of recent entrants had moved from other specialist housing or long-term care in hospitals or residential homes. This was particularly striking in relation to very sheltered housing where the numbers of new entrants from residential/nursing homes has risen from 3% to 11% from 1989 (para 5.30). This increase must be attributable to more general trends in community care, with the closure of long-stay geriatric units in hospitals and Part III accommodation (see Chapter 2).

Overall, some 60% of current residents in council-run sheltered housing were council tenants prior to the move, while Abbeyfields/almshouses and housing associations have the highest proportion of former owner-occupiers (45% and 32% respectively) and local authorities the lowest (16%). The same principles apply in relation to allocation of council-run sheltered housing as to ordinary council tenancies (see **12.4.3**).

Security of tenure and rented sheltered housing

Where the accommodation is provided by a council, the tenancy will be secure under Part IV of the Housing Act 1985. In general, sheltered accommodation has been excluded from the 'right to buy' provisions (see Sch 5, paras 10–11 to the HA 1985, as amended by s 106 of the Leasehold Reform, Housing and Urban Development Act 1993). For housing association accommodation, the tenancy agreement will normally take the form of an assured tenancy under the HA 1988, if granted on or after 15 January 1989. Housing association tenancies entered into before that date are protected by Part VI of the Rent Act 1977 and subject to rent control. Note that residents in Abbeyfields and almshouses are usually licensees, as are residents in residential care homes, and therefore they will not have security of tenure.

Service charges and rents

Affordability of sheltered housing has been recognised as an important issue as it becomes increasingly expensive along the care continuum. However, attendance allowance and housing benefit may be available to cover certain elements of the support services provided in rented sheltered schemes.

Attendance allowance is available to the older disabled people who require care in relation to 'bodily functions' (see further, ss 64–67 of the Social Security Contributions and Benefits Act 1992). Significantly, this benefit is not means tested and thus it may be an important source of income for 'not rich, not poor' residents in 'very sheltered accommodation'.

Housing benefit is means tested, with an upper capital threshold of £16,000. It can be claimed in respect of the rent plus 'eligible' service charges. Falling within the definition of eligible charges are services such as cleaning of communal areas, gardening, removal of refuse, portering, wardens and caretakers as well as general management services. Where emergency alarm systems are provided in sheltered accommodation, that too will be covered. Non-eligible items include water and sewerage charges, fuel costs, laundry services, meals, nursing and personal care. However, if volunteers or staff do provide non-eligible services, no deductions will be made provided that these duties account for less than half of their time and can be described as 'general counselling and support' (reg 10 of the Housing Benefit (General) Regulations 1987 (SI 1987/1971)).

Housing benefit can thus be used to finance some care elements on top of 'pure' housing for low–medium dependency residents. For those elderly people whose income or capital take them just outside entitlement to housing benefit, however, renting sheltered housing may not be an affordable option. More generally, the use of housing benefit to finance care services again illustrates the way housing is not fully integrated into the community care framework.

Service charges for housing association properties may be subject to various statutory controls. First, where there is a Rent Act tenancy, the 'fair rent' procedure will cover service charges where they are part of a fixed rent. Where a regulated tenancy provides for a variable service charge, the rent officer or rent assessment committee may include it as part of a registered rent if 'satisfied that the terms as to variation are reasonable' (s 71(4) of the Rent Act 1977). Variable service charges are also subject to the separate reasonableness provisions of the Landlord and Tenant Act 1985, ss 18–30, as amended by the Landlord and Tenant Act 1987, ss 41–44. These provisions apply to post-1989 assured tenancies and impose machinery for informing and consulting tenants. Note that local authority tenants cannot take advantage of this regime, unless a long tenancy has been granted (s 26 of the Landlord and Tenant Act 1985).

Buying specialist housing

The private sector offers a parallel range of provision to that of the public sector, although private schemes have been increasingly designed to attract particular types of buyer, whether the early retirees, the frail elderly or the very well off. The stagnating housing market has affected this sector in a number of ways. After a period of exponential growth in the 1980s, most companies stopped building during the slump. Nevertheless, the resale market has suffered dramatic price falls, particularly at the bottom end. This is mainly due to beneficiaries selling at knock-down prices in order to avoid paying service charges while the unit remains unsold.

Typically, once the development is complete the builder hands over the day-to-day management of the scheme to a commercial management organisation or to a housing association. The management agency is responsible for employing a warden and running any other services. There is an Association of Retirement Housing Managers which aims to promote and maintain high standards in management and a Code of Practice has been prepared for approval by the Secretary of State for the Environment, under s 87 of the Leasehold Reform, Housing and Urban Development Act 1993.

Tenure can be freehold but is more usually a long lease (99 or 125 years) at a premium with ground rent and service charges. A variety of what are known as 'mixed tenure' schemes are also available aimed at elderly owner-occupiers who have insufficient capital to purchase outright on the open market. For example, some housing association co-ownership schemes have been applied to sheltered housing. Under this arrangement, the elderly person buys a slice of the equity, which might be between 25% and 75%. The balance is funded by a mixture of grant and private loan finance which is serviced by the elderly individual paying rent if the equity purchased is less than 75%. All such mixed tenure schemes still require full payment of their service charges.

Private developers may offer 'discounts' on properties, and the purchaser must be careful to distinguish between cases where this is purely a marketing ploy, with no effect on beneficial ownership, and cases where an equity sharing scheme is being proposed. Again, the elderly person will purchase a slice of the equity outright, and the balance of the purchase price will either be left outstanding as a debt or borrowed from a building society, and secured by a legal charge over the leasehold. The elderly individual will either pay interest as with a normal mortgage or the interest may be rolled up and repaid from the proceeds of sale when the lease is eventually sold.

Some developers in conjunction with finance companies have introduced packages called 'Home for Life' schemes whereby the purchaser acquires a life-share in the whole or part of the property. The amount lent depends on actuarial factors, and on death the whole value of the property passes to the finance company. However, an annuity may be paid to those who surrender the lease, for example to move into a nursing home.

There is no upper age-limit on taking out a loan to purchase property secured by a mortgage and some lenders may be prepared to offer an interest-only loan to an elderly purchaser. Income support may be available to cover the interest payable in spite of the general restrictions which have applied since May 1994 to increased housing costs after obtaining income support. An elderly claimant may take advantage of the exception in the regulations by taking out or increasing a loan 'to acquire alternative accommodation more suited to the special needs of a disabled person'. The definition of 'disabled person' is a person who is getting or who could get an enhanced or higher pensioner premium, or disability premium (Sch 3, para 5A to the Income Support (General) Regulations 1987).

Practical points in relation to the lease or management deed
There are a number of provisions commonly incorporated but peculiar to leases of this type of accommodation and which might therefore require the attention of the elderly person to be specifically drawn to them.

Occupancy and assignment
Typically, there will be a prohibition on occupation of the property by people under a certain age, whether that be 55 or 60 years. There may be a lower age-limit for those sharing the home with an 'elderly person', but it may still be 40 or 50 years. There may be no upper age-limit as such, but depending on the type of scheme, occupancy may be conditional on not requiring permanent nursing care.

There may also be restrictions in relation to the age of assignees, which may prevent assignment of the lease to younger relatives. In some leases there may be provision for an administrative fee payable to the landlord on assignment and a further 'transfer fee'. The level of the administrative fee may vary according to whether the lessor has or has not found the assignee; in the former case it may be equivalent to the standard estate agency fee. The lease may also provide for a 'surrender fee' payable to the managing agents on re-sale.

The warden
While the precise arrangements may vary between schemes, most covenants are expressed in terms that the warden will render 'good neighbourly assistance' to the occupants. This means that the warden's duties are to be on hand in order to call for help in an emergency, to report repair problems to the management and generally keep an eye on residents. Domestic or caring tasks for the residents, such as shopping, cooking or cleaning, are normally specifically excluded as outside the warden's duties.

Service charges
It is important to ascertain what services are provided and what the service charge liability will be. Where the elderly person has to manage on a relatively fixed income, they may be concerned about future increases in the service charges. Long leaseholders in sheltered accommodation flats or bungalows are

protected by ss 18–30 of the Landlord and Tenant Act 1985 (as amended by ss 41–44 of the Landlord and Tenant Act 1987).

All schemes need a 'sinking fund' to cover the costs of long-term repairs, renewals and redecoration. In some schemes, the contribution to the fund is part of the regular service charges, but in others contributions may be deferred and taken as a lump sum out of any proceeds of sale.

In response to concerns about the private market in sheltered housing voiced at the end of the 1980s, the developers opted for self-regulation. The National House Building Council (NHBC) introduced a Code of Practice for new and second-hand sheltered housing sold after 1 April 1990. The Code has two important requirements. First, as soon as a potential buyer has paid a reservation fee, the builder must provide a purchaser's information pack (PIP). This contains detailed information about the builder and management organisation, the purchaser's legal rights, the services provided, the charging system, and the position on resale. Secondly, the Code requires builders to ensure that legally binding management agreements, which comply with the standards set out in the Code, are entered into. The sanction for any builder who does not comply with the Code is disciplinary proceedings and expulsion from the Register of Builders. (The Code of Practice, prepared by the Association of Retirement Housing Managers and currently under consideration by the Secretary of State, is intended to replace the NHBC Code in due course.)

Also, in 1990, Age Concern set up the Sheltered Housing Advisory and Conciliation Service (SHACS) which provides advice and information for prospective purchasers of sheltered housing and a free independent conciliation service for purchasers in dispute with commercial or housing association managers. Alternatively, if the scheme is managed by a housing association, the Housing Association Ombudsman can be approached. In common with most ombudsmen, the Housing Association Ombudsman is concerned with cases of maladministration and insists that complainants have exhausted the relevant association's internal complaints procedure before he will investigate. Few cases get to the formal investigation stage and most are resolved by mediation or arbitration. The remit of the Ombudsman excludes complaints about the level or amount of service charges. However, in his first annual report for 1993–94, the Ombudsman did state that he wished to ensure that leaseholders receive prompt and accurate information from associations and that where errors are made, that would be prima facie maladministration, with the expectation that associations would rectify the matter (para 4.4.27).

12.4.5 Moving in with the family

Most elderly people do retain their own households and only a very small proportion live in the same household as a younger generation of their family. Where the elderly person has children of both sexes, it appears that they are more likely to live with a daughter than a son. There are various possible scenarios in relation to the formation of the new household. The older person's home could be sold and the equity used to make alterations or improvements to the existing home of the relatives. Alternatively, the elderly person may use the equity to make a gift in anticipation of sharing the home. A further possibility is for both homes to be sold and the proceeds invested in a new, bigger house, perhaps with a granny flat.

The dynamics of the family relationships need to be carefully assessed before this type of arrangement is entered into. The implications of declining health of the elderly person should be considered, together with the effects of taking on a caring role on the marriage and children in the household. The need for privacy and personal space should be assessed in the context of the size and layout of the home. Finally, the financial implications both in the short term and the long term if the family cannot provide care and the elderly person needs to enter a care or nursing home should not be overlooked. While it is clear that for some families this type of living arrangement is what they want, for others the strain of living in close proximity can lead to personal relationships breaking down. The vulnerability of the elderly person, should this happen, means that the risks and benefits need to be carefully weighed up at the outset. The economic climate cannot be ignored, and the threat to the security of the older person posed by the redundancy, or bankruptcy of the younger generation and possible repossession proceedings is a further factor to be considered.

Legal advice can be sought at two stages in relation to these arrangements: at the outset or when the arrangement has broken down. The task of the lawyer is rather different depending on when he or she is consulted. If advice is sought before the parties are committed and the understandings and expectations of all concerned are brought to the surface and the arrangements set up accordingly then, even if the worst still happens, at least everyone knows where they stand. If this has not happened and the lawyer is consulted when things have gone wrong, then the task is to unscramble and translate what has happened into the framework of property law.

Where families do seek advice in relation to formalising a home-sharing relationship, then advisers must recognise the risk of conflict of interests between the generations and ensure that separate representation is obtained. This will also reduce the prospect of the transaction subsequently being set aside on the ground of undue influence.

A checklist for the legal adviser in relation to inter-generational home-sharing

(1) In terms of analysing the legal nature of a home-sharing relationship, the starting point is to consider whether the elderly person is putting in capital or not.

(2) If so, then the next question is whether the capital represents:
    (i) a gift;

(ii) a loan;
(iii) payment for a contractual licence; or
(iv) payment to obtain a beneficial interest in the property.

Factors to be considered at the planning stage are that a gift may have potential inheritance tax advantages and may avoid means-tested contributions towards the cost of a care bed. However, the disadvantages are that a gift may be vulnerable to the application of the notional capital rule, and the family may have to meet the cost of the bed anyway. A gift may also leave the elderly donor vulnerable should the donee(s) divorce or become insolvent. A loan or purchase of a beneficial interest may give more security but anticipating the subsequent entry of the elderly person into residential care means that the implications of the means tests applied by the Benefits Agency and the local authority should be considered.

(3) If the plan is for the capital to be used to extend the property or to build a separate self-contained 'granny flat' or annexe, then consideration has to be given to the need for planning permission for form of use and the modification or discharge of any restrictive covenant which otherwise might be breached. In such cases, it may be advisable to convey the 'granny flat' into the name of the elderly person rather than to establish joint ownership over the whole of the property.

If the home-sharing arrangement subsequently becomes unstuck and there is no written documentation dealing with or recording the agreement between the parties, then litigation might be needed to settle the parties' respective rights and interests in the property. Again, there are a range of possible conclusions which a court can reach as to the existence and nature of the interest held by the elderly person.

(1) *Equitable proprietary interest*
In some cases, the elderly person will be held to have acquired a beneficial interest under the doctrine of *implied, resulting and constructive trusts.* Establishing such a claim will require either evidence of an agreement between the parties that the property be shared beneficially and the elderly person having acted to his or her detriment, or the court inferring a common intention to share based on the parties' conduct, for example where the elderly person has made a direct contribution to the purchase price or to improvements carried out to an existing property (*Lloyds Bank v Rosset* [1990] 1 All ER 111).

In other situations, a beneficial interest in the property may be held to have arisen under the equitable doctrine *of proprietary estoppel.* The claimant must be able to show that he or she has acted to his or her detriment in reliance on the belief that he or she will obtain an interest in the property. However, the trend in the courts is to give a remedy which represents the minimum equity to do justice to the claimant and this may mean that a licence for life protected by the estoppel is the outcome rather than a beneficial interest.

(2) *Licence*

If the elderly person does not get beneficial ownership, then his or her occupation of the home must be founded on a licence. If no money has changed hands then it is likely that only a *bare licence* has been created, which can be terminated on reasonable notice. For a *contractual licence* there needs to be consideration, which need not take the form of money; see *Tanner v Tanner* [1975] 1 WLR 1346, where giving up a secure Rent Act tenancy was regarded as sufficient consideration. A contractual licence will be terminable according to its terms, express or implied and it may be that an irrevocable licence for life has been created. If a capital payment has been made which is viewed as a loan, then it will normally be associated with a contractual licence and repayment of the loan will be due upon termination of the licence.

(3) *Tenancy*

A final possibility is that the elderly person may have a tenancy but there would have to be payments which could be regarded as rent and exclusive possession of part of the property. If this inference is drawn, then any capital payment is likely to be a gift. Where a tenancy is created, the elderly person will not be entitled to housing benefit, where living with a 'close' relative and sharing some accommodation other than a bathroom, toilet or hall (reg 7(1)(a) of the Housing Benefit Regulations 1987). A tenancy in respect of a 'granny flat' or annexe therefore might succeed in attracting housing benefit. The elderly tenant will not have security of tenure under the 1988 Housing Act where he or she occupies a 'dwelling house' which is part only of the building, and the landlord has his or her principal home in another dwelling house in the same building (Sch 1, para 10 of the Housing Act 1988). 'Granny flats'/annexes may not be part of the same building if there is no internal means of communication (see *Bardrick v Haycock* (1976) 31 P&CR 420) but this is a question of fact for the judge.

12.5   Conclusion

From this chapter it should be apparent that advice to older clients in relation to housing options can range across a number of discrete legal areas. Housing is increasingly recognised as part of the 'package' of community care, and from the viewpoint of the older individual, any division between housing support, social support or care and health care may be artificial. Legal advice may be relevant both in relation to planning, where the older client anticipates changing housing needs, and in ensuring that any decision is fully informed. Many older people desire independence and a self-determined lifestyle, and legal assistance may be invaluable in dealing with the practical problems, including affordability, that this aspiration for independent living presents.

Chapter 13

CHALLENGING COMMUNITY CARE DECISIONS

'Older people in particular are reluctant to complain, as are – in general – carers. Many people approaching Age Concern are afraid that something adverse will happen to them or their existing service if they complain – feeling that even a bad service is better than none. Many believe that complaining will make little difference. Some are not able to complain for various reasons, and may need support to do so ... Some social services staff – and workers from other agencies – view complaints procedures negatively' (*The Next Steps – Lessons for the Future of Community Care*, Age Concern, 1994).

13.1   Introduction

Users and carers may find themselves in disagreement with local authorities on a wide range of matters in relation to community care decision-making. While many, if not most, complaints will reflect to some extent the limitations on the resources available to social services departments, it is none the less possible in broad terms to classify causes of dissatisfaction as relating to either to 'quality' or 'rationing'. Under the 'quality' heading, the 'problem' may be perceived as the quality of service provided, the appropriateness of the services offered in a particular case or the professionalism of social services staff. In relation to 'rationing' decisions by social services departments, more typically the dissatisfaction will relate to the availability of a service, ie the resources allocated to it and the eligibility criteria used to ration it, or to the operation of financial assessment procedures. Disputes may also relate to the factual basis on which decisions have been made and the legal obligations of the authority.

Historically, the precise nature of the local authority's legal obligations and the gradation between duties and powers has been regarded as central to any analysis of the strength of potential legal challenges in relation to service provision decisions taken on the basis of the availability of resources, or the lack of resources. The distinction has become less significant in the light of the decision in the case of *R v Gloucestershire County Council ex parte Mahfood and Barry* (1995) *The Times*, 17 June (discussed in Chapter 6), particularly as it was always believed that the duty in s 2 of the CSDPA 1970 was the strongest candidate for interpretation as a mandatory duty unqualified by reference to available resources. The legality of taking into account resources both when assessing need and in deciding how to meet those needs was accepted by McCowan LJ in the *Gloucestershire* case. By subjecting such rationing decisions to a standard of *Wednesbury* unreasonableness (see **13.6.3** for a definition) the courts have demonstrated their reluctance to adjudicate on such matters, leaving decision-making power vested in the local authorities. A further consequence, however, is that it will only be in rare circumstances that an individual will be able to successfully challenge a particular rationing decision as 'irrational'.

Different types of complaint may require different considerations and different methods of dispute resolution. From the viewpoint of both service users and providers, informal resolution is preferable and many disputes, particularly of a minor nature, can be, and often are, solved informally. In this context, extra-legal channels such as the local media, community groups, councillors and MPs may be effective in pressing particular cases, especially where the local authority is reluctant to incur bad publicity.

Turning to more formal remedies, there are six potential avenues for challenging community care decisions:

- the local authority complaints procedure;

- the local authority's monitoring officer;

- the local government ombudsman;

- the default powers of the Secretary of State;

- judicial review;

- tort actions for damages.

As will be seen, enforcement in the community care field relies on a mix of self-regulation by authorities, together with non-legal remedies, backed up by formal court-based remedies as a last resort.

13.2   The complaints procedure

The White Paper captured the dual function of complaints procedures when it described them as 'an essential safeguard for users and . . . also . . . an important monitoring and management instrument for social services authorities and service providers alike' ('Caring for People', p 24, para 3.4.10, 1989). The legal framework governing the complaints procedure is located in s 7B of the Local Authority Social Services Act 1970 (inserted by s 50 of the National Health Service and Community Care Act 1990), together with the Local Authority Social Services (Complaints Procedure) Order (SI 2244/1990), and the Complaints Procedure Directions 1990. Practice guidance on how to implement good practice in dealing with complaints has been issued by the Social Services Inspectorate (*The Right to Complain*) and by virtue of s 7B(3) of LASSA 1970 this guidance is mandatory. *The Right to Complain* may be useful as a benchmark in setting standards against which to measure the actual practice of a local authority in a particular case.

13.2.1 Who can complain?

Under s 7B(2) of the LASSA 1970, complaints can be made by a 'qualifying individual' or anyone acting on his or her behalf. An individual qualifies under s 7B if:

'(a) the authority have a power or a duty to provide, or to secure the provision of, a service for him: and

(b) his need or possible need for such a service has (by whatever possible means) come to the attention of the authority.'

Although s 7B permits a wide range of people to use the complaints procedure, it is not comprehensive. For example, it would appear that an individual is not eligible to utilise the procedure in cases where the substance of the complaint is that the authority has declined to carry out an assessment on the basis of its judgement that the individual is not a person for whom it 'may' provide services. This view is supported by reference to the Parliamentary history (HL, 25 June 1990, cols 1396–1397). However, the local authority decision would be susceptible to judicial review in such cases (see *R v Mid-Glamorgan CC ex parte Miles, Legal Action*, January 1994, p 21).

The reference to 'a qualifying individual' would also seem to exclude complaints by a group, such as residents of a particular home, or a class of service users. Some local authorities may be prepared to waive this technical restriction, for example the Social Services Inspectorate (SSI) commended North Yorkshire County Council for using a test case strategy to tackle a group of complaints on a similar issue (*Inspection of the Complaints Procedure – North Yorkshire County Council*, July 1993, para 9.9).

13.2.2 What can be complained about?

Section 7B(1) of the LASSA 1970 states that the statutory complaints procedure operates in relation to complaints about the discharge of, or failure to discharge, social services functions. This is broad enough to cover complaints about day-care, domiciliary services, equipment and adaptations, residential care, and social work services as well as the process of assessment and service determination under s 47 of the NHSCCA 1990. Charges and financial assessments in relation to both domiciliary and residential care would also fall within the procedure. In the first round of a national inspection programme of the procedures, the SSI noted that in the five authorities surveyed, formal complaints about social work services were the most common, followed by complaints relating to residential care and domiciliary services (*Inspection of complaints procedures in local authority social services departments*, SSI, 1993). The second overview report on six further authorities found a similar distribution (*Second overview report of the inspection of the complaints procedures in local authority social services departments*, SSI, 1994).

13.2.3   The procedure for complaining

The procedure is governed by the Directions and has essentially three stages:

–   an informal or problem solving stage;

–   a formal or registration stage;

–   a review stage.

This basic framework should be consistent across all authorities but the precise procedure to be followed may vary considerably from authority to authority and so an up-to-date copy of the authority's rules will be needed in every case. Reference to the local authority's publicity materials on its complaints procedure should indicate where this information can be obtained.

Stage 1: The informal/problem-solving stage of the complaints procedure

At this stage, there is no requirement that the complaint be in writing (*Policy Guidance*, para 6.17). However, if the complaint is made by telephone, then it is important to keep a written record of what is said, the date(s) and the names and roles of the staff spoken to. *The Right to Complain* stresses that the informal stage should not be used as a device to prevent or dissuade users from making a formal complaint and that it is possible to go straight to Stage 2 (paras 4.5, 4.9). Whether it is worthwhile simply to do this and skip the first stage will depend on balancing the delay if a satisfactory resolution of the dispute is not found against the likelihood that it will. This in turn is dependent on the gravity of the complaint and the attitudes of the front-line staff. The SSI inspection of North Yorkshire noted that the defensiveness of some staff pushed some complaints over into the formal stage unnecessarily (para 12.4). If a request has been made for a copy of the complainant's personal social services file then it may be necessary to time the making of a formal complaint to ensure that the file is available as there is a 40-day time-limit for its production (see further the Access to Personal Files Act 1987 and Access to Personal Files (Social Services) Regulations 1989 (SI 1989/206).

Stage 2: The formal/registration stage

Passage to the second stage is marked by the requirement placed on local authorities to give or send to the complainant an explanation of the registration and review stages of the procedure (Direction 5(2)). To 'register' a complaint, it must be put in writing, if this has not already happened at the informal stage (if so, a copy of the original letter will be sufficient). The complaint is 'registered' by the Designated Complaints Officer of each authority and the 'clock' starts running at this point. *The Right to Complain* recommended that the Designated Complaints Officer should be given the power to 'freeze' decisions, which is particularly useful where the complaint relates to changes to services or their location (para 3.10).

At this stage, an investigator may be appointed to look into the complaint. The practice in many social services departments seems to be to appoint an Area or Service Manager outside line management as Investigating Officer. This system of internal investigation has thrown up a number of problems revolving around the role and task of the Investigating Officer, and his or her independence and expertise (see SSI, 1993, para 6.6, and 1994, para 5.60–61).

The Good Practice Guide for Investigators prepared by the Social Services Inspectorate (Appendix A of *The Right to Complain*) recommends that the Investigating Officer should circulate a draft report to the complainant for comment. Local procedures may also require the Investigating Officer to send a copy of his or her final report to the complainant. If this does not happen then it could be argued that the complainant is entitled to the disclosure of the report in order to comment on it prior to the authority's response.

The timescale for this stage of the procedure gives the local authority 28 days from the receipt of the complaint to formulate a formal written response and, where this is not possible, to give an explanation of the position within 28 days and make a full response within three months (Direction 6(1)). The first round of the SSI monitoring found that in four out of the five social services departments inspected these timescales were not being met by a wide margin (SSI, 1993, para 12.10). This was confirmed in the second round of inspections, although overall some improvement was noted (SSI, 1994, para 5.88).

If the complainant is dissatisfied with the authority's response, he or she has a further 28 days to request a review (Direction 7(2)). Again, this must be a formal request in writing, and the authority then has a further 28 days to arrange the meeting of a review panel to consider the complaint (Direction 7(3)).

Stage 3: The review panel
It is at this stage that an independent element is introduced to the procedure. The Directions specify that the panel of three must include at least one independent person, defined as 'a person who is neither a member nor an officer of that authority, nor where the authority have delegated any of its social services functions to any organisation, a person who is a member of or employed by that organisation, nor the spouse of any such person' (Direction 2(1), (3)). The *Policy Guidance* stipulates that the independent person should chair the panel and states that the independent person should have experience relevant to the subject-matter of the complaint (Annex A, paras 3, 4). The precise composition of the panel may vary between authorities. Recent empirical research found that in half of the social services departments surveyed the panel was composed of an independent person and two councillors, with an independent person, a councillor and a senior manager in a further third. Most independent persons were found to come from the voluntary sector (Dean, 'Social care provision: problems of redress', *Legal Action*, December 1995, p 8).

The Directions and the *Policy Guidance* envisage that the review will be initiated by the submission of written submissions followed by an oral hearing. Accordingly, the complainant is entitled to be given 10 days' notice of the hearing and to be invited to attend (*Policy Guidance*, Annex A, para 5). The *Policy Guidance* goes on to state that although complainants are entitled to be accompanied by a representative, that representative 'should not be a barrister or solicitor acting in a professional capacity' (Annex A, para 5). There seems to be an underlying anxiety that the presence of lawyers will convert what should be an 'informal' meeting (see para 6 of the *Policy Guidance*) to a quasi-judicial one. However, this is only guidance and there is no statutory basis for excluding legal representatives from the panel hearings. It has been argued that a decision by a panel that it had no discretion to allow a legal representative to attend might be susceptible to judicial review, particularly if the complaint raised issues of legal complexity (see Gordon, *Community Care Assessments*, p 53) and in practice some panels have ignored the guidance and permitted legal representatives to attend.

Even if there is no objection in principle to a lawyer accompanying the complainant, there may still be a practical obstacle relating to the availability of legal aid. However, the legal practitioner may be able to persuade the local legal aid board, using the analogy of decisions granting legal aid to finance lawyers accompanying parents and children to child protection conferences. This has been justified on the basis that providing assistance at this stage saves costs to the Legal Aid Fund in the long run as the presence of a lawyer diminishes the likelihood of other legal proceedings. In this context, it could be argued that legal representation of the complainant at the panel hearing could prevent the bringing of possible actions for judicial review. The Public Law Project briefing on *Challenging Community Care Decisions* (1994) suggests that a Green Form Extension may cover acting as a 'McKenzie friend' to the complainant at the hearing. The role of the 'McKenzie friend' is limited to advice during the hearing and taking notes but does not extend to advocacy on behalf of the complainant and the point is made that the Legal Aid Board would have to be convinced that the case is of special difficulty or importance or that the person could not act on his or her own without legal help (p 40).

Dean's empirical study found widespread variations in the degree of formality adopted in the oral hearing, both with regard to seating arrangements and procedural conventions (*Legal Action*, December 1995, p 8).

Direction 8(1) refers to the panel making 'recommendations' but there is evidence that some local authorities have effectively conferred decision-making powers on their panels (see SSI, 1993, para 7.1). The SSI has confirmed that the panel should be taking a view on the merits of the complaint and 'whether the action or decision complained about was appropriate and whether it is still appropriate. Considering only whether procedures have been followed seems not to accord with the intention of the DH guidance' (SSI, 1993, para 7.8).

The panel is required to decide on its recommendations and record them in writing within 24 hours of the hearing (Direction 8(1)). The panel must send a copy of its recommendations and the reasons for them to:

–   the complainant and anyone acting on his or her behalf;

–   the local authority;

–   anyone else whom the local authority thinks has a 'sufficient interest' (Directions 8(2), (3)).

The local authority is under a duty to consider what action, if any, should be taken in the light of the panel's recommendations and, within 28 days of the date of receipt of those recommendations, to notify the complainant of its final decision, together with the reasons therefor.

Is the local authority bound to accept the recommendations? In *R v Avon County Council ex parte M* [1994] 2 FLR 1006, Henry J stated that the social services committee 'could not overrule the decision [of the panel] without a substantial reason and without having given that recommendation the weight it requires' (at p 1019). In the subsequent case of *R v North Yorkshire County Council ex parte Hargreaves* (LEXIS transcript, QBD, 30 September 1994), the argument that *ex parte M* established a general principle of universal application in relation to the rejection by local authorities of review panel recommendations was not accepted. *Ex parte M* was distinguished on its facts and it was said that where the review panel endorsed the local authority's position on the subject-matter of the complaint but made recommendations on a collateral issue, the local authority was entitled to make minor modifications to those recommendations without giving reasons for so doing.

13.2.4   Evaluation of the complaints procedure

The complaints procedure, if followed through to the third stage of the panel hearing, is elaborate. Given that throughout it is managed and run by the local authority, complainants may have concerns about the objectivity and independence of the process. The cases of *ex parte M* and *Hargreaves* demonstrate that the operation of the procedure, in itself, may generate grounds for judicial review, particularly in relation to the conduct of the panel hearing. It is suggested that any unfairness should be protested against prior to the conclusion of the procedure and recorded in writing.

The obligation imposed on local authorities to give reasons for their response to the panel's recommendations may have practical significance in the context of seeking judicial review in relation to the initial complaint as opposed to the fairness of the complaints procedure. The reasons may indicate the factors which influenced the local authority and may provide valuable evidence on the way the decision was made and whether it was properly made. Given the absence of automatic discovery of documents in judicial review, it may be difficult otherwise for litigants to establish that an authority has acted irrationally.

The major disadvantage associated with the complaints procedures from the complainant's perspective is the time factor. As noted above, the second round of national inspections carried out by the SSI revealed that most social services departments were still having difficulties in meeting the formal timescales, although the overall picture revealed some improvements compared to the previous year (SSI, 1994). In the six social services departments surveyed, 26% of registered complaints were completed within the 28-day limit and 43% under three months (para 5.81). In 57% of cases, therefore, the process was dragging on and the SSI report does not indicate the maximum time taken. For older clients, in particular, a protracted procedure may not be a suitable mechanism for challenging decisions.

Based on his empirical survey, Dean has criticised the wide variations in the way review panels have interpreted the functions and powers of their role. He also found that although complainants were in general satisfied that they had been properly and courteously treated by the panels, they were not satisfied with the substantive outcome of their complaints (*Legal Action*, December 1995, p 8).

In principle, the complaints procedure would seem to be well suited to handling factual disputes. In particular, the review panel can make detailed findings of fact and take account of the opinions of expert witnesses if necessary. In principle, too, the panel forum should allow for the professional judgements of social workers to be challenged and overturned, where appropriate. However, the procedure seems less well suited to issues arising in relation to rationing, financial assessments and charges. There also appears to be some uncertainty over whether panels can recommend compensation, although some local authorities have been persuaded to make ex gratia payments.

13.3   The local authority's monitoring officer

13.3.1   The function of the monitoring officer

The monitoring officer's role is that of a 'whistle-blower'. All local authorities were required to designate one of their officers as 'monitoring officer' by s 5 of the Local Government and Housing Act 1989. The monitoring officer's duties are triggered when any proposal, decision or omission by the authority, any of its committees, or any of its officers 'constitutes, has given rise to or is likely to give rise to . . . a contravention of any rule of law or any code of practice made or approved by or under any enactment, or any such maladministration or injustice'. The monitoring officer prepares a report which is circulated to those within the authority who are responsible for the matter. Implementation of any decision is frozen while the authority are considering the report, which they must do within 21 days. This temporary reprieve may be useful where the complaint relates to the removal of a service, although the authority are not bound to follow the monitoring officer's recommendations. If the authority decline to act on the report, then it may be worth reporting councillors to the District Auditor.

13.3.2   Evaluation of the monitoring officer

Referral to the monitoring officer is simple, cheap and quick. If difficulties are encountered in getting the name and telephone or fax number of the monitoring officer from local authority staff, then the chief legal officer should be contacted.

Contacting the monitoring officer may be a useful adjunct to the complaints procedure and even if the matter is not resolved satisfactorily, then it will at least be evidence that the local authority were on notice of the existence of a problem in any subsequent judicial review proceedings.

13.4   The local government ombudsman

13.4.1   The jurisdiction of the ombudsman

An individual can complain to one of the three local government ombudsmen, the Commissioners for Local Administration, about injustice sustained as a result of maladministration by a local authority. 'Maladministration' can take various forms such as unreasonable delay, poor communication, incompetence, bias, or a failure to follow proper procedures. The ombudsman does not deal with the merits of a decision unless there has been maladministration in the decision-making process or the decision is *Wednesbury* unreasonable. The complaint must be made within 12 months although the ombudsman may waive this time-limit if there was a good reason for the delay. The requirement that the local authority must have a reasonable opportunity to deal with the complaint first is rigorously applied and such complaints will be treated as premature. Given the existence of the complaints procedure, the expectation may be that it has to be used first, and a strong case may have to be made for not going through it, based on the limits of the procedure such as the absence of financial compensation. The requirement that the complainant must have exhausted alternative legal remedies is a further hurdle, although the ombudsman has a discretion to waive this where it would be unreasonable in the circumstances to expect the complainant to go to court.

13.4.2   The mechanics of complaining to the ombudsman

The Commission of Local Administration (CLAE) has issued a 'how to complain' guide, setting out the three stages in the procedure (*How to complain to the Local Government Ombudsman*, CLAE, 1993). The complaint must be made in writing, either by letter or on the CLAE's standard form, and may be made via a councillor or directly to the Commissioner. At the initial stage, the ombudsman decides whether the complaint falls within the jurisdiction. If it does, then the ombudsman will automatically refer it back to the local authority for the authority's comments on the allegations. Many cases are settled at this second stage. The third stage is a formal investigation by the ombudsman who has the power to require the authority to disclose all relevant information.

At the conclusion of the investigation, the ombudsman will issue a report with recommendations. The recommendations may be directed towards changing procedures to prevent recurrence of the maladministration. Although the recommendations are not directly enforceable, in practice most authorities do comply rather than incur adverse publicity. The ombudsman also has powers to recommend an ex gratia payment to the complainant.

13.4.3   Evaluation of complaining to the ombudsman

The main disadvantage is the length of time taken to deal with complaints, particularly if in due course a full investigation is needed. In 1993/94, these cases took on average 74 weeks to complete compared to an average of 14 weeks otherwise (*Local Government Ombudsmen: Annual Report 1993/1994*, CLAE, 1994, p 39). However, the outcome can be successful in a number of respects. First, ombudsman investigations in relation to social services and housing authorities are relatively wide-ranging and, where they lead to changes in the policies and procedures of particular authorities, can benefit other service-users as well as the individual complainant. Secondly, the report may also provide a useful benchmark of good practice for other authorities to heed. Finally, the possibility of financial compensation may be a further incentive to use this procedure rather than the other avenues for complaint in some cases.

13.5   Default powers of the Secretary of State

13.5.1   Scope of the default powers

Although decisions about community care services are within the control of local, not central, government, the Secretary of State for Health has limited powers to deal with complaints. Under s 7C of the LASSA 1970, he may establish an inquiry into the exercise by a local authority of its social services functions. Where the authority has defaulted on its duties, under s 7D of LASSA 1970, he may make an order with directions which may be enforced through judicial review.

13.5.2   Evaluation of the default powers

It is extremely unlikely that this power will be of assistance in individual cases or even that it will be invoked, given that default powers in other legislation are rarely used. Politically, the Minister would be ill-advised to take action under s 7D as this may simply highlight the problem of inadequate resources available to social services. The limitation in s 7D to the authority's statutory duties means that the Minister's powers will only arise in extreme cases, for example where the authority has failed to set up a complaints procedure. However, the

Department of Health may bring informal pressure to bear on defaulting local authorities without formally intervening.

13.6 Judicial review

Judicial review is the High Court procedure available to individuals or groups for challenging the actions or decisions of local authorities or the Secretary of State. The principal drawback of judicial review from the viewpoint of the litigant is that the role of the court is supervisory, rather than appellate. This means that the function of the court is limited to considering the fairness of the decision-making process rather than the merits of the decision. In terms of remedies, the court cannot simply replace the local authority's decision with its own (as would be possible in an appeal); all the court can do is to quash the decision and remit the matter to the decision-maker. Of course, it is relatively easy for the decision-maker to reconsider 'properly' and then still reach the same decision. A further drawback is that the procedure is primarily concerned with legal issues and it is not geared up to dealing with factual disputes. Unlike normal private law litigation, discovery and cross-examination are not automatic. Yet the limitations of the procedure for individual litigants should not be over-stated. The high proportion of settlements, particularly after leave has been granted, indicates that it can be a valuable tool in negotiating with local authorities. Local authorities may prefer to settle than attract adverse publicity, or bear the costs of litigation. Settlement may also permit the authority to preserve a key policy or procedure by pre-empting a finding of illegality. Equally, judicial review has been used as a 'test case' strategy by those representing the service users in order to challenge local authority policies and procedures. The Public Law Project has been particularly associated with this type of litigation in the community care context ('Annual Report 1994/1995', *The Public Law Project*, 1995).

13.6.1 The requirements for judicial review

The first hurdle for the potential litigant is obtaining leave to proceed to a full, substantive hearing. Leave is not a mere formality: between 40% and 50% of applicants fail at this stage. A court may refuse leave on the ground of delay, as the application must be brought promptly and, in any event, within three months of the date of the decision being challenged (Ord 53, r 4(1)). Where the delay is due to the time taken for the applicant to get legal aid, the court will usually extend the time-limit, as also where the applicant was unsuccessfully pursuing alternative remedies. In the latter case, however, legal advisers for applicants may wish to guard against local authorities taking the time point in subsequent proceedings for judicial review, by extracting a concession to that effect. Alternatively, it may be advisable to lodge an application for leave but invite the court to adjourn it pending the outcome of the other remedies being pursued (see Gordon, 'Challenging community care assessments', *Legal Action*, August 1993, p 8 at p 10).

Applications for leave must, inter alia, specify the grounds upon which the relief is sought and be accompanied by an affidavit (Ord 53, r 3(2)). Leave will be refused if the applicant has not exhausted all alternative remedies or cannot establish an arguable case.

13.6.2　Alternative remedies precluding or delaying judicial review

(1)　*The complaints procedure*
The relationship between judicial review and the comparable complaints procedure under the Children Act 1989 has been examined in the case of *R v Royal Borough of Kingston-upon-Thames ex parte T* [1994] 1 FLR 798. In the *Kingston* case, Ward J, drawing on dicta of Glidewell LJ in *Ex parte Waldron* [1986] QB 824, held that the choice of remedy should depend on whether the alternative remedy would resolve the question fully and directly, whether it was quicker than judicial review and whether it was the most convenient remedy. He found that the complaints procedure met all three criteria on the facts and that the most compelling argument for requiring the complaints procedure to be followed before embarking on judicial review was that this order of priority was consistent with the 'broad legislative purpose' of the Children Act 1989 (at p 815). This approach is likely to prevail in the community care context too, except where the service-user is seeking to challenge the *legality* of the authority's actions, as then the need for authoritative guidance from the courts may make judicial review the more convenient remedy. A further determining factor in the choice may be the availability of interim service provision in judicial review proceedings where the decision being challenged is one not to provide such services under s 47 of the NHSCCA 1990.

(2)　*The default powers*
The availability of the default powers has been considered by the Court of Appeal in *R v Devon County Council ex parte Baker* and *R v Durham County Council ex parte Curtis* [1995] 1 All ER 73. In both cases, elderly residents of local authority homes were seeking judicial review on the ground that the local authorities had failed to consult them prior to taking the decisions to close the homes. The Court of Appeal rejected the authorities' argument that the Secretary of State's default powers constituted an alternative remedy. First, it was doubted whether the duty to consult was a social services function, subject to the default powers contained in s 7D of the LASSA 1970. Secondly, as the issue was entirely a matter of law in a developing field, judicial review was seen as the more convenient remedy.

13.6.3　The grounds for judicial review

To substantiate a claim for judicial review, an applicant must be able to show that the local authority (or Secretary of State in relation to the exercise of the default powers or issuance of *Directions* or *Policy Guidance*) has acted illegally, irrationally or with procedural impropriety (the three-fold classification formulated by Lord Diplock in *Council of Civil Service Unions v Minister for the Civil Service* [1985] AC 374).

'Illegality' in this context means that the authority has acted ultra vires, or outside its powers. An example of illegality would be where the local authority adopts a rigid policy and fetters its discretion in handling individual cases. An authority can adopt a general policy but it must be prepared to consider each case individually and admit exceptions to the general policy. Arguments as to the legality or illegality of an authority's actions frequently turn on the construction of the exact statutory wording. Thus the applicants in the *Gloucestershire* case (above) succeeded on the narrow point that it was unlawful under s 2 of the CSDPA 1970 to cut their services without a reassessment of their personal circumstances. A point of statutory construction was also at issue in *R v London Borough of Wandsworth ex parte Beckwith* [1996] 1 All ER 129. The House of Lords were required to construe ss 21 and 26 of NAA 1948, as amended by the NHSCCA 1990 and the Community Care (Residential Accommodation) Act 1992. Their Lordships held that local authorities are not under a legal duty to maintain some directly provided residential care for the elderly and are entitled to discharge their statutory duties entirely by arrangements with the private sector. Lord Hoffman concluded that the view of the Department of Health, as expressed in para 5 of LAC(93)10, that authorities had to make some provision for residential care, was 'simply wrong' (at p 132).

'Irrationality' refers in essence to decisions that no reasonable authority would have taken. '*Wednesbury* unreasonableness', after *Associated Provincial Picture Houses Ltd v Wednesbury Corporation* [1948] 1 KB 223, is often used as a shorthand description for this ground. Note that the courts are very reluctant to hold that local authorities have acted irrationally and the applicant will accordingly face a high burden of proof. However, *Wednesbury* unreasonableness was the basis on which the decision of the local authority was quashed in *ex parte M* (above), and in the *Gloucestershire* case, McCowan LJ was using the notion of *Wednesbury* unreasonableness when he emphasised that there would be situations where a reasonable authority could only conclude that some arrangements were necessary to meet the needs of a particular disabled person, regardless of a lack of resources.

'Procedural impropriety' occurs where the local authority fails to set up proper procedures, fails to comply with any procedures which have been set up, or fails to observe the rules of natural justice. In the context of community care decision-making, 'natural justice' encompasses the legitimate expectations of individuals in relation to the criteria of eligibility and the practice of conducting assessments. Consultation is a further aspect of procedural fairness (see *R v Devon County Council ex parte Baker* and *R v Durham County Council ex parte Curtis* [1995] 1 All ER 73). A failure to give reasons for decisions may also be susceptible to judicial review under this ground.

13.6.4 Evaluation of judicial review as a remedy

Delay can be a major problem with judicial review. It is possible to apply for an expedited hearing; otherwise there may be a gap of one year or more between the grant of leave and the full hearing. Pending the full hearing, interim relief is available and indeed may justify going straight to judicial review, bypassing the complaints procedure. The applicant has to show that he or she has a real prospect of success at the hearing and that the balance of convenience favours making an interim injunction, for example compelling the local authority to provide services until such time as the case is heard.

Even if the litigant is successful at the hearing, and 'wins' on the law, victory may be illusory as judicial review is discretionary and relief may be refused. It is theoretically possible for damages to be awarded on an application for judicial review but only for breach of a private law duty (see **13.7**).

From the perspective of both applicants and local authorities, the fact that judicial review creates a precedent for the future may be a double-edged sword, depending on the outcome and the politics behind a particular case. As pointed out by Belinda Schwehr, pre-*Gloucestershire*, disabled candidates for services were able to use the legal uncertainty over the relevance of resources in relation to the provision of services under the CSDPA 1970 to their advantage in negotiations with care managers. Post-*Gloucestershire*, that particular bargaining counter has gone. For Gloucestershire Social Services Department the victory was at a price; the cost of re-assessing current users of CSDPA 1970 services was put at £200,000 (*Independent*, 17 June 1995). From a wider perspective, the decision seems unlikely to help local authorities fighting their corner for more funding for community care from central government ('Rational rationing of community care resources', Schwehr, [1995] *Public Law* 374 at pp 380–381).

13.7 Tort action for damages

In theory, a cause of action in private law against a local authority may arise in two possible ways:

– breach of statutory duty;

– common law duty of care in negligence, either by a direct duty of care imposed on the authority or via the authority's vicarious liability in respect of a breach of a duty of care owed by its servants.

On the basis of the current law, however, tortious claims against a local authority in the context of community care remain to be transformed from theoretical possibility into concrete reality. Indeed, the prospect of such a transformation has receded following the decision of the House of Lords in *X (Minors) v Bedfordshire County Council; M (A Minor) and Another v Newham London Borough Council and Others; E (A Minor) v Dorset County Council; Christmas v*

Hampshire County Council; Keating v Bromley London Borough Council [1995] 2 FLR 276 (hereafter referred to as *X v Bedfordshire CC*). Although two of the five cases relate to the duties of social services to protect children from abuse, and the remaining three concern special educational needs, the general approach laid down by their Lordships would seem to reduce the scope for contending that actionable torts arise in relation to the exercise of a local authority's statutory functions in relation to community care services.

13.7.1 Breach of statutory duty

In this context it must be remembered that the NHSCCA 1990 imposes the assessment regime of s 47 as a 'raft' floating on top of pre-existing duties and powers, and that the general approach of the courts in deciding whether a breach confers an action in tort is one of construction of the particular statute. In *Wyatt v Hillingdon LBC* [1978] 76 LGR 727, the Court of Appeal considered whether breach of s 2 of the CSDPA 1970 and s 29 of the NAA 1948 in relation to the level of provision of home help services could give rise to a civil action for damages. Geoffrey Lane LJ roundly rejected this contention, stating:

> 'a statute such as this which is dealing with the distribution of benefits – or, to put it perhaps more accurately, comforts to the sick and disabled – does not in its very nature give rise to an action by the disappointed sick person. It seems to me quite extraordinary that if the local authority, as is alleged here, provided, for example two hours less home help than the sick person considered herself entitled to that that can amount to a breach of statutory duty which will permit the sick person to claim a sum of monetary damages by way of breach of statutory duty' (at p 733).

In *X v Bedfordshire CC*, Lord Browne-Wilkinson, while acknowledging that each case turns on the particular statutory provisions, found it significant that counsel had not referred to:

> 'any case where it had been held that statutory provisions establishing a regulatory system or a scheme of social welfare for the benefit of the public at large had been held to give rise to a private right of action for damages for breach of statutory duty ... The cases where a private right of action for breach of statutory duty has been held to arise are all cases in which the statutory duty has been very limited and specific as opposed to general administrative functions imposed on public bodies and involving the exercise of administrative discretions'.

The duties imposed on social services under the child welfare legislation were held to fall into the latter category and this would seem equally to be the case in relation to community care legislation.

However, it may be possible to formulate a claim based on a derivative statutory duty, ie an implied private law duty to implement a decision, following on from a primary public law duty to make a decision. This line of argument has been successful in relation to a housing authority's duties under the homelessness legislation (see *Cocks v Thanet District Council* [1983] 2 AC 286). In relation to s 47(1) of the NHSCCA 1990, breach of the derivative duty would seem to cover cases where the authority has in fact failed to provide services, having decided as part of its public law decision-making function that such services should be provided to an individual. The *Gloucestershire* ruling that s 2 of the CSDPA 1970 creates an individual and absolute duty to continue to provide services agreed to be necessary, would also seem to be susceptible to this analysis where those services are delayed or withdrawn. However, it would seem that an authority could avoid liability simply by making a further public law decision not to provide services to the individual, resulting in the first decision (which was the condition precedent for the derivative duty) then lapsing.

13.7.2   Common law duty of care in negligence

(1)   *Direct duty of care*
While not definitively ruled out, nevertheless the potential for basing a claim on the existence of a direct common law duty of care owed by a local authority to service users would appear slight post *X v Bedfordshire CC*. The House of Lords distinguished claims based on negligent policy-making from claims based on the negligent operation of policy. Claims in the former category were defined as non-justiciable. Claims falling into the latter category were to be determined by application of the ordinary principles of negligence as laid down in *Caparo v Dickman* [1992] 2 AC 605. Even in respect of this category, the statutory framework is not irrelevant, as Lord Browne-Wilkinson held that a common law duty of care cannot be superimposed on a statutory duty, if the observance of such a common law duty of care would be inconsistent with, or have a tendency to discourage, the due performance by the local authority of its statutory duties (at p 290). On this basis, the House of Lords concluded that it would not be just and reasonable to impose a common law duty of care on either local authorities in relation to the performance of their statutory duties to protect children from abuse, or education authorities in relation to the exercise of their statutory discretions in relation to children with special educational needs. However, the claim that the education authority was directly liable for the way it provided the service of psychological advice was allowed to proceed to trial. It was said that once the decision is taken to offer a service to the public, a statutory body is in the same position as any private individual or organisation and comes under a duty of care to service users (at p 314).

Applying this reasoning to the community care context, it might be argued that failure to carry out proper assessment procedures is part and parcel of the system established by an authority for the discharge of its statutory duty to assess under s 47(1) of the NHSCCA 1990. The courts would therefore approach the question of the existence and scope of any direct duty by assessing whether the imposition of a direct common law duty would impede the due performance of that statutory duty. As in the child abuse and the education cases, the existence of the statutory complaints procedure and the local government ombudsman could well be used to justify the conclusion that a direct duty should not be imposed. However, in other instances the courts may feel that no distinction can be drawn between local authorities directly providing services and their private sector counterparts so that a direct duty could be imposed, for example, where a hoist is badly installed or a bed provided by the authority proves defective and the user is injured.

(2) *Vicarious liability*

In *X v Bedfordshire CC,* a distinction was drawn between the position of the psychologists in the education cases and the doctor and social worker in the child abuse cases, for whom the authorities were held not to be vicariously liable (at p 315). The basis for the distinction was said to be that in the education cases there is no conflict between the professional's duty towards the plaintiff and his duty owed to the authority, nor between the professional being under a personal duty and the discharge by the authority of its statutory duties. Applying this analysis to the community care context might require distinctions to be drawn between care managers and social workers and care assistants/ home helps. Thus, if a care assistant or home help drops an elderly person when lifting them or scalds them in the bath, then the local authority might well be vicariously liable.

13.8   Conclusion

The phrase 'mixed economy' would seem a fairly apt description of the range of enforcement procedures which exist in relation to community care. While the statutory complaints procedure may be regarded as the main avenue for disputes between service users and carers and local authorities, it certainly does not supersede the alternatives in all cases. Those advising and representing users and carers need to be aware of the full range of procedures in order to assess in relation to each individual case which is likely to provide the most responsive means of resolution.

Part II

PAYING FOR CARE

'Effective costing and charging procedures can be valuable in achieving the best use of resources across a range of personal social services and local social services authorities will be expected to develop them' (*Caring for People*, para 3.8.1).

Chapter 14

THE NEW FUNDING ARRANGEMENTS

14.1 Introduction

As has already been noted in Chapter 2, the hidden agenda for the new arrangements for community care was the capping of social security spending on residential care. The transfer of funding to local authorities via the STG has been explained in Chapter 2, and the effect of the NHSCCA 1990, with related changes in the benefits rules, has been to make it impossible in future for local authorities to shift costs over to central government via the benefits system. 'Local government's great and final opportunity' (Bottomley, 1993) was in fact to spend rather less in implementing the full range of community care policies than central government had previously laid out in the residential sector alone.

Clients will notice three main financial consequences of the legislative changes.

(i) Local authorities, through the assessment process (see Chapter 5), have become 'gatekeepers' of public funds. People who feel that they need services at home, or who wish to enter residential care homes or nursing homes, and who are not in a position to purchase their requirements in the open market, must 'pass' the needs test in order to qualify for local authority commissioned services, which now include all residential care arrangements. Services are supposed to be needs-led, but, as explained in Chapter 6, this does not necessarily mean that people get what they want. Even if needs do match wants, however, services will have to be paid for, as far as users are able to do so.

(ii) Local authorities are now operating means tests for most services. People going into residential care by arrangement with the local authority will always be subject to a statutory means test. Where home care arrangements are being made, local authorities will undoubtedly charge users, as they have power to do, and may either operate a means test or use some other charging device. Health care services, whether delivered in hospital or via community health providers, will still be free of charge to users. It is apparent, however, that the demarcation line between the different community services is shifting. Services previously labelled 'health' and so free of charge are being re-labelled 'social care' and are having to be paid for by users. There is a more extensive discussion of this issue in Chapter 2.

(iii) Income support rules have changed. Elderly people who are on very low incomes, or without resources at all, can still claim means-tested benefits to raise their resources to a basic subsistence level, but the enhanced payments of income support which used to be available for residential care have stopped. People who entered residential accommodation before 1 April 1993 could claim an accommodation allowance of between £175 and £280 per week (1992/93 rates) plus a personal expenses allowance. Claimants living in their own homes received, generally speaking, less than half that amount. The changes in the law now mean that residential care no longer carries a benefits incentive.

In order to understand the implications of these changes, it will be helpful briefly to consider the legal position as it was before April 1993, and then to fit the new rules into context.

14.2　Paying for residential care before 1 April 1993

As explained in Chapter 9, residential care arrangements before April 1993 were made either by local authorities, in pursuit of their responsibility under Part III of the NAA 1948, or by individuals purchasing on their own behalf. Local authorities owned and managed their own Part III accommodation and, in addition, there was a flourishing independent sector in which authorities were permitted to sponsor beds as an alternative means of discharging their statutory responsibility. They had no explicit duty to make arrangements for nursing home care. Individuals could, of course, enter nursing homes by their own arrangement, and health authorities had power to commission beds in independent nursing homes.

The residential care system was largely funded by central government through social security benefits. Those placed in local authority Part III accommodation, or in sponsored beds elsewhere, had to be charged for their accommodation, under s 22 of the NAA 1948. Those with means would be asked to pay a standard charge which was related to the economic cost of providing the bed. The local authority's responsibility was always in the nature of a safety net, however, and so most people placed were at poverty level. A means test was prescribed by charging regulations, and a minimum contribution was payable which could be met either by paying over the basic retirement pension, or by claiming income support (previously supplementary benefit) which was available at a special 'Part III' rate.

Establishments in the independent sector would set their own fees. Residents who had insufficient income to pay the fees, and who were without capital of at least £8,000, could claim income support at the enhanced level. During the early 1980s, rates for income support matched home fees. In 1986, the link was broken and regulations set maximum fees for different categories of residential home accommodation. In March 1993, the benefit payments ranged from £175 (outside Greater London) per week for residential care homes for elderly people with a physical disability to £280 per week for nursing homes for elderly people with mental health problems. Residents were not asked to establish need for a particular type of residential care, or indeed for care at all. This created a 'perverse incentive' so far as the Audit Commission was concerned (see Chapter 2).

Thus, the benefits system funded independent sector beds in both residential care homes and nursing homes. In particular, it allowed health authorities to camouflage the gradual reduction in continuing care provision within the NHS by discharging elderly patients from hospital into nursing homes, where their care could be paid for by the DSS rather than the NHS. In 1993, this convenient practice was questioned when the Court of Appeal ruled that an arrangement to place former long-stay hospital patients in a nursing home was nothing more than an extension of NHS hospital care, and could not be funded through income support (*White and Others v Chief Adjudication Officer and Another*, (1993) *The Times*, 2 August). The implications of this decision were considerable, but relatively unexplored, because soon afterwards implementation of Part III of the NHSCCA 1990 turned the whole system on its head.

14.3 Paying for services delivered at home before 1 April 1993

Local authorities have a long-standing power, not a duty, to charge users for non-residential social services. The power emanates from s 17 of the Health and Social Services and Social Security Adjudications Act 1983.

The power to charge applies to the following community care services:

–   services provided under s 29 of the NAA 1948 (welfare arrangements for the disabled);
–   services provided under s 45 of the HSPHA 1968 (welfare of old people);
–   services provided under Sch 8 to the NHSA 1977 (prevention of illness; care and after-care; home help facilities).

In addition, it seems clear that s 29 of the NAA is an umbrella provision, which covers and incorporates s 2 of the CSDPA 1970 so that the power to charge extends to the services provided under s 2.

Local authorities are not empowered to impose charges in respect of social work support services, occupational therapy, or advice and assessment of client needs. Assessments carried out under s 47 of the NHSCCA 1990 will therefore be free of charge. In addition, there is no power to charge for services provided under s 117 of the MHA 1983, which requires social services and health authorities to provide after-care to people discharged from hospital after being detained under the Act.

By comparison with the residential sector, regulation was minimal before April 1993. Section 17 of the HASSASSAA 1983 permits the imposition of 'reasonable' charges, but without direct reference to either the economic cost of providing services or to users' ability to pay. It was left open to local authorities to impose flat rate charges, adopt means tests and/or establish hardship policies. Some authorities made no charges at all, and generally speaking there were considerable variations in charging practice up and down the country.

14.4   Charging policies from April 1993

For the residential sector, a new statutory means test has been introduced to determine an individual's ability to contribute towards the cost of accommodation and care, and it is now clear that the principle of means testing will eventually be extended across the whole range of community care services. This fits in with the view that all local authority provision is a safety net extended to those who are vulnerable and in need. For this client group, the rationale is that the poorest should have free services, and those with modest resources should make a contribution towards the costs of their care. In practice, it will mean that social security benefits available to the poorest and most in need will be effectively appropriated by the local authority to help make its resources stretch further.

The White Paper on community care emphasises that the ability to pay for services in full or to make a contribution towards costs should not in any way influence provision itself. This is also clear as a matter of law; there is no rule which makes the duty to provide services conditional upon payment of charges. However, the new duty to assess need under s 47 of the NHSCCA 1990 raises a very obvious conflict for local authority care managers, in that where needs are bound to exceed budgets, awareness of means may taint the assessment process and render it susceptible to challenge. There is explicit reference to this point in the *Policy Guidance.*

> 'Assessments of financial means ... should ... follow the assessment of need and decisions about service provision' (para 3.31).

> 'The provision of services, whether or not the local authority is under a statutory duty to make provision, should not be related to the ability of the users or their families to meet the cost.'

Advisers will wish to check that a clear line is indeed drawn, in practical terms, between the assessment of need and any subsequent financial assessment. Best practice requires the assessment to be finalised and communicated before any financial investigation is undertaken.

There is now some anecdotal evidence that local authorities are declining to assess the needs of individuals with substantial means on the basis that, as they will become private purchasers of care, an assessment wastes precious time and resources. As has already been noted, however, s 47 of the NHSCCA 1990 creates a general entitlement to assessment, as a specific service, so that a refusal to assess, on financial grounds alone, is probably unlawful.

14.5   Paying for residential care after April 1993

For anyone requiring financial support entry to all residential care homes and nursing homes is subject first to an assessment of need under s 47 of the NHSCCA 1990, and, secondly, to a means test conducted by the local authority under new assessment regulations. Chapter 15 considers the law in some detail.

Local authorities use their transferred funding either to purchase care beds in the independent sector or, to a lesser extent, to maintain beds in what is left of their own Part III accommodation, but, either way, they are required to seek contributions from residents. 'Sponsorship' by local authorities of independent sector beds is no longer possible. Private arrangements are, of course, still available to individuals with substantial means. Those with modest means, whose funds may, in time, become exhausted, will need advice on whether to seek a s 47 assessment at an early stage, or whether to wait until financial assistance is actually required (see p 64).

14.6 Preserved rights

The new legislation is not retrospective in its effect. People already resident in independent sector care homes or nursing homes before 1 April 1993 now have 'preserved rights' which enable them to continue claiming income support at the old enhanced rates. Those who do not yet qualify for income support will be able to claim benefit, at the enhanced rates, once their capital has been depleted beneath the new £16,000 threshold. This means that, for at least the next generation, three separate financial regimes, two of them based on different forms of State subsidy, will co-exist in the same residential establishments:

– residents with preserved rights, who entered residential care by 31 March 1993;

– new residents who are being funded by the local authority and who are making an assessed contribution towards the overheads;

– new residents who are funding themselves and who have made their own arrangements with the establishments concerned.

In addition, there will be a small, and rapidly declining number of people who occupy beds contracted by the NHS. These people will not be paying for their accommodation, but if they are income support claimants their entitlement to benefit will be substantially less than that of other residents (see p 23).

Before 1 April 1993, preserved rights status was perceived as potentially favourable, and there was pressure to place elderly people in residential care beds before the new legislation took effect. Local authorities, for obvious reasons, set out to mitigate their financial responsibilities by making placements before the implementation date. Now, however, it looks as though preserved rights are creating very serious problems for some elderly clients and their families. The legal position is analysed in detail in Chapter 16.

14.7 Paying for home care services after 1 April 1993

The law has not changed, but practice has changed considerably. New DoH Guidance (LAC(94)1) has emphasised the expectation that users should be

required to pay for services, subject to their ability to do so. Guidance issued by
the Association of County Councils recommends that authorities adopt flexible
charging policies which are not seen as a deterrent to the take-up of services or
as causing hardship to those in need. On the other hand, increasing financial
pressures on local authorities have quite evidently forced up charges over the
past few years, and community care policies themselves expressly encourage
the provision of more elaborate, and more expensive, domiciliary services.
Clearly, regulation is likely to be needed before long in order to ensure equality
of treatment across the country and to bring practice into line with residential
care, where the charging process is standardised and highly regulated (see
Chapter 15). A report recently published by the National Consumer Council
indicates that there are 'unacceptable disparities' between the charging
policies of different local authorities (*Charging Customers for Social Services*, NCC,
1995).

Current law and practice is discussed in more detail in Chapter 17.

14.8   Essential reference materials for the legal adviser

Apart from the primary legislation and the various regulations referred to in
Chapters 15 to 19, advisers on financial matters should have access to the
following:

(a) the 'Charging for Residential Accommodation Guide' ('CRAG'). The
     Government has produced this guidance for local authorities on the rules
     for the means test set out in the National Assistance (Assessment of
     Resources) Regulations 1992 (see **15.1**). Copies of the CRAG may be
     obtained from DoH publications (see List of Useful Addresses), quoting
     reference LAC (95)7, LAC (95)21 and LAC (96)9.

(b) The 'Adjudication Officers' Guide' ('AOG'), HMSO. This is a loose-leaf
     work in ten volumes which covers all social security benefits. Volumes 3
     and 4, which deal with income-related benefits, will be particularly useful.
     The Guide is usually available in central reference libraries, university
     libraries or benefits agency offices;

(c) *Income Related Benefits: The Legislation* by J Mesher and P Wood (Sweet &
     Maxwell). This work comprises annotated primary and secondary
     legislation. It is used by social security appeal tribunals;

(d) A general guide to welfare benefits law and practice. For example: *Welfare
     Benefits Handbook* (Child Poverty Action Group); *Rights Guide to Non-means
     Tested Benefits* (Child Poverty Action Group); *Disability Rights Handbook*
     (Disability Alliance);

(e) 'Decisions of the Social Security Commissioners'. These are available from
     Harp House, 83 Farringdon Street, London EC4A 4DH.

Chapter 15

THE LOCAL AUTHORITY'S MEANS TEST FOR RESIDENTIAL CARE

15.1   What is the legal basis of the means test?

Section 22 of the NAA 1948 remains the source of the local authority's legal obligation to recover the costs of residential accommodation. That provision must now be read alongside s 26 of the NAA 1948 (substantially amended by s 44 of the NHSCCA 1990). The combined effect is as follows:

(a) Local authorities must fix and recover charges in respect of placements which they provide directly in their own, maintained Part III accommodation, and in respect of placements which they arrange with independent providers in either residential care homes or nursing homes.

(b) Section 22(5) contains power to make regulations prescribing a means test of the resident in question. The current regulations are the National Assistance (Assessment of Resources) Regulations 1992 (SI 1992/2977).

(c) The previous central government subsidy for residential care arrangements, paid through income support, is still available but is considerably reduced. Benefit may be claimed by residents entering Part III homes or independent residential care homes or nursing homes after 1 April 1993, and will be taken into account in the local authority's means test. Higher levels of benefit are payable to claimants placed in the independent sector. This means that there is a financial incentive for local authorities to purchase beds from the independent sector and a disincentive for them to assume the provider role. This pressure operates alongside the requirement that 85% of the STG funding should be spent in the independent sector (see Chapter 2).

The National Assistance (Assessment of Resources) Regulations 1992 are modelled on the Income Support (General) Regulations 1987. Many provisions of the 1987 regulations are applied directly. Thus, the means test is complex, technical and difficult for clients to understand. It will generally be administered by local authority finance officers, who may have little understanding of legal concepts and certainly lack the long experience of the Benefits Agency in operating the income support rules. To help them, the Department of Health has published the 'Charging for Residential Accommodation Guide' (CRAG) (see **14.8**), which provides an authoritative explanation of the regulations themselves. In practice, the CRAG is the common currency and it is essential that legal advisers have access to it (see **14.8**).

The legislation does not provide any direct means of appealing against local authority financial assessments. The complaints procedure is available, but is not well suited to interpreting black letter law. Two consequences flow from this:

(i)   clients may benefit considerably from legal advice given at the time of the financial assessment. At this point, there may be scope for correcting errors and for discussion and even negotiation on difficult conceptual issues, such as beneficial entitlement under trusts;

(ii) there will be no opportunity to develop case-law concerning the interpretation of the regulations. This means that, for guidance, advisers will have to rely on analogous decisions of the Social Security Commissioners interpreting the income support rules (see, for example, the discussion at **18.2.8**).

Even though the means tests for residential accommodation and income support are substantially similar, there are no prescribed links between local authorities and the Benefits Agency. The CRAG emphasises, however, that the quality of liaison between social services departments and the Benefits Agency will play an important part in ensuring that benefits are claimed when there is entitlement and that there is no misuse of public funds. It recommends that local authorities should establish, at senior level, a main channel of contact between social services departments and Benefits Agency offices. Channels of contact do not, however, appear to have simplified the system. Where a prospective resident is likely to be eligible for income support, two financial assessments will have to be made and two bureaucratic processes endured. In addition, as will be described in detail later on, there are certain crucial distinctions between the two sets of regulations, which are likely to generate confusion for individuals and confront local authorities with some hard decisions.

15.2   How does the means test operate?

Sections 22(2) and 26(3) of the NAA 1948 require people placed by local authorities in residential accommodation to repay the full economic cost of the accommodation if they are capable of doing so. Technically, the onus is then on a resident with limited means to satisfy the local authority that he or she is unable to meet accommodation fees in full, and in such cases the authority will assess his or her ability to pay a lower rate. If a resident withholds necessary financial information, so that the means test cannot be carried out, the local authority may charge him or her for the full cost of the accommodation.

The financial assessment is applied to both capital and income. From April 1996, individuals with capital of more than £16,000 will be expected to pay for their own care in full, irrespective of the amount of their income (s 134(1) of the SSCBA 1992, and reg 20 of the NA(AR) Regs 1992). Since the cost of a residential care home or nursing home bed is probably between £15,000 and £20,000 per year (subject to considerable regional variations), few elderly people who are above the capital threshold will be able to pay for their care from income alone, and some will be forced to draw heavily on savings to fund their placements.

Where it is immediately clear that an individual resident's capital exceeds £16,000, the local authority need not make a wider assessment of his or her ability to pay for the bed (reg 20). Sections 21 and 26 of the NAA 1948 clearly contemplate that the local authority may still make the accommodation arrangements, thereby using its superior purchasing power, but require a full contribution to the costs from the resident. In practice, however, where no public subsidy is involved, and particularly where the private funds are substantial, the local authority may suggest that the individual makes his or her own arrangements directly with a provider.

If the client's capital is less than £16,000 at the outset, or is later reduced below that threshold, the local authority must apply the regulations in order to determine the resident's income resources. If those resources do not meet the full cost of the bed, the local authority itself must nevertheless meet its contractual obligation to the provider to pay the full fee for it. The authority must then calculate and recover the appropriate contributions from the resident. This process highlights the potential conflict for a social services care manager, operating a cash limited budget: the greater the contributions made by individual residents, the further the local authority's resources will stretch. It is very easy to see how the process of assessing need could be construed as tainted by financial considerations.

When an assessment has been completed, the local authority should provide a resident with a written statement of his or her contribution and how it has been calculated.

15.3 How is capital assessed?

15.3.1 The new capital limits

In his November 1995 Budget, the Chancellor of the Exchequer announced increases in the upper and lower capital limits prescribed by the NA(AR) Regs 1992. The upper capital limit is raised from £8,000 to £16,000 and the lower capital limit from £3,000 to £10,000. These increases took effect in April 1996. Residents whose capital assets are valued at less than £16,000 are now eligible for financial assistance from the local authority. Capital assets of between £10,000 and £16,000 are subject to the tariff income calculation (see **15.4**).

In addition, there have been corresponding changes to the income support capital limits affecting people who are in residential care. Older people who have preserved rights to income support (see Chapter 16) are affected, as are those admitted to residential care since 1 April 1993 who are entitled to top-up low incomes with income support. For claimants living in the community, however, the limits remain at £8,000 and £3,000 (regs 45 and 53(1A), (1B), (1C) and (4) of the ISG Regs 1987).

15.3.2 Method of valuation

Neither the regulations nor the CRAG go into details as to how the assessment of capital is to be conducted. There is no explicit duty for residents to disclose assets and no explicit powers for assessors to force disclosure. However, the rule that the onus is on a resident to show why he or she should not pay for a bed in full means that clients should be advised that it is in their interests to respond to requests to see bank books, building society passbooks and other relevant sources of financial information. Where residents are unable to handle their own affairs, the local authority should find out if anyone has a power of attorney or has been appointed receiver and, if so, should seek information from that person. The CRAG stipulates that the local authority should also identify any DSS appointees although, as a matter of law, their power to provide information is strictly limited to benefit matters.

The regulations contain no definition of 'capital' or 'income'. Therefore, a common sense approach has to be adopted, even in the face of arcane provisions which allow income to be treated as capital or capital as income (regs 16 and 22). Where capital assets are held by a resident, they must be valued at current market or surrender value less 10% of the valuation for the expenses of realisation, where that would be necessary, and less the value of mortgages or other encumbrances, but not ordinary unsecured debts (reg 23).

Market value is considered to be the price a willing buyer would pay to a willing seller (CRAG, para 6.012).

The CRAG gives examples of capital assets which assessors will commonly have to deal with (para 6.002):

– buildings;

– land;

– national savings certificates;

– premium bonds;

– stocks and shares;

– capital held by the Court of Protection or by a receiver;

– any savings held, for example, in building society accounts;

– bank accounts;

– unit trusts;

– trust funds;

– cash.

15.3.3 Ownership of assets

The NA(AR)Regs 1992 require the whole of a resident's capital to be taken into account (reg 21). This includes interests held on trust for the resident. Sometimes difficult questions of trust law will be raised during an assessment where, for example, the nature of the beneficial interests subsisting in a particular asset are unclear.

In principle, where a resident has an interest under a fixed trust that will be assessed as actual capital. The same applies to interests under resulting or constructive trusts, although these may not, in practice, be easily identifiable or quantifiable. The normal market value rule will operate and the local authority may ask for written evidence of the value of the trust fund. Contingent interests in capital will be regarded as having a discounted market value, and so will be taken into account as actual capital.

Where a resident receives trust income, that will, of course, be taken into account in the assessment of income. The right to receive the income also has a value, as capital, but the regulations provide that this will be disregarded in the assessment (see **15.3.5**).

Discretionary trusts cause some difficulties in practice. In principle, the discretionary beneficiary has no *entitlement* to capital before it is appointed, and the assessor should therefore take into account only payments out of the trust fund. If the trustees exercise their discretion not to make payments out, the beneficiary will have no actual capital which is capable of assessment. Legal advisers should resist the argument that regular discretionary payments have created a quasi-entitlement to a proportion of the trust capital. Not only does this argument seek to go behind the discretionary trust principle, but also a potential interest under such a trust is unlikely to have a market value (R(SB)25/83).

Where a fixed trust contains an express discretionary power to advance capital, or where s 32 of the Trustee Act 1925 applies, it may be argued that the value of the underlying contingent interests is enhanced (*Peters v Chief Adjudication Officer*, R(SB)3/89). Legal advisers should seek to negotiate with finance officers where the valuation seems to be excessive. The CRAG gives little guidance on this point, and the regulations none at all.

15.3.4 Co-ownership of assets

Where a joint beneficial interest in personal property is being assessed, reg 27(1) requires normal equitable principles to be ignored. Instead, assessors must assume that the property in question is owned in equal shares.

Example:
Mr and Mrs Scott have £9,000 in a joint building society account. According to equitable principles, the beneficial shares are:

Mrs Scott – £3,500
Mr Scott – £5,500.

Mrs Scott is about to go into a nursing home. Regulation 27(1) applies and the local authority finance officer, when conducting the financial assessment, will conclude that the building society account is to be treated as owned in equal shares and that Mrs Scott has £4,500 capital available to her. Anticipating this decision, Mrs Scott's solicitor may advise that the joint account should be closed and two separate accounts opened, in one of which Mrs Scott has £3,500 in her sole name. This would not constitute a 'deprivation' of capital by either Mr or Mrs Scott, because each has received no more than his or her beneficial entitlement. The action would, therefore, avoid the notional capital rule being applied (see **15.3.6** and Chapter 18).

Regulation 27(1) does not, however, apply to land. Therefore, the precise extent of a beneficial interest must be established before it is given a market value. Resulting and constructive trust principles may be relevant, as will express declarations of trust. There will be difficulties in some cases because the Benefits Agency, when assessing capital for income support purposes, is required to assume that *all* jointly owned capital assets are held in equal shares, irrespective of actual agreement and ignoring actual documentation (ISG Regs 1987, reg 52). This means that the Benefits Agency will adopt a different approach from the local authority when valuing an interest in a jointly owned house.

Regulation 27(2) provides that a resident's share in jointly owned land must be valued at an amount:

> 'equal to the price which his interest in possession would realise if it was sold to a willing buyer (taking into account the likely effect on that price of any incumbrance secured on the whole beneficial interest), less 10% and the amount of any incumbrance secured solely on the resident's share of the whole beneficial interest.'

This is a gloss on the rule that assets are to be valued at market value and raises difficult questions about what sort of market might exist in these circumstances. It is clear, for example, that the value of a resident's interest will be very much influenced by the possibility of a market among his or her co-owners, since outsiders are unlikely to be particularly interested in an investment of this kind.

The recent decision of the Court of Appeal in *Chief Adjudication Officer v Palfrey* (1995), *The Times*, 17 February illustrates circumstances in which it may be appropriate to bring a resident's part share in a house into account at a nil valuation. Mr Palfrey, an elderly widower, and his daughter were beneficial joint tenants of a former council house. When Mr Palfrey's failing health forced him to go into a nursing home his half-share in the house was assessed by the district valuer, on behalf of the benefits agency, at £16,000, one-half of the net estimated selling price. Miss Palfrey made it clear that she had no intention of buying out her father, preferring to rely on her right of survivorship on his death, and it was also highly unlikely that any outsider would be willing to buy into a house where occupation would have to be shared. There was, therefore, no 'market' in Mr Palfrey's equitable interest.

The ISG Regs 1987, on which the appeal in *Palfrey* was based, contained no equivalent to reg 27(2); at that time, the market value principle was simply not elaborated in the context of shared property interests (but see **15.3.7**). Regulation 27(2) does, however, obliquely raise the possibility of a nil valuation, and local authority finance officers should also be familiar with para 7.014 of the CRAG, which states:

> 'Where an interest in a property is beneficially shared between relatives, the value of the residents' interest will be heavily influenced by the possibility of a market amongst his fellow beneficiaries. If no other relative is willing to buy the residents' interest, it is highly unlikely that any "outsider" would be willing to buy into the property unless the financial advantages far outweighed the risks and limitations involved. The value of the interest, even to a willing buyer, could in such circumstances effectively be nil.'

The Court of Appeal did, however, underline the point that there is no exact formula for establishing the market value of joint interests, and that legal advisers must be prepared to negotiate on behalf of their clients if they consider that the extent of the 'market' has been overestimated.

There is further discussion of this issue at **15.3.7**, and the example on p 187 which shows the inter-relationship between reg 27 and the market valuation principle highlights some important issues for individuals who are being assessed.

15.3.5   Disregarded capital

Schedule 4 to the NA(AR) Regs 1992 lists various types of capital which will be ignored in the financial assessment. It repays detailed consideration because it offers significant opportunities for financial planning. This point is discussed more fully in Chapter 18.

The most important and best known disregard applies to the capital value of a home, which is occupied by a third party (for example, the resident's spouse), and will be considered separately (see **15.3.7**). Other disregards include:

- the capital value of an annuity;

- the surrender value of a life policy;

- personal possessions (except those purchased with the intention of reducing other capital and so mitigating charges for accommodation);

- the capital value of an occupational pension;

- the value of a reversionary interest; this would include a reversionary interest under a trust but not the landlord's interest in freehold property which is subject to a lease or tenancy. (The NA(AR) Regs 1992 have recently been amended on this point, as have the ISG Regs 1987, see NA(AR) (Amendment No 2) Regs 1995 (SI 1995/3054));

- the capital value of a life interest, whether in land or in a trust fund;

- the capital value of an interest under a personal injury trust.

In addition, Sch 4, para 6 to the NA(AR) Regs 1992 provides that arrears of, or compensation for non-payment of certain social security benefits will be disregarded for a maximum of 52 weeks. The list includes arrears of attendance allowance, disability living allowance, income support and housing benefit.

Example:
Mr West is being assessed by the local authority for a nursing home placement. He has the following assets:

  (i) an occupational pension producing £120 per week;

 (ii) a State retirement pension of £61.15 per week;

(iii) a life interest in the house in which Mr West lives. The house was owned by his late wife, who left it in her will to Mr West for life, with remainder to their grandchildren;

 (iv) some valuable antique furniture;

  (v) £5,000 in a building society account.

Mr West's only immediately assessable capital will be £5,000, and his income (dealt with later) will fall short of the average fee for a nursing home bed (see **15.4**). Therefore, the local authority will initially assess his income contribution, but will have to subsidise the placement.

15.3.6   Notional capital

In some circumstances, a resident may be treated as possessing a capital asset where he or she does not actually possess it (NA(AR) Regs 1992, reg 25). The local authority may include this notional capital as part of its assessment. A very similar rule applies to income support claimants (ISG Regs 1987, reg 51). There is an extensive discussion of the notional capital rules in Chapter 18.

Where a resident has been assessed as having notional capital, that capital will be notionally reduced under reg 26 by the difference between the resident's assessed contribution and the weekly amount he or she would have been paying if he or she had not been treated as possessing notional capital.

Example:
Mr Crane is assessed as having notional capital of £8,000 plus actual capital of £10,000. He has been placed by the local authority in a residential care home. The contracted fee is £300 per week. Without the notional capital, Mr Crane's assessed contribution towards the cost of his bed would be £200 per week.

With notional capital added on, Mr Crane is above the £16,000 limit, and will be responsible for the full cost of his bed. Because he cannot 'spend' notional capital, it is reduced, week by week, under the reg 26 formula:

Assessed contribution without notional capital:	£200.00
Full residential home fee:	£300.00
Notional capital reduced by £300 – £200	= £100.00

15.3.7   The resident's own home

Policy

For many people entering residential care, their home will be their only substantial capital asset. The State – represented either by the local authority or by the Benefits Agency in some cases – will have an interest in using this capital value in offsetting the costs of care or of benefit, but this interest has to be balanced against the interests of other people who occupy, or have proprietary rights in, the property.

Disregarding the capital value of the home

The NA(AR) Regs 1992 require the local authority to ignore the capital value of a resident's home in the following circumstances:

(a)   where the resident is only temporarily in residential accommodation and either:

- intends to return home; or
- is taking reasonable steps to dispose of the house in order to acquire another property to return to (Sch 4, para 1).

The house must still be 'available' to the resident. Here the parallel income support regulations are more prescriptive in specifying that the property must not be let (ISG Regs 1987, Sch 10, para 1 and Sch 3, para 3(8)). Although the meaning of 'available' is not wholly clear, clients who enter residential care on a temporary basis should be advised against letting their homes, because loss of the capital disregard will have serious financial consequences;

(b)   where the resident has entered residential accommodation on a permanent basis, but where the house is still occupied by a spouse or partner (except an estranged or divorced spouse/partner) or by certain specified relatives of the resident or of members of his or her family (Sch 4, para 2). In these circumstances, the benefit of the disregard continues until such occupation ceases. Relatives (but *not* spouses or partners) must be aged 60 or over; under 16; or incapacitated. The regulations do not define 'incapacitated', but the CRAG suggests that it should be taken to mean being in receipt of a social security benefit for incapacity (for example disability living allowance, attendance allowance or severe disablement allowance), or having an equivalent level of incapacity. The same interpretation is used by the Benefits Agency for income support purposes (AOG, para 30237);

(c)　in addition, the local authority has discretion to ignore the capital value of premises owned by the resident if they are occupied by any third party (Sch 4, para 18). If, for example, an elderly person is admitted to a nursing home, leaving behind in his house a long-term carer or housekeeper, who has no other available accommodation, the local authority may decide to ignore the resident's interest in the house. The disregard will not be indefinite: the authority will review the situation from time to time, and will, of course, assess the capital interest when the carer dies or moves elsewhere.

The Benefits Agency has no such discretion. In equivalent circumstances, it *must* assess the resident's interest in premises as capital.

In applying its discretion, the local authority will have to balance a concern for the circumstances of the third party occupant of the home against the need to ensure that residents with assets are not maintained at public expense. Where, for instance, an assessment would result in the house having to be sold to meet the cost of residential care, so that the occupant would become homeless and might become the responsibility of the housing authority, then it would seem reasonable for the social services department to exercise its discretion in favour of continuing the capital disregard. It appears that practice varies between local authorities, and that discretion is being used less freely now than immediately following implementation of the regulations. Advisers should expect discretion to be exercised fairly and objectively, in accordance with declared criteria.

Homes subject to co-ownership

Where a resident has a joint beneficial interest in his or her former home, which the local authority is not prepared to disregard in the assessment, the value attached to the interest will be critical and good legal advice may produce substantial benefits for the client. In principle, a market valuation (reg 23) depends on:

(i)　there being a 'market' – ie, there exists a willing buyer;

(ii)　the ability of the resident to transfer his or her interest to a willing buyer.

Since co-ownership confers the right to occupy the property in question, any sale of his or her interest by one of the owners is subject to the occupation rights of the other(s). It is likely, therefore, that (notwithstanding the ultimate possibility of an application for sale under s 30 of the LPA 1925) the only person(s) interested in acquiring such an interest would be the other co-owner(s).

For these reasons, the value of a share in a jointly owned house could, effectively, be nil, as is conceded by the CRAG (para 7.014) or, at most, what another co-owner would be prepared to pay. This was confirmed by the Court of Appeal in a benefits case, *Chief Adjudication Officer v Palfrey* (see **15.3.4**).

The *Palfrey* decision indicated that the Benefits Agency should adopt the same approach to valuation of co-owned property as the local authority, under reg 27 of the NA(AR) Regs 1992. However, reg 52 of the ISG Regs 1987 prescribes that all shares in jointly owned property will be treated as equal shares, irrespective of basic equitable principles or of specific agreement between the co-owners. For the Benefits Agency, therefore, the starting point in applying the market value test was often different from the local authority's starting point under reg 27(1) of the NA(AR) Regs 1992 (see **15.3.4**). Nevertheless, *Palfrey* confirmed that a nil valuation would be appropriate in some cases.

Since *Palfrey*, however, reg 52 has been amended, with effect from 2 October 1995. It now reads as follows:

> 'Where a claimant and one or more persons are beneficially entitled in possession to any capital asset they shall be treated as if each of them were entitled in possession to an equal share of the whole beneficial interest therein; and the value of that equal share shall be calculated by taking the value of the whole beneficial interest, as though—
> (a) that interest is solely owned by the claimant; and
> (b) in the case of a dwelling, none of the other joint owners occupying the dwelling concerned, and dividing the same by the number of persons who have a beneficial interest in the capital in question' (Income Related Benefits Schemes and Social Security (Claims and Payments) (Miscellaneous Amendments) Regulations 1995 (SI 1995/2303)).

The effect of para (b) is to require the Benefits Agency to value a share in a house by taking the appropriate fraction of the market value of the whole property. At the time of writing, there were no plans to amend the NA(AR) Regs 1992 similarly, although advisers must be alive to that possibility, which would have very serious implications for some older clients and their families. There is now a substantial difference of approach between local authorities and the Benefits Agency on valuation, which is best understood by reference to the Case study 3 on p 187).

Effect of taking the value of the home into account
Where the capital value of the resident's home is taken into account by the local authority, so that the £16,000 capital threshold is exceeded, the resident will be expected to pay the full cost of the care bed out of capital, plus whatever income he or she has available.

Legal advisers should note the following points:

– The resident will be expected to pay the full cost of the bed as soon as he or she enters residential care on a permanent basis. The local authority has no power to postpone levying its charges until, for example, a property is sold.

– The local authority has, however, no power to enforce sale of the property, nor may it withdraw services if its charges are not met. The duty to make residential provision where need exists is not conditional upon payment of an assessed contribution (ss 22(1) and 26(2) of the NAA 1948).

– Where the house is occupied by a third party, the local authority may place a charge on the resident's interest in the property to secure fees which the resident is unable to meet without selling the house over the occupant's head (s 22 of the HASSASSAA 1983; see **15.11.1**). Where the resident and an occupant or occupants of the house share the beneficial interest, valuation will, therefore, be an important issue.

– Income support will not be available where a resident's capital exceeds £16,000. If the resident has been claiming before entering residential care, by taking advantage of the occupation disregard on the capital value of the home, benefit will stop (but see p 187).

– Exercise by the local authority of its discretion to disregard the value of a house which is occupied by a non-prescribed third party (Sch 4, para 18 to the NA(AR) Regs 1992) has important financial consequences. The placement is bound to be more expensive to the local authority than if the resident's capital assets are used to the full extent that the regulations allow. In addition, however, the Benefits Agency, having no discretion in such cases, will always refuse income support, so that there will be no central government subsidy to help the local authority meet its financial obligations.

– Where it is clear in advance that the value of the resident's house will be taken into account, and that the resident will have to fund his or her own placement, two options are available:

   (i) The resident may elect 'to go private': to make his or her own arrangements direct with a residential establishment, and to remain outside the local authority's sphere of influence. The advantages of this course of action are that the resident will have an unrestricted choice of home, and that the attendance allowance may be available to help meet the home fees (see Chapter 19). The disadvantages are that if the resident's capital is eventually exhausted, the local authority will have to take over the care responsibility and may not be prepared to subsidise home fees which it regards as excessive (see **9.2.4**).

   (ii) The resident may elect to ask the local authority to assess his or her needs under s 47 of the NHSCCA 1990 (see Chapter 5) and may subsequently ask the local authority to make residential care arrangements under s 26 of the NAA 1948. The advantage of this course of action is that the local authority will be able to negotiate a more competitive price with care providers than is likely to be available to a lone individual. The resident will also have the benefit of the quality standards imposed by the local authority on providers of residential accommodation (see Chapter 10). The disadvantage is that the resident's choice of accommodation is likely to be restricted (LAC(92)27).

Dealing with sale

Where an elderly person who has entered residential care is taking reasonable steps to dispose of an empty property, the Benefits Agency will disregard its capital value for at least 26 weeks from when he or she first took those steps, and for such longer period as is 'reasonable' in the circumstances to enable him or her to dispose of the premises (ISG Regs 1987, Sch 10, para 26). If no steps are taken, for instance by putting the property on the market, the capital disregard will immediately cease. It may, however, be revived if steps towards disposal are subsequently initiated. The resident may claim income support throughout the period allowed for sale of the property unless his or her other capital or income resources are above the statutory limits. The net proceeds of sale will then be assessed as capital by the Benefits Agency. The Benefits Agency has generally been willing to exercise its discretion to extend the initial 26-week period during the recent recession in the housing market, and this has been helpful for claimants.

The local authority has no equivalent powers under the NA(AR) Regs 1992. Once the decision is taken to include the value of a property within the financial assessment, so pushing the resident above the £16,000 capital threshold, he or she will immediately become responsible for the full weekly cost of the care bed. The availability of income support for at least 26 weeks (see above) may help to cushion this financial burden, as may the possible availability of attendance allowance (see Chapter 19). There will, however, be pressure on the resident to realise the capital because he or she will be in debt to the local authority and, as time goes by, there will also be pressure to reduce the asking price for the property, particularly once the Benefits Agency takes its value into account. Attorneys dealing with sales in these circumstances should be aware that the local authority will almost certainly use its charging power under s 22 of the HASSASSAA 1983 if payments fall into arrears. The attorney may, nevertheless, choose to sell the property when he or she judges the time is right.

Case study 1

Bill Simpson, a 78-year-old widower, entered a nursing home six months ago following an assessment by the local authority. At that time his wife was living alone in their home, which they bought as beneficial joint tenants 30 years ago. Mrs Simpson has just died. On her death, Mr Simpson became the sole beneficial owner of the house which is now worth £80,000 and is mortgage free. Mr Simpson's income consists of £61.15 State retirement pension and £50 occupational pension. He has capital of £2,500.

(a) While Mrs Simpson was alive the local authority disregarded Mr Simpson's interest in the house. Now, however, they must take it into account, and must re-assess his capital resources. They cannot directly force him to sell the property, but they will base their assessment on the price quoted by an estate agent for a quick sale. From the date of the assessment, the local authority will require Mr Simpson to pay his own nursing home fees in full.

(b) Mr Simpson will have been claiming income support before his wife's death because his income is relatively low. The Benefits Agency will allow at least 26 weeks for the sale of the property before taking its capital value into account.

After 26 weeks, or whatever reasonable period the Benefits Agency allows for sale of the house, Mr Simpson's capital will increase by the net proceeds of sale of the house, or by its estimated market value if still unsold, and he will no longer be entitled to income support.

(c) Neither the local authority nor the Benefits Agency can directly enforce the sale of the house. If, however, Mr Simpson is unable to meet his assessed payments to the nursing home, the local authority will seek to secure its position by imposing a charge on his house pending sale, under s 22 of the HASSASSAA 1983.

(d) Had the beneficial joint tenancy been severed before Mrs Simpson died, only a half share in the house would have been available for nursing home fees, unless Mrs Simpson left her estate to her husband. Valuation of that half share would have been governed by reg 27 of the NA(AR) Regs 1992.

Case study 2
The facts are as in Case study 1, except that Mr Simpson has been a patient in a private nursing home since January 1993.

(a) Mr Simpson will have preserved rights to income support at an enhanced level because he was in residential care before 1 April 1993 (see Chapter 16).

(b) On his wife's death, the Benefits Agency will take into account the value of his interest in the house, but will allow 26 weeks for the sale to take place. If sale proves difficult the Benefits Agency may be prevailed upon to exercise its discretion to extend the 26-week period (ISG Regs 1987, Sch 10, para 26).

(c) Once 26 weeks (or an extended period) have elapsed, the capital disregard will cease and Mr Simpson's income support payments will stop because his capital will exceed the £16,000 threshold. There will then be considerable pressure to undersell the house.

(d) In such cases, proprietors of residential accommodation are in a difficult position. If the house is not sold within the time allowed by the Benefits Agency, and benefit is stopped, their fees may not be met. They will, however, be reluctant to take steps to evict frail elderly residents. The local authority will have no power to assist in this situation by taking over the arrangements for Mr Simpson's nursing home care, and those advising him may have to consider other possible sources of financial support. This issue is discussed in some detail in Chapter 16.

Case study 3

John Wilson, a widower aged 79, has lived in the same council house for 30 years. Ten years ago, his 40-year-old daughter, who now lives with him, helped him to exercise his right to buy under the Housing Act 1985 and the house was conveyed to them as legal and equitable joint tenants. The house is worth about £60,000 net.

Mr Wilson has been admitted to a nursing home following an assessment of his needs. His pension income is about £100 per week and his only savings are £2,000 in a building society account.

(a) The local authority is not required to disregard Mr Wilson's capital interest in the house because his daughter is under 60 and, it seems, in good health (Sch 4, para 2 to the NA(AR) Regs 1992). It has discretion to disregard that interest, because Mr Wilson's daughter remains in occupation (para 18), but is unlikely to do so in the given circumstances.

(b) Mr Wilson's income is low and he will qualify for income support if his capital is below £16,000. The Benefits Agency *must* assess his interest in the house in the present circumstances.

(c) Both the local authority and the Benefits Agency would take the view that Mr Wilson has a 50% interest in the house. A valuer for the local authority, setting out to quantify this interest, would have to express a view on the existence of a 'market'. Clearly, it would not be in the daughter's interests to indicate a willingness to buy out her father.

(d) Mr Wilson's advisers should argue for a nil valuation by the local authority based on para 7.014 of the CRAG and on the Court of Appeal's decision in *CAO v Palfrey* (see **15.3.4**). The Benefits Agency must now bring in a valuation of £25,000 less 10% under the amended reg 52 of the ISG Regs 1987.

(e) Mr Wilson will not therefore be able to claim income support, as his actual capital will exceed £16,000.

(f) If the local authority were to put a value of, say, £20,000 on Mr Wilson's half share in the house, he would then have to meet the cost of his bed from total capital of £22,000 until this was reduced to £16,000, when the local authority would be able to assist with fees. £2,000 is now free and available. Mr Wilson's daughter might have to consider raising the other £4,000, possibly by mortgaging the house. Alternatively, the local authority could place a charge on the property in respect of any unpaid contributions.

(g) It is clearly essential that Mr Wilson's legal advisers seek to negotiate with the local authority finance officer for as low a capital valuation as possible. Because there is no direct right of appeal against the financial assessment, negotiations must take place at an early stage. The value to the client of a favourable settlement will be considerable.

15.4   How is income assessed?

The NA(AR) Regs 1992 make detailed provision for different types of income to be taken into account in the financial assessment. With older people, the following are most commonly encountered:

–   retirement pensions;

–   other social security benefits, such as attendance allowance, disability living allowance (care component), severe disablement allowance, and incapacity benefit;

–   occupational pensions;

–   annuity income;

–   trust income.

In addition, capital below the £16,000 ceiling but above £10,000 is considered to give rise to a 'tariff income' of £1 per week for every complete £250 or part of £250 capital over £10,000 (reg 28). Accordingly, capital of £12,000 would give rise to a tariff of £8 per week; capital of £12,005 would give £9 per week. Clearly, the chosen tariff represents a (currently) highly inflated hypothetical return on capital. The tariff is supposed to equate with an amount which a resident with some capital should be able to contribute towards accommodation costs, but since it is applied in exactly the same way to income support claimants, the rationale is obviously fluid. The resident's capital is deemed to produce income at the tariff rate; if it does produce actual income the tariff will apply none the less and the actual income will be treated as an addition to the capital (reg 22(4)).

15.4.1   Disregarded income

The NA(AR) Regs 1992 list sources of income which will be wholly or partially disregarded in the assessment (Sch 3). Fully disregarded income includes:

–   income in kind, for example food, clothing, personal items;

–   disability living allowance (mobility component);

–   any income support which is referable to a resident's home commitments; this can apply only during the first 52 weeks in residential care;

–   Christmas bonuses;

– charitable payments which are intended for and used to top up home fees which are set at a higher level than the local authority would normally pay;

– payments by charities which are intended for specific items not covered by the home's fees (for example payments to enable a resident to have his or her own telephone or television set).

Partially disregarded income includes:

– income from a home income plan annuity, provided that one of the annuitants is still occupying the house which is the subject of the scheme, and subject to conditions specified in para 12 of Sch 3;

– war disablement pension (£10 disregarded);

– war widow's pension (£10 disregarded).

15.4.2 Rental income

Under income support rules, rental income is treated as capital, and disregarded as income (ISG Regs 1987, reg 48). The same is true for the local authority assessment. Although the CRAG glosses over this point (para 6.042), reg 22(4) of the NA(AR) Regs 1992 addresses it directly: '... any income of a resident which is derived from capital shall be treated as capital, but only from the date on which it is normally due to be paid to him'.

15.4.3 Notional income

In some circumstances, a resident will be treated as having an income which he or she does not actually receive. In a sense, the tariff income previously described falls into this category, but reg 17 refers specifically to several categories of notional income which the local authority is required to take into account in its financial assessment:

(a) income of which the resident has deprived himself or herself for the purpose of decreasing the amount that he or she may be liable to pay for his or her accommodation (reg 17(1)).

This paragraph would cover the conversion of income into capital – for example, the sale of the right to receive annuity income. Since receipt of such income will increase an individual's contribution towards the costs of a care bed, conversion may seem an attractive idea, particularly where a resident has no other capital.

Example:
Mr Pearson sells the right to receive income under an annuity of £10 per week for £2,000. He already has other capital of £10,100, which is, therefore, producing a tariff income of £1 per week. The £2,000 consideration for the sale of the annuity will increase the tariff income by £8, and, in addition, a notional income will be attributed to Mr Pearson.

He will not lose out both ways, however; the notional annuity income will be offset by the increase in the tariff income. Nevertheless, the net effect will be to give him a notional income of £10 per week;

(b) income which would become available to the resident upon application being made. The CRAG suggests that unclaimed social security benefits – for example, retirement pension – would fall into this category. This is debatable, however, because only where entitlement is absolutely straightforward can a benefit properly be regarded as 'available' to the claimant. Income which may be payable under a discretionary trust is not to be regarded as 'available';

(c) income which is due to be paid to the resident, but has not yet been paid. This could include unpaid superannuation or unpaid earnings. It would also include trust income to which a resident is entitled but which has not been applied by the trustees. Again, the distinction between a fixed trust and a discretionary trust is important; income which is payable at the trustees' discretion is not 'due';

(d) 'top-up' payments towards the cost of residential accommodation made by a third party to the local authority. This rule is meant to ensure that the local authority takes these payments into account when assessing the resident's contribution. Payments made to the local authority in respect of arrears of charges will not, however, be regarded as notional income (reg 17(4) and (5)).

If the local authority comes to the conclusion that reg 17 applies, it will assess the accommodation charge taking account of the notional income. In some cases, the local authority may seek to transfer liability to a third party under s 21 of the HASSASSAA 1983 (see **18.3**).

15.5   The personal expenses allowance

Section 22(4) of the NAA 1948 requires local authorities to allow residents to retain specified amounts out of their assessable resources for personal expenses. Regulations made each year (National Assistance (Sums for Personal Requirements) Regulations 1996) specify a minimum amount for 1996/97 of £13.75 per week.

The allowance is supposed to be inalienable. It is intended that residents should spend it as they wish on stationery, toiletries, treats, presents and other personal items.

In the view of the DoH it would be unlawful for a local authority to allow a resident to use the allowance, even on his or her own initiative, to help pay for more expensive accommodation than the local authority is prepared to subsidise (see LAC(94)1). Instances have been reported of homes seeking to charge residents separately for services which either ought to be covered by local authority contracts, or ought to be part of community health provision. Charges are not infrequently made for incontinence or chiropody services.

As a general rule, attempts to relieve residents of their personal expenses allowances should always be questioned, whatever explanation is offered.

Section 22(4) of the NAA 1948 allows local authorities to raise the personal expenses allowance above £13.75 where they consider it appropriate to do so. There is no prescribed ceiling. Advisers should be aware of this power, and should be prepared to ask the local authority to use it. The CRAG suggests that the allowance could be increased to help residents with learning disabilities to live more independently (para 5.005). A further example is discussed below.

15.6   Married or unmarried couples

15.6.1   Assessing one partner

The local authority has no power under the NA(AR) Regs 1992 to take account of the combined resources of married or unmarried couples when assessing one partner for residential care. Income and capital have to be allocated to the individual being assessed either according to normal proprietary rules or as prescribed by the regulations. The approach will be the same for both temporary and permanent placements. When income support is being claimed, the Benefits Agency takes a rather different approach for temporary placements. Here, income support will be assessed for the couple, and will be paid to one partner in respect of both, as is normal when partners are living together in the same household. Usually, payments will be made to the partner who is still at home, in the community.

One problem with the approach prescribed for the local authority will arise where the partner in residential accommodation is technically entitled to income which is really intended to meet the needs of both partners. Occupational or personal pensions, often payable to a husband, provide a good example. The husband's income may be so substantial that he will be required to pay the full cost of a care bed, whilst his wife, living at home, is impoverished. The regulations allow no discretion in such circumstances, but the local authority may consider using its power under s 22(4) of the NAA 1948 to raise the husband's personal expenses allowance (see **15.5**) beyond the present statutory minimum of £13.75 per week, so that he can then support his wife at home. This is a very convoluted way of dealing with a serious problem, and advisers or attorneys must be alive to the need to negotiate with the local authority in such circumstances. Quite reasonably, the local authority may be reluctant to use its discretion if the result would simply be to reduce the income support already being paid to a wife in the community (CRAG, para 5.005).

As a result of strenuous lobbying by the Alzheimer's Disease Society, together with Age Concern, the Government has now agreed to an amendment to the

Pensions Act 1995, which will require local authorities to disregard one half of a resident's occupational pension where it is paid to a spouse who remains at home. Unmarried partners will not have the benefit of this dispensation. The change in the law will alleviate to some extent the difficulty described above. It is expected to come into effect from April 1996.

15.6.2 Assessing both partners

Where both partners are admitted to residential accommodation, the local authority will always assess them separately, according to their individual resources (CRAG, para 4.005).

Where both partners enter the same residential accommodation, the Benefits Agency has discretion as to whether to assess them as two separate individuals or whether to aggregate their resources and assess them as a couple. The approach adopted by the agency will depend on the arrangements in the home; for instance, whether the partners share a room; whether, in dual-registered accommodation, one is placed in a different wing from the other. Advisers should be aware that the income support personal allowance for an individual is £47.90 per week for 1996/97. The allowance for a married or unmarried couple is £75.20.

15.6.3 Liable relatives

Section 42 of the NAA 1948 makes spouses (but not cohabitants) liable to maintain one another. Section 43 permits enforcement via the magistrates' court. Whenever one spouse's accommodation in a registered care home or nursing home is provided wholly or partly at public expense the local authority may seek reimbursement from the liable relative. There seems to be no authority as to the extent of this liability, but it must be presumed that it is to provide 'reasonable maintenance'. Anachronistically, however, the liability will be affected by matrimonial conduct.

The liable relative rule does not allow local authorities to assess the means of anyone apart from the person for whom care arrangements are being made. Spouses of those being assessed can be asked to contribute to the cost of a care bed, but they cannot be asked to disclose information about their own resources. Residents should be advised not to complete assessment forms which seek to elicit financial information about their spouses. A local authority has to make a judgement on what a spouse could be expected to contribute (based, perhaps, upon previous standards of living) and must then seek to negotiate reasonable maintenance payments. Ultimately, the court could be asked to order appropriate payments, but, as always with enforcement measures, local authorities will have to weigh the adverse publicity which court proceedings may bring against the need to recoup expenditure.

Where a resident is receiving income support, the assessing local authority may draw the conclusion that the liable relative obligation has already been explored by the Benefits Agency, since social security law also requires spouses (and cohabitants) to maintain one another (Social Security Contributions and Benefits Act 1992, s 106). Any payments subsequently exacted from the liable relative, unless very substantial, will simply reduce income support and will not benefit the local authority. In such cases, it will not be worthwhile pursuing maintenance at all.

15.7 Calculating the local authority's charge

Residents must contribute to the cost of their accommodation the whole of their assessed weekly income, as calculated in accordance with the regulations, (ie including their actual and notional income but ignoring any disregarded income). They are, however, permitted to retain a specified amount for personal expenses (see **15.5**).

Where the individual's weekly income is below income support level, the local authority will expect him or her to claim benefit. However, nothing in the regulations directly requires a resident to make a claim. If income support could be regarded as income which 'would be available' to a resident if application were made, it would then be notional income under reg 17 and the local authority's assessment could take it into account irrespective of the resident's willingness to claim it.

Bearing in mind the complexity of the means test for income support, however, it is doubtful whether reg 17 would apply to unclaimed benefit. In addition, the local authority will always be liable for the full cost of a residential care bed under its contractual arrangements with the provider, and by virtue of s 26(2) of the NAA 1948. It will have to meet from its own budget whatever costs it is unable to recoup from the resident or from central government.

15.8 The residential allowance

Since April 1993 a new residential allowance has been payable to those in independent residential care homes and nursing homes who need to claim income support. It is part of the new applicable amount for income support (ISG Regs 1987, regs 17(1)(bb), 18(1)(cc) and Sch 2, para 2A (see **14.1**)).

For the financial year 1996/97, the allowance is set at £54 per week, or £60 for homes situated in the Greater London area. The home must be registered, or deemed to be registered, under the Registered Homes Act 1984 (see Chapter 10). (Abbeyfield Homes only qualify if registered under the 1984 Act.)

The allowance is not, therefore, available to residents in Part III accommodation owned or managed by the local authority. This disentitlement extends to residents of former Part III homes which have been transferred to the independent sector after 12 August 1991 (ISG Regs 1987, reg 21(3A)).

The legislation does not require that the local authority should necessarily finance the care arrangements. Residents who, for example, elect to fund their own placements, using available benefits plus financial assistance from relatives may, therefore, take advantage of the residential allowance (see Chapter 19).

Residents with preserved rights do not, however, benefit from the residential allowance. As noted in Chapter 16, their income support payments are differently prescribed.

The residential allowance stops if a resident is absent from the home for more than 21 days, or six weeks if he or she is admitted to hospital. Where the local authority has made the care arrangements it will remain liable to the provider for the full contractual price and is therefore likely to impose terms in respect of temporary absences (see Chapter 8).

15.9   Placements in local authority managed homes

The NA(AR) Regs 1992 apply to placements made in old-style Part III accommodation owned and managed by the local authority. The financial disincentives to such placements are noted at **15.8** and Chapter 2, and the recent decision of the House of Lords in *R v Wandsworth London Borough Council ex parte Beckwith* [1996] 1 All ER 129, has now given local authorities carte blanche to close or sell off all their own residential homes. Nevertheless, politics will ensure that some local authorities will continue to maintain the option of using their own accommodation to discharge their responsibilities under s 21 of the NAA 1948, rather than relying exclusively on contractual arrangements with the independent sector.

The local authority must purport to charge a resident for the full economic cost of providing the placement (s 22(3) of the NAA 1948). Before April 1993, local authority beds were traditionally cheaper than beds in the independent sector, but the extension of the NAA 1948 regime to all residential placements has ensured that pricing in the different sectors has been brought into line.

Section 23 of the NAA 1948 allows local authorities to make rules regarding the management of their Part III accommodation. In particular, they may provide for accommodation charges to be waived in part where residents assist in running homes (s 23(3)). This section does not apply to independent sector homes.

The financial regime for Part III accommodation now differs in one important respect from the (preferred) regime for independent sector placements. Income support is only available to top up a resident's resources to the basic

State retirement pension level. No premiums, and no residential allowance are available.

As the Case studies below demonstrate, the effect is to diminish central government support for these placements and to make them considerably more expensive for local authorities to maintain than contracted placements in the independent sector.

15.10   Case studies: calculating residents' contributions

(a)   The local authority has agreed to arrange a place in a private residential home for Mrs Anna Jones, aged 81. Her only sources of income are her State retirement pension, and an occupational pension of £30 per week. She has £11,000 in savings. The contracted fee for the bed is £250 per week.

Cost to the local authority of providing the bed		£250.00
Mrs Jones's weekly income:		
retirement pension	£61.15	
occupational pension	£30.00	
tariff income	£4.00	
income support	£28.05	
(personal allowance, (£47.90)		
enhanced pensioner premium (£21.30)		
residential allowance (£54.00)		
less other income)		
TOTAL INCOME	£123.20	
Less personal expenses allowance	£13.75	
Mrs Jones's contribution		£109.45
Cost to the local authority		£140.55
TOTAL FEE		£250.00

(b)   The local authority has agreed to arrange a place in a nursing home for Mr Jim Craven, aged 75. The local authority would normally expect to pay £340 per week for someone with his care needs. Mr Craven has chosen, however, to enter a home with more facilities, which costs £400 per week, and his daughter has agreed to pay the extra £60 per week. Mr Craven transferred his house to his daughter some years ago, and she has been caring for him up to now. His assessable capital is £13,000.

Cost to the local authority of providing the bed	£400.00
What the local authority would normally have paid	£340.00
Mr Craven's weekly income:	
retirement pension	£61.15
occupational pension	£250.00
tariff income	£12.00
daughter's contribution towards extra fees	£60.00
TOTAL INCOME	£383.15

Less personal expenses allowance	£13.75	
Mr Craven's contribution		£369.40
Cost to the local authority		£30.60
TOTAL FEE		£400.00

Note:

(i) The cost to the local authority of meeting the needs of a particular individual is always unpredictable because it depends on the extent of the individual's own resources. The temptation to allow the assessment of need to become tainted with financial considerations is quite evident.

(ii) Mr Craven's right to choose which nursing home he enters is discussed in some detail in Chapter 9. In this example it must be assumed that the local authority is satisfied as to the financial standing and integrity of Mr Craven's daughter. The fact that Mr Craven's income is relatively high will doubtless have influenced this judgement. The family must be made aware, however, of the possible consequences of failure to meet the top-up payments.

(iii) It is highly unlikely that the local authority will seek to open up the possibility of assessing the value of Mr Craven's former house as notional capital. The ambit of the notional capital rules, together with possible planning options are explored, in detail, in Chapter 18.

(c) The local authority has agreed to arrange a place for Mrs Eva Stowe, aged 70, in one of their own homes. Her only income is the married woman's pension of £36.60. In addition, she has £1,000 savings.

Cost to the local authority of providing the bed		£250.00
Mrs Stowe's weekly income:		
pension	£36.60	
income support (up to full pension level)	£24.55	
TOTAL INCOME	£61.15	
Less personal expenses allowance	£13.75	
Mrs Stowe's contribution	£47.40	£47.40
Cost to the local authority		£202.60

Note:

Income support level for Mrs Stowe is £61.15 per week. Compare Mrs Jones. The local authority's financial subsidy for Mrs Stowe is much higher than for Mrs Jones.

15.11 Enforcing payment of assessed contributions

Although there is no contractual relationship between a local authority and residents in respect of whom it makes arrangements under s 21 or s 26 of the NAA 1948, s 56 of that Act provides that any sum due 'under this Act to a local authority (other than a sum due under an order made under section 43 of this Act) shall be recoverable summarily as a civil debt'. Orders made under s 43 for contributions from liable relatives towards the cost of a spouse's care (see **15.6.3**) will be enforceable like any other maintenance orders made by the family proceedings court.

Section 56 allows the local authority to take the same steps as any commercial creditor to enforce payment of assessed contributions and, in some cases, the final outcome may be proceedings under the Insolvency Act 1986. How readily local authorities will take such steps is hard to predict. There is undoubtedly a cultural antipathy towards enforcement against service users who are frail and vulnerable, and the cost of recovery may also deflect local authorities in cases where the debt is small and prognosis for the resident perhaps limited.

Unpaid contributions are most likely when the value of a resident's home is taken into account in assessing a contribution. Since the local authority has no power to waive its charges pending sale of the property, a debt will build up very quickly unless the resident has other resources from which to meet the care fees. In these circumstances, a further statutory remedy is available which carries attractions for local authorities and is now routinely used.

15.11.1 Section 22 of the HASSASSAA 1983

Section 22 applies where a person fails to pay an assessed contribution and has a beneficial interest in land in England or Wales. In such circumstances, the local authority may create a charge over that interest by executing a written declaration to that effect, and may register the charge as a class B land charge in the case of unregistered land, or as a charge by way of legal mortgage where the title is registered.

This power was expressly introduced to assist local authorities who are reluctant to obtain a court order to compel sale of a defaulting resident's property, or other assets. The charge covers the resident's indebtedness to the local authority at any one time and crystallises on the death of the resident in the sense that interest starts to run from that date (s 24 of the HASSASSAA 1983). At that point, the local authority would normally expect the deceased resident's personal representatives to arrange for the property to be sold. If, however, a caring friend or relative were still in occupation of the property, there might be further postponement of sale. The local authority itself has no power to sell a property without first obtaining a charging order from the court.

Where the resident is co-owner of a property, s 22(3) of the HASSASSAA 1983 provides that his interest under the statutory trust for sale is to be treated as an interest in land for the purposes of imposing the charge. The charge may not, of course, exceed the value of the resident's beneficial interest.

Imposition of a charge does not sever a beneficial joint tenancy (s 22(5)) and, on the death of a resident who is a joint tenant, the operation of the right of survivorship will pass his or her beneficial interest, still subject to the charge, to the remaining joint tenant or tenants.

Example 1:

Robert Black owns a house valued at £40,000. He also has pension income amounting to £120 per week. The local authority arranges accommodation for him in a nursing home at a cost of £320 per week. There is no reason to disregard the value of the property, so Mr Black should pay the full cost of the bed because he has more than £16,000 capital.

He refuses to sell the house, with the result that he is only able to pay £120 per week, less his personal expenses allowance. The local authority places a charge on the property as soon as the first payment falls due and, on Mr Black's death, six months later, the debt is paid.

Example 2:

Henry Green, aged 65, enters a private nursing home under arrangements made by his local authority. He owns a house in which he has lived with his younger sister, Muriel, for the past ten years. Muriel is 55. An estate agent has valued the house at between £50,000 and £60,000, and it is mortgage free. Mr Green's only income is his State retirement pension.

The local authority has assessed Mr Green as having capital of £55,000, and he is therefore expected to pay in full for his nursing home place.

(a) The CRAG indicates that if the local authority is considering placing a charge on a resident's interest in property, he should be advised/assisted to seek advice from a solicitor.

(b) Henry's solicitor should ask the local authority why it has not exercised its discretion to disregard his capital interest in the house, because his sister still lives there (Sch 4, para 18 to the NA(AR) Regs 1992; see **15.3.6**). The local authority should be prepared to state its reasons and, if it has acted arbitrarily or without due consideration, Mr Green may challenge the decision.

(c) Otherwise, the imposition of the local authority's charge will be unavoidable.

(d) If Henry dies after three years, Muriel will presumably inherit the house, subject to the charge, and interest will run from the date of Henry's death. The local authority's concern will then be whether to dispossess Muriel, or whether to postpone enforcement of the debt until after her death.

Chapter 16

PRESERVED RIGHTS TO INCOME SUPPORT

'A little-discussed legacy of the Government's Community Care Reforms is the provision of "preserved rights" to higher rates of Income Support for people resident in independent sector residential and nursing homes on or before 31 March 1993. For some, entitlement to "preserved rights" has protected their place in a care home; for others, the provision is like a sentence to worry and despair about how care home fees will be paid' (*Preserved – and Protected?*, Age Concern, 1994).

As has been seen, the community care reforms gave local authorities financial responsibility for making residential care arrangements from 1 April 1993. The old system of funding through DSS benefit payments continued to apply, however, to people who were living permanently in registered residential care homes or nursing homes on 31 March 1993. It has been estimated that at that date there were 350,000 such people. They have 'preserved rights' to income support (ISG Regs 1987, reg 19(1ZB)) which is payable at the enhanced rates which were previously available to all residents in the independent sector who needed financial assistance with fees. The rates are nationally defined, and vary according to age and disability.

In the 1996/97 benefit year, the enhanced rates range from £203 weekly for a registered care home bed to £304 weekly for a bed in a nursing home offering care to patients with Alzheimer's disease. For homes in the London area, there is a supplementary payment of £43. The payments described are maximum payments, and are not directly related to the fees charged for residential accommodation.

Two categories of people have preserved rights:

(i) those who were claiming income support before 1 April 1993 in order to maintain their residential placement;

(ii) those who were funding themselves on 1 April 1993 but who have subsequently claimed benefit, or may in the future claim benefit, once their capital assets are reduced to £16,000 or less and they cannot sustain their placements out of their weekly income.

All residents with preserved rights will have made their own arrangements with providers of residential or nursing home care. They will not have been assessed by the local authority, and the local authority will not have made care arrangements on their behalf.

Elderly people resident in local authority maintained accommodation ('Part III' accommodation) do not have preserved rights. As previously explained (at **15.10**), the NHSCCA 1990 has not substantially altered their financial regime.

Example:
Mrs Wainwright entered a nursing home in April 1992. At that time she had substantial capital assets of some £100,000, and a small pension. In April 1996 her remaining capital amounts to £16,000, and she is entitled to claim income support. She has preserved rights.

Her income support will consist of:

Nursing home bed	£304.00
Personal expenses allowance	£ 13.75
Total income support payment	£317.75

Mrs Wainwright's pension will be taken into account. It will reduce her income support, as will a notional tariff income on her remaining capital in excess of £10,000 (see **15.4**).

Before implementation of the community care legislation, it was generally considered that preserved rights status would carry advantages. For this reason, considerable efforts were made to arrange residential placements before 1 April 1993. Certainly, assessments of need were avoided, and individual residents were able to exercise a free choice in respect of their accommodation because income support payments were then, and still are, based on categories of accommodation and not on an individual's actual needs. Local authorities, in particular, had a hidden agenda: to ensure that central government took over the ultimate financial responsibility for as many people as possible before the transferred funding became effective in April 1993. It is now apparent, however, that preserved rights status is likely to give rise to considerable individual hardship over the next few years, and it is difficult to understand how legislators could have seen fit deliberately to create a highly disadvantaged minority of vulnerable elderly people.

16.1   Why do 'preserved rights' cause problems for clients?

Although the relatively high levels of benefit payments were available to residents before April 1993, the DSS has not since 1986 purported to match benefit rates with actual fees charged. By the early 1990s, there was considerable evidence that, in some areas of the country, the national limits did not in fact cover home fees. In 1992/93, for example, there was, nationally, an average gap between benefit payments and actual fees of about £40 per week. Many placements depended, therefore, on top-up payments typically made by residents' relatives or, as a last resort, by charities.

When community care funding was restructured in April 1993, the Government did not bring benefit rates into line with bed prices. Clients who have preserved rights and are actually claiming income support must, therefore, still rely on top-up payments to meet their care bills. The situation has been exacerbated in some areas by the fact that local authorities are purchasing beds from residential care providers at fees higher than the preserved right rates of income support. It is also clear that some providers are trying to increase fees charged to people with preserved rights. Overall, there seems to be a widening gap between fees and the benefits available to meet those fees.

16.2 Can the local authority help?

Section 26A of the NAA 1948 (amended by s 43 of the NHSCCA 1990) expressly prevents local authorities from arranging residential care or nursing home accommodation for people already resident in private or voluntary homes on 1 April 1993. If, for example, an elderly person is evicted, or threatened with eviction from a nursing home because relatives have failed to meet top-up payments, it will be ultra vires for the local authority to purport to intervene and support the placement. Similarly, where an elderly person in a residential care home now needs more specialised nursing home care, but has no access to top-up payments, the local authority cannot offer financial assistance.

However, s 26A(3) empowers the Secretary of State to exempt certain residents from this general exclusionary rule. The Residential Accommodation (Relevant Premises Ordinary Residents and Exemption) Regulations 1993 (SI 1993/3182) have been made under s 26(A)(3) and offer limited relief. Regulations 8 and 9 provide that, notwithstanding the general prohibition in s 26(A), local authorities may still make residential arrangements for people over pensionable age who have been evicted or are about to be evicted from residential care homes (whether because the home is closing down or the fees have not been paid). In order to avoid undue pressure on local authorities to take on such additional responsibility, reg 8(2) states that new placements may not be made in premises within the same ownership or management as the original home unless that home has been, or is about to be, closed down. This proviso hits at evictions which are 'contrived' in order to make the local authority financially responsible for a placement, but it means that elderly residents will have to be moved, even if that is not in their best interests, and even if higher fees have to be paid in a new placement.

16.3 Does the health authority have any responsibility?

Local authorities have no power to make arrangements in nursing homes for people over pensionable age with preserved rights. As has been seen (Chapter 2), health authorities have power to purchase nursing home places for patients (s 23 of the NHSA 1977), but they have no specific powers to protect those facing eviction from nursing homes or to top-up inadequate levels of income support. In any event, the decision in *White v Adjudication Officer* (1993) means that, if health authorities purport to make top-up payments, placements so supported will become 'health' placements, and enhanced income support will be lost (see **2.4.3**).

Joint finance arrangements under s 28A of the NHSA 1977 offer some possibility, but intervention may also be inconsistent with the new NHS *Guidance* on continuing health care responsibilities (see **2.5.2**).

Earlier DoH *Guidance* states that, where the health authority originally purchased the nursing home place, it should take responsibility for finding alternative accommodation for a resident threatened with eviction or home closure. It is not clear, however, whether the NHS is expected to fund the alternative placement. Where, as is often the case, a resident has entered a nursing home under private arrangements, the *Guidance* places the onus firmly on the resident, his or her relatives, and the home-owner to negotiate the placement or find alternative accommodation. Local authorities are expected to assist by providing 'advice and guidance' to help people in difficulty to find alternative accommodation using their preserved rights and 'any other resources available to them' (Circular LAC(93)(6)). Some local authorities are advising residents and their families to try to negotiate with home-owners wherever possible with a view to securing a reduction of fees, perhaps by virtue of an agreement to share rooms. Community care plans may be expected to lay down protocols for dealing with home closure or evictions, in order to minimise possible disruption and distress to residents.

16.4 Are there any other options?

It is always worthwhile for advisers to try to tap the resources of charities or benevolent associations on behalf of elderly clients who are in financial difficulties. They may also be able to negotiate fee reductions with home-owners on behalf of clients. Clients may, of course, draw on their remaining capital and utilise all or part of their personal expenses allowance in order to top-up the income support payments.

Beyond that there are two further options:

 (i) Although the lifeline offered to residents with preserved rights by regs 8 and 9 of the 1993 regulations is clearly very limited, reg 5 offers another approach. It states quite explicitly that s 26A(1) of the NAA 1948 shall not apply to any person who has ceased to have a preserved right by virtue of reg 19(1ZF) or (1ZG) of the ISG Regs 1987.

  Regulation 19 indicates that a resident will normally retain preserved rights for the rest of his or her life. Rights will persist, for example, if a resident moves from one independent sector home to another, or from a care home to a nursing home. The same is true if ownership of the home itself changes. Short absences from registered accommodation have no effect on preserved rights. If, however, a resident is absent from a residential care home or nursing home for a period exceeding 13 weeks (or 52 weeks where he or she has been in hospital) preserved rights will be lost, and s 26A(1) of the NAA 1948 will cease to apply. As a result, the local authority will be empowered to make new residential care arrangements.

(ii) Section 135(3) of the SSCBA 1992 allows the Secretary of State for Social Security, when prescribing the amounts of enhanced income support payments for residential care, to take into account information provided by local authorities regarding fees which they have negotiated with providers of residential accommodation in their areas. Where contractual fees have outstripped income support payments, local authorities may take the opportunity to present relevant information to the Secretary of State, to influence his decision on income support levels. Section 135(3) indeed suggests that the Secretary of State may prescribe different benefit levels for different parts of the country.

Example:

Your client, Jane Walsh, aged 55, has just retired early from her clerical job with the local authority, on account of ill health. She is unmarried, and her only close relative is her elderly mother, aged 83, who has been in a nursing home since 1991. Mrs Walsh has Alzheimer's disease.

Until her retirement Jane was topping-up her mother's income support payments to meet the nursing home fees. Currently Mrs Walsh's income support is £304 per week plus £13.75 personal allowances. The nursing home fees have just been increased to £375 per week. Jane is now unable to afford the top-up payments. Her mother's capital is almost exhausted.

(i) It may be possible to obtain charitable assistance for Mrs Walsh, although this particular source of funds is now more limited than it once was. Charities like the Alzheimer's Disease Society should be contacted, together with local charities or benevolent associations with which Mrs Walsh may have had connections before she became ill. (For other sources of advice on funding, see List of Useful Addresses.)

(ii) If Jane fails to make the top-up payments, her mother could face eviction from the nursing home for non-payment of the fees. How soon this is likely to happen will depend on the financial pressures faced by the management of the home. The local authority should, at least, offer advice and general assistance, but it may not assist in paying the fees. The community care plan should be inspected, and approaches made to the health authority. It may be helpful to enlist support from the local media.

(iii) If Mrs Walsh is 'evicted' from the nursing home and returns home to live with Jane for at least 13 weeks, her preserved rights status will be lost (reg 5). Jane may then ask the local authority to assess her mother under s 47 of the NHSCCA 1990, and to arrange a nursing home placement for her. The local authority will be responsible for the home fees and will recover a contribution from Mrs Walsh, who will be in a position to claim income support at the new, reduced level which applies to all placements made after 31 March 1993. Jane will not be required to make a financial contribution. Subject to the fees charged being acceptable to the local authority, there is no reason in law why Mrs Walsh should not return to the previous nursing home.

(iv) If the local authority is aware of other cases where nursing home residents face financial hardship it may decide to make representations to the Secretary of State, and urge him to use the discretion afforded to him by s 135(3) of the SSCBA 1992. Legal advisers of clients like Jane Walsh may wish to encourage their local authority to pursue this course of action.

Chapter 17

PAYING FOR NON-RESIDENTIAL SERVICES

'Authorities are locally accountable for making sensible and constructive use of the discretionary powers they have, in order to prevent avoidable burdens falling on council and national taxpayers. Authorities are reminded that the standard spending assessment formula for domiciliary care for elderly people does not take account of the level of income from charges actually received by each authority. This means that any authority which recovers less revenue than its discretionary powers allow is placing an extra burden on the local population or is forgoing resources which could be used to the benefit of the service' (LAC(94)(1), para 18).

Since April 1993, most local authorities have reviewed their charging policies in respect of non-residential care services. As a result, there have been dramatic increases in fees and many recorded instances of users declining services which they need, but can no longer afford. The switch in focus from health to social care, described in Chapter 2 is part of this picture: as free services previously delivered by the NHS have been withdrawn, gaps in provision have been filled by local authority commissioned services, for which users are expected to pay.

A recent report prepared by the National Consumer Council highlights this point:

'For 30 years we have had care from the district nurses and doctors . . . Now after all these years we have been put to home carers for bathing and nursing. The local council now demand *payment* for this service!! I have contested this as Mrs T requires total nursing. We now need *more* money, not *less* . . .' ('Charging Consumers for Social Services', NCC, 1995).

The *Policy Guidance* on community care published in 1990 emphasised the expectation that users should be required to pay for services subject to their ability to do so (para 3.31) and, as outlined above, a more recent Circular reiterates that message. Since 1993, funding has been allocated by central government on the assumption that local authorities will raise a proportion of their revenue through charges. The 1994/95 figure is said to have been 9% (NCC 1995, p 21). There has been, however, no clear guidance as to the legal, practical or operational issues posed by the pressure to charge. Section 17 of the HASSASSAA 1983 remains the enabling provision but does not purport to regulate charging methods, or ways and means of promoting openness, equity or fairness in the practice of charging.

17.1 Section 17 of the HASSASSAA 1983

As noted above, local authorities derive their power to impose charges for non-residential services from s 17 of the HASSASSAA 1983. Section 17(1) states that 'an authority providing a service . . . may recover such charge (if any) for it as they consider reasonable'.

The draftsman of the time clearly contemplated that local authorities might elect not to recover charges at all, and until April 1993 this was indeed the approach adopted in some areas.

Section 17(3) states:

> 'If a person—
> (a)   avails himself of a service to which this section applies, and
> (b)   satisfies the authority providing the service that his means are insufficient for it to be reasonably practicable for him to pay for the service the amount which he would otherwise be obliged to pay for it, the local authority shall not require him to pay more for it than it appears to them that it is reasonably practicable for him to pay.'

Comparing subs (1) with subs (3), it appears that s 17 is purporting to impose two separate tests of reasonableness. Section 17(1) expects the local authority to make a judgement as to what is reasonable, based, presumably, on the overall needs and financial circumstances of its local population, coupled with the perceived need to recover costs as far as possible.

Section 17(3) postulates a test of reasonableness which is focused on the individual, and which would indicate the need for procedures to review charging decisions on the basis of individual circumstances. It carries also the underlying implication that the application of a means test, as for residential care services, may commend itself to local authorities as a way of achieving reasonableness and equity across the population of service users.

17.2   Charging strategies

It seems that many local authorities interpret 'reasonableness' in s 17 of the HASSASSAA 1983 as meaning 'affordable' (NCC, 1995, p 42), and so will seek to match charges with users' ability to pay. Flat rate charges which were commonly fixed before April 1993 are less favoured now because of their regressive nature. Means-tested schemes vary from authority to authority, but generally involve an assessment of a service user's available capital and income and of allowances to meet the costs of daily living. For each individual, the balance between these two figures is then regarded as a 'disposable' resource from which care fees can be met. In the absence of detailed regulation, however, there are considerable differences in approach to the basic calculation. Sometimes all 'disposable' resources are judged to be available to meet charges; sometimes a fixed percentage of such resources is taken; sometimes a sliding scale is adopted, relating disposable resources to the service provided. Approaches to the assessment of income and capital resources are variable. Inevitably, too, there are different perceptions as to what level of basic resources should be exempt from any charge, although it is clear that many local authorities relate their living allowances to income support, as a measure of the ability to pay.

The National Consumer Council gives an example of one local authority's five-band charging scheme ('Charging Consumers for Social Services', NCC, 1995, at p 47).

Band 1: People getting income support alone, or people with income support and lower-rate disability living allowance (care component).
Upper charge limit: £3.20 per week.

Band 2: People with income support and lower-rate attendance allowance or middle-rate disability living allowance (care component).
Upper charge limit: £10.00 per week.

Band 3: People with income support and higher-rate AA or higher-rate DLA (care).
Upper charge limit: £15.00 per week.

Band 4: People with a disposable income of £50.00 per week or less pay up to one-third of that disposable income as the charge.

Band 5: People with a disposable income of over £50.00 per week are considered to have available to meet charges one-third of the first £50 and one-half of all income in excess of £50.

In Bands 4 and 5, the disposable income is calculated by adding together actual income and then deducting a basic allowance equivalent to income support rates, excluding the severe disability premium, plus extra expenses arising from disability. If no surplus income is available the charges are then as for Bands 1 to 3. If there is a surplus, AA/DLA (care) is added to it, to produce a total disposable income.

It will be noted that this scheme is heavily based on entitlement to welfare benefits, and the implication is that the local authority's assessors will seek to identify benefit entitlement and promote take-up.

17.3   Welfare benefits and charging

Nothing in s 17 of the HASSASSAA 1983 prevents local authorities from charging recipients of social security benefits for community care services. Those dependent on income-related (means tested) benefits are, however, already on the poverty line and to charge them is arguably objectionable in principle. This was acknowledged during the passage of the HASSASSAA Bill in 1982.

Nevertheless, Government policy has shifted over the years, and the latest opinion expressed through the SSI is that:

'the Government does not consider that there should be an automatic exemption from charges for people receiving social security benefits such as income support

... housing benefit, Social Fund payments ... or disability working allowance'
(Advice Note, 1994).

All the benefits referred to are means tested. On the ground, there is evidence
that some income support claimants are expected to pay standard charges for
services out of their benefit. Given that such claimants are not required to pay
council tax it may be argued that local authorities are now seeking to collect, by
indirect means, local taxes which they are not permitted to levy directly (NCC,
1995, at p 52).

Other benefits, particularly those targeted at disability, and payable
irrespective of claimants' financial circumstances, may invite recoupment.
Within this category are the attendance allowance and the disability living
allowance (DLA) (care component). Both are payable to claimants who can
establish a need for personal care. Neither is means tested. The maximum rate
for both benefits is currently £48.50 per week (1996/97 rates).

Most local authorities will now assume that AA and DLA (care component) are
available to pay for services and that it is reasonable to take them into account.
They see these benefits as designed to enable claimants to purchase additional
care from the local authority or elsewhere. In practice, however, users who are
otherwise on low incomes spend this extra money on meeting the other
unavoidable costs of disability, which will not be met by the local authority.

Again, charging practice varies. Some authorities, for example, impose flat rate
charges on all users who are in receipt of AA or DLA (care component). Others
will include the value of the benefit, or a proportion of it, in their calculation of
a user's income resources. In some areas the charge is based on the percentage
of assessed care needs met by the local authority.

The disability living allowance (mobility component) is a linked benefit, which
is payable to those unable or virtually unable to walk (s 73 of the Social Security
Contributions and Benefits Act 1992). It may not, however, be taken into
account for charging purposes under any means test, discretionary or not
(s 73(14)). Whether for this reason, or because of the highly specific definition
of 'need' for this benefit, there is no evidence that it is treated as available to pay
local authority charges.

17.4   Treatment of capital for charging purposes

In the absence of legal regulation in this area, it is nevertheless clear that, in
practice, local authorities take account of users' capital assets in setting fees for
non-residential services. Given that capital is taken into account for means-
tested social security benefits and in the means test for residential care (see
Chapter 15) it is not surprising that local authorities seek to follow suit, but,

once again, the fact that there are differences in approach to this very contentious question may be seen as unfair or inequitable.

It seems that local authorities have regularly imposed a tariff income on capital in excess of £3,000 and have also expected service users with capital above a set threshold (often £8,000) to pay for their services in full. Such practices run in parallel with the National Assistance (Assessment of Resources) Regulations 1992 which govern residential care arrangements (see Chapter 15). Following the recent raising of the capital limits for residential care, it remains to be seen whether similar adjustments will be made in respect of homecare charges.

The NCC Report gives examples of hardship caused by setting capital limits:

> 'I have been informed that I will be charged £56 a week (because our savings are more than £8,000). The help provided is eight hours per week. Home help (cleaning) one hour per week. The position is going to be reviewed because I have refused to pay £56 a week, which is more than the weekly attendance allowance, and, quite frankly we cannot afford it' ('Charging Consumers for Social Services', 1995, p 62).

As regards the value of the user's own home, it has become the received wisdom that an elderly person needing care may decide to remain in the community in order to avoid having to use the value of his or her home to pay for residential care. At the same time, there is an incentive for local authorities to place such people in residential care because the NA(AR) Regs 1992 allow them to recover their costs from the value of a property. It can be argued that the only position which is consistent with community care policies is to take account of capital tied up in the house in all circumstances. Given the current intense debate as to how far the value of the home should be available to meet residential care fees (see Chapter 18) there is an urgent need to clarify how far it is lawful, or acceptable, for local authorities to seek to access the capital value of a service user's home whilst he or she continues to live there.

17.5   Couples and non-residential charges

As noted at **15.6**, the NAA(AR) Regs 1992 make it clear that local authorities may only assess and charge individuals who are being provided with residential care and not their spouses or partners, and s 42 of the NAA 1948 (the liable relative provision) applies only where residential accommodation arrangements are made. Section 17(3) of the HASSASSAA 1983 also refers only to the circumstances of the 'person who avails himself of the service'. In practice, however, there is a great deal of confusion among local authorities as to whether or not they have the power to take account of resources owned by users' spouses or partners, and the NCC research highlights a wide divergence of approach. Some authorities routinely assess couples, whilst others make it clear that they are interested only in the financial circumstances of service users.

17.6   Inability to pay

Section 17(3) of the HASSASSAA 1983 implies that service users who feel that it is not reasonably practicable to pay service charges should have a right of review or appeal against a decision to impose them. Once again, local authorities are left to their own devices in this area but basic public law principles would require that service users should be made aware of their right to make representations about their ability to pay charges and that local authorities should lay down adequate criteria to enable them to consider 'reasonableness' in individual circumstances on a review.

It is important to notice that, as with residential care, the local authority has no power to withdraw a service which has been provided on the basis of need, if the user is unable or unwilling to pay charges. Best practice would also require local authorities to investigate circumstances where users decline services because they cannot afford to pay for them. If a request to review service charges is unsuccessful, or if the service user is unaware of the possibility of a review, the complaints procedure is still available in respect of any question connected with the provision of community care services. It is not, however, well adapted to handle financial questions. There is an extended discussion of this, and other remedies in Chapter 13.

17.7   Collecting charges

Section 17 of the HASSASSAA 1983 empowers only local authorities to recover charges in respect of non-residential services. Where, consistently with the new philosophies of care, the local authority commissions services from independent providers, difficulties may arise in terms of how charges are to be paid. Collection of fees by providers raises questions of confidentiality and it seems inappropriate that this should be done without sanction from service users. Direct billing by local authorities will be the most appropriate procedure, but where service users do not have bank accounts or where they live in isolated areas, cash payments to service providers will often be the only practicable option.

The collection of residential care charges is now governed by statute, and is discussed in Chapter 9.

17.8   Practice points

(a) Legal advisers should obtain information about their local authority's scale of charges for non-residential services. In some areas, services may be purchased more cheaply from friends, neighbours, voluntary agencies or independent commercial providers.

(b) Where clients may be entitled to welfare benefits, advisers must be prepared to assist them to claim, or to refer them to someone else who has the necessary skills. Where non-residential services are needed it will be very important to maximise a client's entitlement to benefits.

(c) Advisers should ask the local authority for information about its charging procedures, how charges will be collected and whether the spouse's or partner's resources will be taken into account in any assessment. If, given what is said in this chapter, the local authority's practice appears to be unfair, or possibly unlawful, it may be necessary to initiate the complaints procedure (see Chapter 13).

(d) Attempts by a local authority to take account of the value of a property in which a client is still living should be firmly resisted as being objectionable in principle. A local authority may also need to be reminded that service provision, based on assessed needs, may not be made conditional on the payment of fees. It may be argued that excessive charges are unlawful because any rationing of services should be based on levels of need, not on individual resources (*Policy Guidance*, para 3.1).

(e) Respite care arrangements may cause problems, because although charges for permanent residential care arrangements are regulated, s 22(5A) of the NAA 1948 allows local authorities to charge 'reasonable' amounts for temporary stays up to eight weeks. In practice, there are wide variations in respite charging policies, and many authorities will assess the resources of carers in fixing charges. There are dangers in creating disincentives to use respite care, because non-residential arrangements may break down altogether as a result, and legal advisers should be prepared to challenge policies which appear to have this effect.

Chapter 18

PRESERVING ASSETS FROM THE STATE

'The gradual realisation that they must not only support their aged relatives, but also take out long term insurance for their own old age may lead the middle classes back into the welfare state' ('A Crisis in Care', FPSC, 1994).

'The main thing we get correspondence on is people trying to preserve their property from being taken over by the local authority or being sold to defray the cost of care' (NOP Survey, March 1994).

Although we have noted elsewhere that relatively few people over pensionable age are at the moment in a position to pay for their own care, it is nevertheless apparent that clients are increasingly seeking advice on how, if at all, they may be able to mitigate what are seen as the very onerous costs of residential care. As more of the over-60s become owners of their own homes and, consequently, of capital assets which may be available to meet care fees, it is likely that planning for residential and, ultimately, home-based care will become as commonplace as tax planning.

In both cases, the client may be seeking to preserve his or her assets from the State. For inheritance tax or capital gains tax, this means ordering his or her affairs in order to pay as little tax as possible. Planning for care has another dimension, however, which comes from expectations about the balance of expenditure as between the State and the individual.

There is much evidence that elderly people are experiencing a sense of betrayal by the welfare State, in which they invested such high hopes and expectations during the 1940s. What gave meaning and purpose to the huge sacrifices made by armed forces and civilians alike during the Second World War was the understanding that a more just and equal society would be created when the war was over. This 'social contract' – quite alien to the political climate of the 1990s – was seen as fundamental to the war effort, and led directly to the setting up of the income welfare State and the National Health Service in 1948. The political and cultural change needed to deliver such radical legislation was unprecedented, but the consensus on which it was based endured through many governments, of different persuasions, until the Thatcher administration in the 1980s attacked the social policy which underpinned this collectivist approach, and set about pushing back the frontiers of the welfare State.

The commitment by the post-war State to care for its citizens from 'cradle to grave' sounds increasingly hollow in the 1990s, but for older clients that has been a fundamental expectation, on the strength of which National Insurance contributions will have been paid for many years (see Figure 6 below). Such clients find it unacceptable that, when they are frail and in need of care, modest wealth will quickly be exhausted by nursing home fees; that partners may suffer financial hardship; and that the younger generation may lose an inheritance in

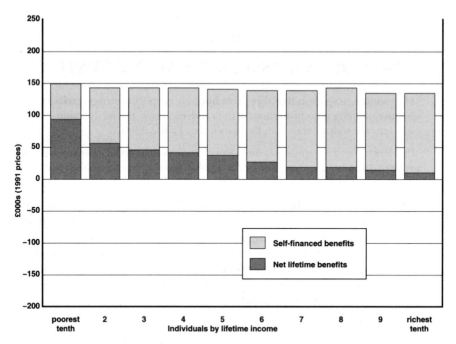

Figure 6. Lifetime benefits and taxes.
People pay themselves for around three-quarters of the welfare benefits they receive
over their lives; the 'lifetime rich' are net contributors to the system, the 'lifetime poor'
are net gainers.

Source: Falkingham and Hills. Results derived from LIFEMOD simulation model.

Notes: 1.   Individuals are ranked by lifetime equivalent net incomes.
       2.   Calculations allow for share of tax bills necessary to pay for cost of welfare
           benefits (23% of gross incomes).
       3.   Results use structure and relative generosity of 1991 tax and benefit systems.

(From John Hills, *The future of welfare: A guide to the debate,* Joseph Rowntree Foundation,
1993.)

respect of which financial sacrifices have been made by their parents. In a study
of financial decision-making by people over pensionable age commissioned
recently by the DSS, most respondents expressed a predominant wish to have
'something to pass on' to future generations. This wish was often held despite
contrary persuasion from children and others (Finch and Elam, *Managing
Money in Later Life,* DSS 1995).

The desire to leave an inheritance is of course linked to the fact that the vast
bulk of care is provided within the family, not by the State.

> 'Rather than, as is sometimes suggested, occupying a monopoly or near monopoly
> position in the provision of care to older people, the public health and personal
> social services are, in fact, junior partners' (Walker, *The Future of Family Care for
> Older People,* Allen and Perkins (eds), HMSO, 1995).

There is little evidence, for example, of extensive packages of care being provided for elderly people where they have relatives to care for them, and most of the research shows that family commitment to caring for elderly people is as strong as it has ever been. Within this culture it is clear that the expectation of inheritance may be an important element of the inter-generational social contract upon which the family care system depends. 'Policy-makers tinkering with it should exercise extreme caution' (Walker, 1995).

In addition, the preliminary findings of a national survey carried out in 1995 by the Nuffield Community Care Studies Unit at the University of Leicester shows that most people believe that the prime responsibility for the costs of residential care lies with the government, that people should be able to pass on property to their children and that elderly people should not have to sell their homes to finance their care.

18.1 Professional issues

Preservation of assets is a concept which has caught the attention of the media in recent months and has, in consequence, become overlaid with emotional or even ethical concerns which legal practitioners find extremely taxing. The fact that The Law Society has recently seen fit to issue guidelines entitled *Gifts of Property: Implications for Future Liability to Pay for Long-term Care* (Mental Health and Disability sub-committee, September 1995) is evidence enough that advice giving is considered to be a professional minefield. Given the level of client demand for advice, this is an unfortunate situation.

In fact, to a large extent, the debate is about nothing more than sensible financial husbandry. Advice about making wills, creating enduring powers of attorney, equalising assets between spouses or partners, and severing joint tenancies should enable clients to put their affairs in order and, in some cases, to mitigate possible care fees. There is also a growing market in financial services packages designed to help clients to plan for care fees in a tax-effective way, and the needs of many clients will be met by sound advice in this area. Finally, there is no doubt that clients may benefit very considerably from simple advice and information about community care and particularly about the financial assessment for residential care. Such advice, in itself, may alleviate concerns which frequently arise from reading inaccurate press reports or listening to gossip. In some cases, however, a client's instructions will be that he or she wishes to dispose of assets in order to put them beyond the reach of the State in the event of residential care becoming necessary.

Some legal practitioners maintain that such instructions pose ethical questions for them as professionals.

> 'There is of course a moral question about whether it is right that an individual should be able to dispose of assets which would otherwise be used to pay for care and thereby load the cost on to tax payers generally' (Prouse: *EAGLE*, August 1994).

Most private client advisers engage, however, without embarrassment, in inheritance tax planning or advise clients on how to manipulate the tax exemptions available through the middle-class welfare State, and it is difficult to see why the ethical position here should be different. Provided that he or she is not being asked to endorse false accounting, failure to disclose assets, or misrepresentation, is it really part of the legal adviser's job to pass judgement on where the balance should lie between the interests of the individual client and the interests of the State?

It is worth emphasising that the legal provisions which will be the focus of the advisers' attention in these cases, are neutral in their terms. Both the ISG Regulations 1987 and the NA(AR) Regulations 1992 permit capital which has in fact been disposed of to be treated nevertheless as the notional capital of the donor and to be included in a financial assessment. The regulations are not penal in nature; they have to do simply with the definition of capital and how it is assessed. Even the Insolvency Act provisions which permit certain gifts to be set aside when the donor becomes bankrupt and which may be invoked, exceptionally, by local authorities are similarly non-judgemental.

A more serious concern focuses on how to assess risk where clients do decide to embark on schemes aimed at shedding capital. Unlike tax law, the relevant provisions in the social security legislation, and now in the assessment regulations made for local authorities, are still relatively undeveloped through case-law. It may be difficult, therefore, to advise with certainty on the likely outcome of proposals put forward by clients, and it is of the utmost importance that clients are made fully aware of this fact. It is not unknown for social workers to suggest to older clients that they take advice on disposal of capital before a financial assessment is made, and such referrals can raise particular problems where advisers feel that they cannot recommend watertight solutions.

Above all, the challenge for the legal adviser will be how to balance the client's wish to protect assets, particularly the home, against the possibility of residential care, and how to protect the client against possible hardship brought about by the misfortunes, or even the fecklessness or abuse of the younger generation. Here, The Law Society's new guidelines (see below) seek to clarify and explain further the existing professional conduct rules.

It is important, however, to maintain a sense of proportion. The Law Society highlights the possibility that donees of property may become involved in divorce or bankruptcy proceedings or may simply become estranged from the donor. When the subject of a gift is the donor's home, any of these eventualities may cause considerable problems. The guidelines do not, however, present the alternative perspective which is that informal care by family members overwhelmingly outweighs State provision (see Chapter 11) and that inheritance, or the disposal of assets *inter vivos* is very much part of the network of intergenerational relationships and obligations on which this informal system is based. Disposal of assets by the older generation may well be perceived primarily as the recompense for family caregivers who have assumed, perhaps over many years, a responsibility which the State would otherwise have had to meet.

18.1.1 The Law Society's guidelines on gifts of property

The new guidelines emphasise the following points:

(a) the need for good legal advice. Here, The Law Society quotes examples of non-solicitor advice services which are marketing schemes to elderly people on the back of unjustified claims as to their effectiveness;

(b) the need for the legal adviser to be clear about whom he or she is acting for and where potential conflicts of interest may lie, particularly when a relative purports to be giving instructions on behalf of an elderly person;

(c) the need to ensure that the client understands the immediate effect of making a gift and the possible long-term risks of doing so;

(d) the need to clarify the client's objectives in making the gift and to explain the implications and possible consequences of what is being proposed. This would include weighing possible benefits to the client against possible risks. Evaluation of risks would, in some cases, necessarily involve advising the client as to the possibility of a disposition becoming subject to the notional capital rules and of any consequent enforcement proceedings being taken at the instigation of the local authority (see below).

(e) the solicitor's duty, which is expressed as follows:

> 'The Solicitor's role is more than just drawing up and registering the necessary deeds and documents to effect the making of the gift. S/he has a duty to ensure that the client fully understands the nature, effect, benefits, risks and foreseeable consequences of making the gift. The solicitor has no obligation to advise the client on the wisdom or morality of the transaction, unless the client specifically asks ... Solicitors will want to satisfy themselves in each individual case that no breach of the law is involved in the proposed transaction. Having advised the client as to the implications and possible consequences of making the gift, the decision whether or not to proceed remains with the client' (paras 20 and 21).

18.2 The notional capital rule

Wherever direct or indirect State subsidies are available to the individual citizen, he or she may seek to maximise or accelerate entitlement. If entitlement is based on a capital threshold – as with income support or local authority help with the costs of residential care – the State will have an interest in preventing individuals from disposing of resources prematurely in order to qualify. The income support rules (and the supplementary benefit rules before 1988) have therefore sought to control claimants who dispose of capital or income in order to maximise entitlement to benefit. The same is now true of the assessment regulations operated by local authorities when they arrange residential placements.

Such controls exist throughout the benefits and the tax systems. In all cases, the citizen is permitted to organise his or her affairs so as to mitigate tax liability or maximise benefit entitlement provided that he or she acts within the law.

In analysing the notional capital rules, the starting point must be reg 51 of the ISG Regs 1987. Regulation 25 of the NA(AR) Regs 1992 simply replicates reg 51, and such judicial authority as exists relates to the former.

18.2.1   Regulation 51 of the ISG Regulations 1987

Unlike its predecessor in supplementary benefit law, reg 51 is now mandatory rather than permissive. Paragraph 1 provides:

> '(1) a claimant shall be treated as possessing capital of which he has deprived himself for the purpose of securing entitlement to income support or increasing the amount of that benefit except:
>> (a) where that capital is derived from a payment made in consequence of any personal injury and is placed on trust for the benefit of the claimant; or
>> (b) to the extent that the capital which he is treated as possessing is reduced in accordance with regulation 51A (diminishing notional capital rule).'

Paragraph 2 adds a gloss by prescribing that capital which would become available to the claimant upon application is to be treated as possessed by him. Here, as a matter of law, a distinction must be drawn between capital in which the claimant already has a beneficial interest but which he may have to take steps to realise (for example, an interest under a trust; money held in client account by his solicitor; money held by the court) and capital which is not regarded as owned by him until an application has been made (for example an unclaimed prize on the national lottery). The former is *actual* capital, and only the latter is covered by para 2.

Paragraph 3 goes still further in providing that, subject to some exceptions, payments made to third parties in respect of a claimant shall be treated as belonging to the claimant. This would catch, for example, household fuel bills paid by a relative in order to help out an elderly claimant. Lump sums paid to providers of residential accommodation to top up income support payments for residents with preserved rights also fall within para 3. There is an important planning point here, in that such capital payments may pose problems for residents by taking them over the £16,000 capital threshold or by triggering a tariff income (see **15.4**), whereas income top-ups are expressly disregarded (ISG Regs 1987, Sch 9, para 30A).

In practice, it is para 1 which provides the focus for those who seek to gain entitlement to income support. If it applies, its effect will be to cause capital of which a claimant has 'deprived' himself to be returned, notionally, to his ownership, even if he has no actual means of recovering it. For a long time this was the ultimate 'catch 22' in that claimants could be denied benefit on the basis that they could be expected to rely for their subsistence on capital which either did not exist or was irrecoverable.

Example:

Mr Ian Hamilton has been in a nursing home for 4 years, and is claiming income support at the enhanced rate for residents with preserved rights. He has pension income of £160 per week and £5,000 free capital. His wife has just died and her half share of their former home (now valued at £60,000) has passed under her will to their son. Immediately before his wife's death, Mr Hamilton assigned his interest in the home to their son.

–   the Benefits Agency will expect to assess Mr Hamilton's capital interest in the house on his wife's death (see **15.3.6**);

–   in these circumstances, a market valuation would be in the order of £30,000 less certain allowances (see **15.3.6**);

–   if the Benefits Agency considers that the terms of reg 51(1) are met, Mr Hamilton will have notional capital in excess of £16,000, and will therefore lose his income support. Unless his son is prepared to meet the home fees there will be considerable difficulties ahead. The Benefits Agency has no power to take any action against third parties, and no interest in doing so. The local authority is not empowered to take over the residential care arrangements because Mr Hamilton still has preserved rights to income support (see Chapter 16).

18.2.2   Reduction of notional capital

Notional capital can, however, be 'notionally' spent. Before 1990, the regulations did not make explicit provision for this, but it was accepted that notional capital could be reduced over time by reasonable weekly living expenses. Now, however, reg 51(1A) lays down an express diminishing notional capital rule, which is linked to the income support that would have been available to the claimant had reg 51(1) not been applied. It is, therefore, possible to calculate and advise as to the moment when notional capital will be deemed to have been reduced sufficiently to allow income support to be claimed.

18.2.3   Regulation 25 of the NA(AR) Regulations 1992

The local authority's approach to notional capital differs from that of the Benefits Agency in one important respect. Regulation 25(1) states that: 'a resident *may* be treated as possessing actual capital of which he has deprived himself for the purpose of decreasing the amount that he may be liable to pay for his accommodation'.

Paragraph 2 incorporates reg 51(2), (3) of the ISG Regs 1987, and reg 26 introduces a diminishing notional capital rule based on the difference between a contribution assessed to reflect notional capital, and an assessment which ignores notional capital.

Clearly, the substitution of the word 'may' in reg 25 for 'shall' in reg 51(1) has considerable significance. The local authority is given discretion whether or not to apply the notional capital rule. The same discretion also existed under the old supplementary benefits system, but was removed, so far as income support is concerned, after 1988.

This discretion makes sense for local authorities because their duty to make arrangements for residential care is independent of their duty to charge for services and of the users' duty to pay assessed charges. If, for example, a frail, elderly resident effectively deprives himself of all his capital, the local authority may take the view that, unless the capital is recoverable by the resident, applying reg 25 will serve no useful purpose. A mounting debt resulting from unpaid contributions may well not be enforceable even on the death of the resident, and resources are therefore needlessly wasted on administration. Far better, perhaps, just to assess the resident's income and ignore the notional capital. In such cases, the local authority will have to take account of the Benefit Agency's lack of discretion and the fact that, if income support is denied to the resident, the authority's own financial responsibility will increase.

Example:
Mr Joseph Bean, a pensioner, gives £20,000 (his life savings) to his son. He retains £2,000 only. He has a retirement pension of £61.15. The son invests the capital in his business. Soon afterwards, Mr Bean enters a nursing home.

–   in carrying out its assessment of Mr Bean's resources, the local authority finds out about the gift. Mr Bean tells the social worker that he wanted his son to have the money, not the Government;

–   the local authority decides not to seek to apply reg 25. If it takes the £20,000 into account, Mr Bean will be required to pay for his care in full for a few months. Because his resources, apart from notional capital, are very limited, a large debt will build up. There are no easy options for recovery open to the local authority and their responsibility to make care arrangements for Mr Bean persists regardless of the financial circumstances;

–   the Benefits Agency could apply reg 51 and take the £20,000 into account as Mr Bean's notional capital. In these circumstances, no income support will be payable until the notional capital is reduced to the £16,000 threshold through the operation of reg 51A.

18.2.4 What determines the application of the notional capital rule?

Manifestly, one or other of the notional capital rules will inhibit individuals who may wish to distribute assets before claiming income support or entering residential care. On closer analysis, however, it becomes apparent that the precise scope of the rules is far from certain.

The Adjudication Officers' Guide (para 30312) states that the following questions must be addressed when the State is considering the application of reg 51(1):

(1) Was the claimant the beneficial owner of the capital asset?
(2) Has deprivation occurred?
(3) What was the purpose of the deprivation: was it in order to obtain entitlement to income support?
(4) Can the notional capital be disregarded?

The CRAG does not offer such a clear analysis of the relevant issues, but it should always be argued that an analogous approach by the local authority is appropriate. It cannot be acceptable that the approach of two public agencies to the interpretation of virtually identical regulations should diverge.

Issues arising from (1) above are considered in Chapter 15; (2), (3) and (4) will now be discussed in turn.

18.2.5 Deprivation

Neither reg 51 nor reg 25 offers a definition of 'deprive', and the term must therefore be given its natural meaning (ie to bring about a situation where a capital asset previously possessed is no longer possessed). The Adjudication Officers' Guide (para 30317) gives the following as examples of deprivation:

– payment of a lump sum to a third party, either as a gift or in repayment of a debt;

– incurring substantial expenditure – for instance, on an expensive holiday;

– creating a trust;

– pursuing an extravagant lifestyle;

– converting money into personal possessions, which would normally be disregarded capital (see below);

– transferring a house to a third party when it has ceased, or will shortly cease, to be the claimant's home.

The CRAG cites the same examples (para 6.061).

Given any one of these events, the State may take the view that the claimant or resident has deprived himself of actual capital. The State must then prove the specified purpose.

18.2.6 Purpose

The issue here is often presented, simplistically, as: did the claimant/resident *deliberately* give away assets in order to achieve the specified result? In fact, the analysis of 'purpose' is complex, and given that the onus of proof is always on the State, those advising individual clients must expect the State to justify conclusions which are adverse to their clients. Local authority assessors in particular are likely to experience difficulties with the structured decision-making which is indicated here.

Once again, the Adjudication Officers' Guide provides a helpful analysis. Para 30336 states that, if the evidence shows that a claimant has,

(1) requisite knowledge, and

(2) has exercised choice in depriving himself of an asset with at least a significant purpose of securing entitlement to income support,

then the adjudication officer is entitled to take that asset into account as notional capital. The requisite knowledge referred to is of the relevant capital limits.

The adjudication officer or the local authority assessor must prove such knowledge and it is not enough that an individual ought to have known of the relevant rule. Social Security Commissioners have suggested that the existence of some limit might be said to be common knowledge (R(SB)40/85), but they have also made it clear that the individual's whole background must be considered, including experience of the relevant system, and advice which is likely to have been received from the family or elsewhere. Research published in 1995 by the DSS indicates that older people have very considerable misconceptions about the capital limits for means-tested benefits. In particular, many are unclear about the precise threshold figure (Finch and Elam, *Managing Money in Later Life*, DSS, 1995). Again, an opinion poll conducted in March 1994, one year after the community care changes, revealed that more than 60% of the respondents were unaware of, or vague about the then £8,000 threshold for local authority assistance with the cost of care. These findings are significant, given the importance for the State in establishing knowledge, and could be used on behalf of a client to help rebut any suggestion that knowledge should be inferred.

It is now established that securing entitlement to income support need not be the predominant purpose of a deprivation, but must be a 'significant operative purpose' (R(SB)40/85), and the CRAG adopts the same approach for local authority assessments. Paragraph 6.062 states 'avoiding the charge need not be the resident's main motive but it must be a *significant* one'. If direct evidence of purpose is not available, the assessor must find primary facts from which to draw an inference as to purpose. There is an obvious temptation for the assessor to employ a 'but for' test: to say that, if obtaining benefit or mitigating care charges are foreseeable consequences of deprivation, then it is reasonable to conclude that there was a significant operative purpose. The Adjudication Officers' Guide emphasises, however, that the assessor must look at all the circumstances, and that he is not entitled to conclude that a significant purpose of a deprivation must have been to secure benefit solely because entitlement was a foreseeable consequence (para 30328). The same principle must apply to assessment by a local authority.

Each case will, therefore, turn on its own facts and the Social Security Commissioners have mentioned a number of relevant factors, for example whether a gift is made in return for a personal service; the claimant's health or personal needs; whether a loan is immediately repayable. The Adjudication Officers' Guide emphasises that the Benefits Agency must look at what motivated the individual in the given circumstances, and that the choices open to the individual at the time must be considered. Were creditors pressing for repayment of a debt, for instance? Was the claimant in fact doing no more than satisfying his need for one of the 'necessities of life'? (para 30320).

The CRAG introduces, in addition, a test of reasonableness:

> 'If, for example, a person has used capital to repay a debt, careful consideration should be given to whether there was a need for the debt to be repaid at that time. If it seems unreasonable for the resident to have repaid that debt at that time, it may be that the purpose was to avoid a charge for accommodation' (para 6.063).

Two examples are given:

– A person has £9,000 in the bank. He is about to move permanently to a residential care home, and before doing so, pays off £3,500 outstanding on a loan for home improvements. It would be reasonable in these circumstances not to treat him as having deprived himself of the £3,500 deliberately in order to reduce his residential accommodation charge.

– A resident has £5,000 in a building society. Two weeks before entering the home he bought a car for £10,500 which he gave to his son on entering the home. If the resident knew he was to be admitted permanently to a residential care home at the time he bought the car, it would be reasonable to treat this as deliberate deprivation. However, all the circumstances must be taken into account. If he was admitted as an emergency and had no reason to think he would not be in a position to drive the car at the time he bought it, it would not be reasonable to treat it as deliberate deprivation.

These examples cause difficulties because reg 25 itself carries no suggestion that a deprivation should be subjected to a test of reasonableness. The Social Security Commissioners have clearly interpreted 'purpose' subjectively, and a foreseeability test is only relevant when direct evidence as to purpose is lacking. In CIS 62/1991, for instance, where the claimant had been warned about the consequences of a proposed disposition by the local DSS office, but still went ahead, the inference was drawn that the securing of entitlement to benefit could not have been a significant operative purpose. Nevertheless, both examples do emphasise the point that the facts must not be regarded as speaking for themselves, but must be fully investigated.

18.2.7   Timing

Neither reg 51 nor reg 25 specifies time-limits for the operation of the notional capital rule. Practitioners familiar with IHT planning are sometimes surprised to find that there is no 'safe period' within which disposals of assets may be made. Where there is a 'deprivation' immediately before a claim for benefit or entry into residential care, the facts may then speak for themselves in giving an indication of whether or not a significant purpose existed (AOG, para 30329). In these circumstances, the State is entitled to ask: would this elderly person have engaged in this transaction, at this moment, had he or she not intended to claim benefit or avoid care charges? In R(SB)9/91, for example, the Social Security Commissioner looked at an existing claimant's gift of her house to her two daughters just before she entered a nursing home. He held that the gift was caught by reg 51 because, although the claimant always intended that her daughters should have the house, since its capital value would remove her right to benefit once she became a permanent patient in a nursing home, the timing suggested that obtaining benefit was a significant operative purpose.

Nevertheless, the facts of the individual case will still be crucial and it is not appropriate to draw inferences from the timing of a gift if there is evidence which points in a different direction. In CIS 242/1993, the Commissioner reached the opposite conclusion on the facts. Here, the claimant's son had cared for his mother for 15 years, and when she went into residential care she gave her share of the proceeds of sale of their jointly owned home to him to be used towards the purchase of a flat. It was accepted that the transfer had been made out of gratitude and not with a significant operative purpose of securing income support. The CRAG underlines this approach, stating that it would be 'unreasonable to decide that a resident had disposed of an asset in order to reduce his charge for accommodation when the disposal took place at a time when he was fit and healthy and could not have foreseen the need for a move to residential accommodation' (para 6.064).

Where, on the other hand, a substantial period has elapsed between a deprivation and a claim for benefit or entry to residential care, it will be difficult for the State to discharge its burden of proof by making the necessary connection between the two events. Planning to cover a possible eventuality which may or may not arise is one thing; disposing of property with a significant operative purpose is something else. Since both regulations suggest that the purpose of a deprivation must be directed at an event which is clearly foreseen and anticipated, timing is extremely relevant. Nevertheless, advisers are still faced with a problem of quantifying the risks involved in disposing of assets at a particular moment, and this is not helped by the fact that the practice of the benefits agency and of local authorities up and down the country appears to lack consistency.

18.2.8 Disregarded capital

Regulation 46 of the ISG Regs 1987 and reg 21 of the NA(AR) Regs 1992 provide that specified assets will be disregarded by the State in assessing whether an individual has capital in excess of the £8,000 threshold. Schedule 10 to the ISG Regs and Sch 4 to the NA(AR) Regs contain extended lists of such assets. The best known disregarding provision applies to the value of an interest in a home occupied either by the claimant or by the claimant's partner or other specified relative (see **15.3.6**). The Schedules repay detailed attention because, as for inheritance tax, sensible planning may involve an appropriate arrangement or rearrangement of assets. Particularly useful examples are as follows:

(a) the capital value of the home or former home as outlined above;

(b) the value of the right to receive any income under a life interest or from a life rent (ISG Regs 1987, Sch 10, para 3; NA(AR) Regs 1992, Sch 4, para 11).

(c) personal possessions, except those acquired with the intention of reducing capital for the purpose of claiming benefit or reducing residential care fees (Sch 10, para 10; Sch 4, para 8);

(d) reversionary interests.

In the past, there has been some debate as to what is meant by 'reversionary interest'. It has always been accepted that the term would include equitable future interests, but more recently the Court of Appeal held, in *CAO v Palfrey* (1995) *The Times*, 17 February, that the landlord's freehold reversion on a lease was also included. The DSS reversed this decision, however, with effect from 2 October 1995 and Sch 10, paras 5 and 24 to the ISG Regs 1987 have been amended to make it clear that properties held subject to tenancies are not 'reversionary interests' (Income Related Benefits Schemes and Social Security (Claims and Payments) (Miscellaneous Amendments) Regulations 1995 (SI 1995/2303)). The NA(AR) Regs 1992 were similarly amended from 20 December 1995 (NA(AR) Amendment (No 2) Regs 1995 (SI 1995/3054)).

The importance of disregarded capital lies in the fact that the regulations appear to encapsulate the principle that notional capital may be disregarded in the same way as actual capital. Regulation 51(6) of the ISG Regs 1987 states for example:

> 'Where a claimant is treated as possessing capital under any of paragraphs (1) to (4), the foregoing provisions of this Chapter (including reg 46) shall apply for the purpose of calculating its amount as if it were actual capital which he does possess.'

In the past, there has been some disagreement amongst the Social Security Commissioners on this point, but the prevailing view now supports this interpretation (CIS 81/1991; CIS 562/1992).

The Adjudication Officers' Guide states unequivocally that notional capital is calculated in the same way as actual capital and that appropriate disregards should be applied (para 30337). An example is given:

> 'A claimant gave away her interest in the property occupied as her home. She did this to retain entitlement to income support when she entered a nursing home. Although she was treated as having a sum of notional capital which represented the value of her former interest the notional capital was disregarded whilst she lived in the property.'

Regulation 21 of the NA(AR) Regs 1992 states that the capital of a resident to be taken into account shall be the whole of his capital. The CRAG makes no direct reference to this point, but the same reasoning ought to apply given that reg 21 appears to have the same effect as reg 51(6).

The conclusion must be that, so long as capital which could legitimately be assessed as notional capital is held in disregarded form, then its value cannot be taken into account. Furthermore, in a robust decision a Social Security Commissioner has held that it is not necessary for the disregarding provision to have been applicable to capital before the act of deprivation (CIS 231/1991). In this case, the appellant transferred his former home to his parents in consideration of natural love and affection three months before claiming income support. He had by that time moved to a new home which was disregarded in the assessment, but the value of the transferred property was taken into account by the Adjudication Officer as notional capital. The Commissioner held that Sch 10 'applies to notional capital just as it applies to actual capital. It is not necessary that the disregard under Schedule 10 should have been applicable before the claimant deprived himself of the capital ... It is ... plain that, even if the claimant had deprived himself of the former home for the purpose of obtaining income support, that former home fell to be disregarded under para 4 of Schedule 10' (because it was occupied by elderly relatives of the claimant).

Example 1:
Mr and Mrs Clark are legal and equitable joint tenants of their home. Mrs Clark has lived in a nursing home since February 1993 and has preserved rights to income support. She severs the equitable joint tenancy and transfers her interest in the house to her son.

  (i) Mrs Clark's capital interest will be disregarded for income support purposes as long as her husband remains in occupation of the house (Sch 10, para 4 to the ISG Regs 1987).

 (ii) Mrs Clark's gift to her son is technically a 'deprivation' within reg 51(1). At present, however, the substance of the gift is in disregarded form and will remain so as long as Mr Clark is alive and is living in the house. It appears that Mrs Clark has no duty to disclose to the Benefits Agency the change in her circumstances since it will not affect her entitlement to benefit for the time being. If Mrs Clark predeceases her husband the Benefits Agency will have no interest in the gift.

(iii) If Mr Clark predeceases his wife, the Sch 10 disregard of her interest in the house will cease to operate unless another elderly or incapacitated member of the family continues to be in residence (Sch 10, para 4). Mrs Clark should notify the Benefits Agency of Mr Clark's death. At that point, her gift may be disclosed and the adjudication officer may seek to apply the notional capital rule. Depending on how much time has passed, however, the case may not be clear cut. Can the officer establish, for example, that Mrs Clark had the necessary 'significant operative purpose' when she made the gift, bearing in mind that it was by no means evident that she would outlive her husband?

Example 2:
Mrs Brown, a widow, settles her house worth £75,000 on herself for life, with remainder to her two adult children. One year later she goes into a nursing home.

(i) Mrs Brown's occupation of the house is protected, for as long as is necessary, by virtue of her equitable interest as tenant for life.

(ii) The settlement falls within reg 25 of the NA(AR) Regs 1992 because Mrs Brown has deprived herself of her beneficial interest in the house by giving away the equitable reversionary interest and converting her equitable fee simple into an equitable life interest.

(iii) The capital value of the life interest is, however, disregarded capital under Sch 4, para 11, as is also the reversionary interest (para 24).

(iv) The value of the life interest will continue to be disregarded after Mrs Brown goes into the nursing home; para 11 imposes no time-limits on this disregard.

(v) If, at this point, the local authority assessor seeks to raise reg 25, there will be two arguments in Mrs Brown's favour:

 – after 12 months, the local authority may have some difficulty in establishing the necessary significant operative purpose. If, for example, Mrs Brown's children have cared for her and the settlement was made in consideration of natural love and affection, the likelihood must be that the local authority will accept the situation;

 – if the equitable reversionary interest were regarded as Mrs Brown's notional capital it would be disregarded indefinitely under Sch 4, para 10 (CIS/231/91 is directly relevant here).

Conclusions
So long as the regulations remain unaltered it appears that schemes which take advantage of the disregarded capital rules may enable clients to avoid notional capital. The regulations create other possibilities too. For example, although the creation of a trust is clearly an act of deprivation, where the trust is discretionary beneficiaries have no 'entitlement' to capital so long as the

property remains within the trust. Even if there is a significant operative purpose in setting up the trust, there may be no assessable interest to which the label notional capital can be attached unless payments out are made. This model forms the basis of some of the off-the-shelf schemes which are now being marketed by non-solicitor services. The Law Society is concerned that some of these schemes fail to take into account clients' individual circumstances, and warns against them in its recent guidance. Nevertheless, discretionary trusts are extremely flexible vehicles for protecting both individuals and assets, given appropriately skilled draftsmanship.

18.3   Rights of local authorities to recover gifts from third parties

Application of the notional capital rule is likely to have one of two outcomes for the elderly client:

(a) it may prevent entitlement to income support. This will be particularly problematic for clients who have preserved rights to income support;

(b) it may trigger indebtedness to the local authority because the fee charged for residential accommodation will reflect notional capital.

In addition, further sanctions are possible in that the local authority may consider using its statutory power to recover the costs of care from third parties, or may consider invoking the anti-avoidance provisions in the Insolvency Act 1986. Such possibilities are considered, in turn, below and at **18.4**. For reasons which will be explained, the risk for the client that either section will be applied appears at present to be relatively low. However, the ever increasing pressure on community care resources may, inevitably, mean that local authorities will in future have to consider their enforcement options more cynically than, on the evidence, they have done so far.

Section 21 of the HASSASSAA 1983, which was brought into force on 1 April 1993, provides a new and effective remedy for local authorities where dispositions of property are made with the intention of avoiding, or reducing residential care fees.

Section 21(1) refers to a person who 'avails' himself of Part III accommodation and who knowingly and with the intention of avoiding charges for the accommodation transfers an asset to a third party by way of gift, or for a consideration which is less than the value of the asset. In such circumstances, the transferee 'shall' be liable to pay to the local authority the 'difference between the amount assessed as due to be paid for the accommodation by the person availing himself of it and the amount which the local authority receive from him for it'. This wording seems to imply that the local authority must make an initial decision to treat the subject matter of the gift as notional capital under reg 25 of the NA(AR) Regs 1992 in order to be able to make an assessment which includes the value of the property disposed of. The CRAG confirms this interpretation, emphasising that the local authority should only consider using its powers under s 21 if the asset disposed of is one which 'would have been taken into account for the purposes of assessing the charge' (Annex D, para 2.2). It would follow from this statement that local authorities will not use s 21 where the subject matter of a gift is disregarded under Sch 4 to the NA(AR) Regs 1992.

Section 21 can only be used in respect of gifts which are made not more than six months before the donor begins to reside in Part III accommodation or after admission to such accommodation. In such circumstances it will often be relatively easy for the local authority to show the deliberate intention required for both s 21 and reg 25.

It should be noted, however, that the drafting of s 21 creates a clear loophole for those seeking to avoid charges. The reference to 'Part III accommodation' links with s 21 of the NAA 1948, and must be taken to mean accommodation which is arranged by the local authority. Consequently, if a resident enters a home on a self-funded basis, makes a gift, waits for more than six months and then asks for an assessment with a view to the local authority making the care arrangements, s 21 is excluded. Equally, however, there is, as already noted, no time-limit on the operation of the notional capital rule and the local authority could, in such circumstances, assess the value of the gift if it could establish the necessary significant operative purpose under reg 25. It is sometimes said that gifts made more than six months before entering residential care are 'safe'; this view is quite clearly incorrect.

There is in fact no express time-limit on the local authority's right to seek recovery under s 21, assuming that the gift itself is made within the statutory period. The extent of any liability is limited to the benefit accruing from the gift, and where there are joint donees the liability is proportionate to the benefit received. The value of any asset will be the amount which would have been realised on the open market at the time of the gift. The previous discussion of shared interests in property will be relevant here (see **15.3.4**). Secured debts and reasonable expenses of sale will be allowable (s 21(7)).

Section 21 appears to offer local authorities a realistic method of recovering costs where a deprivation of capital has taken place. Given the limited resources available to local authorities for enforcement, it would, for instance, seem reasonable to use the discretion not to apply reg 25 unless the case is clear cut, unless substantial funds are at issue, and, particularly, unless s 21 is also available. In fact, the evidence is that, up to now, local authorities have signally avoided using s 21. This position may change in the future as resources diminish and pressure mounts to recover contributions wherever possible.

Example:

One year ago, Mr and Mrs Carruthers transferred their jointly owned home to their daughter, Margaret, by deed of gift, in consideration of their love and affection for her. Three months later, Mrs Carruthers, who suffers from Alzheimer's disease, entered a nursing home under a private arrangement.

Seven months after that her capital was reduced to £16,000, and Margaret asked the local authority to assess her mother's needs under s 47 of the NHSCCA 1990. There is no doubt that she needs nursing care.

(i) Given the relatively short time between the gift and Mrs Carruthers entering the nursing home, the local authority may draw the conclusion that the gift was made in order to avoid care fees. The burden of proof is, however, on the local authority to show that this was Mrs Carruthers' significant operative purpose. It may be, for instance, that the transfer was initiated because Margaret had made financial sacrifices to care for her parents and they, in return, wished to offer her financial security.

(ii) Even if the local authority decides to pursue an assessment of notional capital it will come up against the further problem that, were Mrs Carruthers's interest in the house still owned by her, it would be disregarded for as long as Mr Carruthers remains in occupation of the house. By the same token, if the subject of the gift to Margaret is regarded as notional capital, it too will be disregarded under the same rule (reg 21 of the NA(AR) Regs 1992).

(iii) Furthermore, since, as a matter of law, Mrs Carruthers no longer has an equitable interest in the house, it will not be possible for the local authority to place a charge on it under s 22 of the HASSASSAA 1983 in respect of unpaid care fees (see **15.11.1**).

(iv) Although the gift was made within six months of Mrs Carruthers entering the nursing home, it was not made within six months of her 'availing' herself of Part III accommodation as required by s 21 of the HASSASSAA 1983. The local authority does not, therefore, have the option of recovering care fees from Margaret.

18.4   Setting aside dispositions under the Insolvency Act 1986

Section 56 of the NAA 1948 allows local authorities to recover residential care fees as civil debts. Ultimately, therefore, they may initiate bankruptcy proceedings and ask for a trustee in bankruptcy to be appointed. Section 17(4) of the HASSASSAA 1983 is in similar terms to s 56 of the NAA 1948 and it must, therefore, be concluded that local authorities also have that option in respect of unpaid home care charges.

18.4.1   Section 339 of the Insolvency Act 1986

In most cases, the only purpose in forcing bankruptcy would be to enable the trustee in bankruptcy to use his powers to set aside voluntary dispositions under s 339 of the Insolvency Act 1986.

Section 339 provides that a trustee in bankruptcy may apply to the court for an order to set aside a gift or other transaction entered into for a consideration, the value of which is significantly less than the value of the consideration provided. Dispositions made up to five years before presentation of the bankruptcy petition are open to attack in this way. Where, however, the transaction takes place within the five-year period but more than two years before the petition is presented, the trustee has no powers unless the bankrupt was insolvent at the time of the transaction or become insolvent in consequence of it. Insolvency is presumed where the transaction is with an associate (including spouse/partner or relative) and the contrary must then be proved in order to avoid s 339. If the trustee's challenge is upheld the court may make such order as it thinks fit for restoring the position to what it would have been prior to the transaction. It may, but is not necessarily obliged to set the transaction aside.

In its recent guidance on Gifts of Property (September 1995), The Law Society warns of the possibility that local authorities may seek to utilise s 339. In appraising this risk it is important to reflect on the decision-making process which would lead to such action:

(i) the assessor identifies the fact that a gift has been made, and raises requisitions. As a result, notional capital is included in the assessment;

(ii) the resident's solicitor argues against the assessment. If the local authority will not change its position the solicitor may invoke the complaints procedures. Given that the residential placement must be maintained in any event, the local authority is unlikely to take further steps until the complaint is resolved;

(iii) the local authority may consider recovering care fees from third parties under s 21 of the HASSASSAA 1983 if the gift was made within the statutory time-limit;

(iv) otherwise, the local authority will proceed to seek an assessed contribution based on notional capital. It may charge a resident's interest in land under s 22 of the HASSASSAA 1983 in order to secure payments;

(v) as a last resort, once the resident has fallen into debt to the extent of £750 the local authority may commence bankruptcy proceedings. The trustee in bankruptcy having been appointed, he or she may seek to set the gift aside under s 339. One question for the court may be whether the care provided for the donor by a donee can be regarded as consideration in money or money's worth. In view of the importance of family care within the system as a whole, the argument could be made, and there is some support from the case-law. In *Re Kumar (A Bankrupt) ex parte Lewis v Kumar* [1993] 2 FLR 382, the court accepted that the compromise of a claim for family provision within matrimonial proceedings can be money or money's worth for the purpose of s 339. Ferris J also accepted, implicitly, that the assumption of responsibility for children, within a marriage, is capable of forming the subject of a 'bargain' between husband and wife, and so provide consideration for a transfer of property (at p 397).

The issues are not straightforward, but there will be pressure on local authorities to act quickly since most donors will probably have been solvent when making gifts, so that the trustee in bankruptcy's powers extend only two years back from the presentation of the bankruptcy petition. Some donors will have taken the precaution of executing declarations of solvency. In the final analysis, too, the court has discretion and the local authority may not achieve the desired outcome. Costs may be substantial whatever the outcome.

In addition, public opinion is sensitive on this issue, and by adopting a stance which is seen as overly aggressive a local authority may incur criticism from the community which it serves. This, too, will be a factor in the decision on whether or not to use s 339.

18.4.2   Section 423 of the Insolvency Act 1986

Section 423 of the Insolvency Act 1986 allows the court to set aside at any time a gift or transaction at an undervalue where it is satisfied that it was entered into for the purpose of putting assets beyond the reach of a person who is making or may at some time make a claim against the donor. This provision does not hinge on bankruptcy proceedings.

The High Court recently reviewed the law in *Midland Bank plc v Wyatt* [1995] 1 FLR 696 and made it clear that the meaning of 'purpose' in s 423 is much the same as for the notional capital rule, 'It is a question of proof of intention or purpose underlying the transaction' (DEM Young QC, at p 709). The onus of proof is on the creditor, but, as with notional capital, it is enough if the 'dominant' purpose of the donor can be shown to have been the removal of assets from creditors in cases where there was also an intention to benefit a third party.

Nevertheless, it is not a foregone conclusion that s 423 is applicable to a disposition which has the effect of reducing or avoiding residential care fees. There has been little case-law, but in *Midland Bank v Wyatt* the bank challenged a trust arrangement whereby the defendant gave the equity in the family home to his wife and daughters shortly before setting up a new business, in order to protect them from long-term commercial risk. The judge commented (at p 709):

> 'I consider that if the purpose of the transaction can be shown to put assets beyond the reach of future creditors, s 423 will apply whether or not the transferor was about to enter into a hazardous business or whether his business was as a sole practitioner or as a partner or as a participant in a limited liability company. It is a question of proof of intention or purpose underlying the transaction. Clearly, the more hazardous the business being contemplated is, the more readily the court will be satisfied of the intention of the settlor or transferor.'

These words emphasise the business context of the transaction and the commercial nature of the risks which the defendant sought to avoid.

It may be argued that s 423 is not appropriately used by a local authority which has acted under a public law duty in arranging residential care, and is seeking to recover fees under s 22 of the NAA 1948 from a resident with whom it has no contract at all, let alone a business relationship.

In addition, the 'proof of intention or purpose' is always going to raise problems for a local authority. Advisers to elderly clients may take some comfort from recent dicta of Millett LJ in *Tribe v Tribe* [1995] 2 FLR 966, CA:

> 'It is, of course, perfectly legitimate for a person who is solvent to make a gift of his property, particularly the matrimonial home, to his wife in order to protect her against the possibility of future business failure' (at p 987).

Can it not be assumed, therefore, that it would be equally legitimate to make a gift which seeks to protect the beneficiary against the possibility that the donor might have to go into residential care, and against the adverse financial consequences of such an eventuality? If so, then surely s 423, or indeed, reg 25 require evidence of more than the 'possibility' of residential care at the time of the disposition?

Chapter 19

USING WELFARE BENEFITS TO FUND RESIDENTIAL CARE

The importance of identifying entitlement to certain welfare benefits for clients living in the community has already been noted (see Chapter 17). Once clients enter residential care homes or nursing homes, the interface between the rules for claiming certain benefits and the local authority's assessment regulations becomes very complex. Good and timely advice in this area will often result in measurable value for clients.

19.1 What benefits?

The benefits to be considered here are the attendance allowance; the disability living allowance (care component) and (mobility component) and, to a lesser extent, income support. A full discussion of eligibility for these benefits lies beyond the scope of this book, and readers are referred to the various benefit guides listed at the end of this chapter for more detailed information. The relevant legal rules are to be found in ss 64–67 and 71–76 of the Social Security Contributions and Benefits Act 1992 and in the Social Security (Attendance Allowance) Regulations 1991 and the Social Security (Disability Living Allowance) Regulations 1991. The scope for entitlement is, however, as follows:

(i) *Attendance allowance and disability living allowance (care component)*
Both these benefits are available for people who need personal care. The former can now be claimed only by elderly people over the age of 65, whilst the latter is available to any claimant below the age of 66 who meets the prescribed conditions. Once a successful claim has been made, both benefits will continue in payment as long as the claimant lives, unless circumstances change. Most of the entitlement rules are identical for both benefits. In each case, the maximum benefit payment will be £48.50 per week (1996/97 rates). The majority of elderly people who fall within the conditions of entitlement are in fact paid the highest rate of benefit.

Both attendance allowance and DLA care component are non-contributory, and are available, therefore, irrespective of a claimant's other resources.

(ii) *Disability living allowance (mobility component)*
The DLA (mobility component) is available for people who are unable to walk or who have difficulty in walking. The present rules cover physical disability and also some types of mental incapacity. Older people with

Alzheimer's disease may, for instance, establish entitlement to this benefit alongside entitlement to either attendance allowance or DLA (care component).

The mobility component is non-contributory and non-means tested. Entitlement must be established before the claimant's 66th birthday, but may then continue until the claimant dies, assuming that the disability remains.

The higher rate of the mobility component is now £33.90 per week (1996/97 rates).

(iii) *Income support*

Unlike the other benefits described in this chapter, income support is 'income related' or means tested. It is available for those whose resources fall short of their 'applicable amount' as determined by the legislation.

The applicable amount for a person entering a registered residential care home or nursing home after 1 April 1993 comprises three elements:

(a) a fixed personal allowance – currently £47.90 for an individual and £75.20 for a couple (1996/97 rates);

(b) premiums, that is payments targeted at certain types of need. Elderly people are favoured above other groups in the system in that they are eligible for several premiums which are capable of raising their applicable amount very significantly in some cases;

(c) relevant housing costs. A flat rate residential allowance of £54 per week (£60 per week for placements in the London area). This allowance is not available for people living in unregistered private sector homes or in local authority Part III accommodation (see **15.8**).

This model of entitlement closely resembles that for elderly people living in the community whose resources are limited (see Figure 7). For people with preserved rights, however, the applicable amount consists simply of a fixed allowance based on the type of residential accommodation plus a small personal expenses allowance. There is a further prescribed variation of the applicable amount for people resident in Part III accommodation (see **15.9**). In addition, the recent raising of the capital limit for claimants in residential care, but not for other claimants, has created an imbalance which could be represented as a revival of the pre-1993 'perverse incentive' towards residential care (see **2.4.2**).

19.1.1 Income support premiums

The key to maximising income support entitlement on behalf of an elderly client lies in identifying premiums which may be available. These are as follows:

INCOME SUPPORT

APPLICABLE AMOUNT

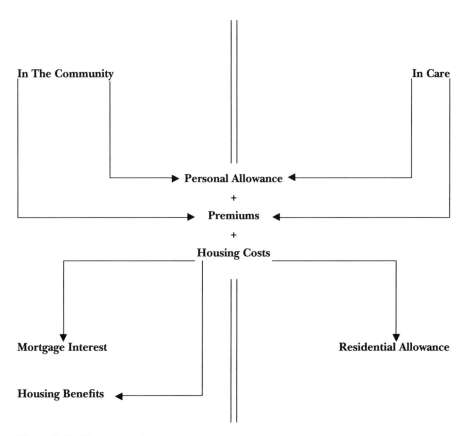

Figure 7. Entitlement to income support.

(a) Pensioner premium, which is available simply on the basis of age. There are two bands: age 60–74 and age 75–79 (Sch 2, paras 9 and 9A to the ISG Regs 1987).

(b) Higher pensioner premium. The qualifying conditions are either advanced age (claimant or partner is aged 80 or over) *or* old age (60–79) together with disability signified by receipt of a qualifying benefit for disability (Sch 2, para 10 to the ISG Regs 1987).

(c) Severe disability premium. Here the claimant must be in receipt of attendance allowance or one of the higher rates of DLA (care component) and must not have an adult non-dependant residing with him or her. In addition, no one must be receiving invalid care allowance in respect of care given to the claimant.

Only *one* of the pensioner or higher pensioner premiums (whichever is the greater) can be claimed at the same time. Severe disability premium may, however, be paid in addition to either pensioner premium (Sch 2, para 13 to the ISG Regs 1987).

(d) In addition, a carer's premium is available to those caring for elderly and disabled people, who are receiving the invalid care allowance, but need to top up their income with income support. It should be noted that where a carer lives with the disabled person who is receiving care, a claim in respect of carer's premium will involve the loss of severe disability premium for the disabled person. Advice on this point can help clients maximise entitlement (Sch 2, para 14ZA to the ISG Regs 1987).

19.2 Availability of disability benefits to those in residential care

Two questions arise here:

(i) Is entitlement to any benefit affected if a claimant or prospective claimant enters a residential care home or nursing home?

(ii) How far will a disability benefit be means tested where a resident is also claiming income support?

On the first question, it is necessary to consider the benefits in turn.

19.2.1 DLA (mobility component)

For this benefit, the present legal position is relatively straightforward. A resident who meets the legislative requirements of being unable or virtually unable to walk, and who is within the prescribed age-limits, may claim benefit whilst in residential care, whilst in hospital, and whilst in hospice care.

In no circumstances will the DLA (mobility component) be means tested (s 73(14) of the Social Security Contributions and Benefits Act 1992). Consequently, whenever a placement is funded or partly funded by the State, whether through the local authority or the DSS, receipt of the DLA (mobility component) will leave the resident with a weekly sum (£33.90 maximum) which cannot be recouped to meet the costs of the care. Where, on the other hand, a resident is privately funded, receipt of this benefit will decelerate the rate at which his or her assets are depleted.

The Government has now given notice of its intention to amend the rules of entitlement to the DLA (mobility component) so that this benefit will cease to be available to patients who have stayed in hospital for more than four weeks.

19.2.2 Attendance allowance and DLA (care component)

The rules which affect claims made by residents in respect of either of these two benefits are anything but straightforward. The difficulties derive from the fact that both benefits are targeted at an individual's need for personal care. Given that provision of such care is the function of residential accommodation, there is a policy objection to double funding, by public bodies, of the same need. As a result, regulations prevent either benefit being claimed in any circumstances by people for whom residential accommodation is provided under certain statutory responsibilities, in particular Part III of the NAA 1948. There is also disentitlement in other circumstances where the cost of the accommodation is or may be borne wholly or partly out of public or local funds 'in pursuance of those enactments or of any other enactment relating to persons under disability' (regs 7 and 8 of the Social Security (Attendance Allowance) Regulations 1991; regs 9 and 10 of the Social Security (Disability Living Allowance) Regulations 1991). Residents in Part III accommodation managed by the local authority, or residents in respect of whom the local authority has made accommodation arrangements with independent providers under s 26 of the NAA 1948 are therefore disentitled to either benefit (*Chief Adjudication Officer v Kenyon* (1995) *The Times*, 17 October, but see **19.4**). The same applies to nursing home residents in respect of whom their health authority has made care arrangements. All such people are prevented from making first-time claims after they have entered residential care, and previous entitlement ceases, subject to dispensation in respect of the first 28 days in the residential establishment.

The words 'could be borne' in the regulations are problematic because it is clear that, given a need for residential care, a local authority always 'could' make arrangements for any individual under s 21 or s 26 of the NAA 1948. It has been accepted, however, that the statutory power is of last resort because it is to be exercisable only in respect of those who need care 'which is not otherwise available to them' (s 21(1)(a) of the NAA 1948). Consequently, where an elderly person is willing and able to make his or her own care arrangements, and does so, the cost 'cannot' be borne by the local authority (*Steane v Chief Adjudication Officer* (1995) *The Times*, 19 December).

Some residents may wish to fund their placements out of a combination of benefits, including income support. The possible advantages of such a course of action are explained at **19.3**. The original intention of the DSS seems to have been that those who are subsidised by central government funds through income support should be treated in the same way as those subsidised by local authorities. In other words, neither attendance allowance nor DLA (care component) should be available after the first 28 days. Regulation 8(6) of the Social Security (Attendance Allowance) Regulations 1991 provides that the 'could be borne' provision (reg 7) does not apply where the resident 'is not entitled to income support . . . and the whole of the cost of the accommodation is met out of his own resources . . .', implying that it does not cover those who claim income support. Regulation 10(8) of the Social Security (Disability Living Allowance) Regulations 1991 is in identical terms.

Since 1994, however, an extra-statutory concession has applied, in that a person who enters residential care, without a local authority financial assessment, and claims income support to fund the placement, may also claim attendance allowance or DLA (care component). For some residents this option offers a means of bypassing the local authority's assessment process and so of extending personal choice. The DSS is currently monitoring the effects of this 'loophole' and benefits claims made in such circumstances will be referred to the Benefit Agency's Disability Benefits Unit. Benefit payments are suspended pending referral, but should subsequently be reinstated (IS Bulletin 68/95).

Residents who have preserved rights to income support (see Chapter 16) may claim attendance allowance or DLA (care component) because they have, in the past, made private care arrangements with a provider and are, therefore, outside the scope of the regulations.

19.2.3   Means testing of attendance allowance and disability living allowance (care component)

On the second question, it is the general rule that neither benefit is taken into account for the income support means test, although receipt of either benefit will usually affect the level of a local authority's charges for social services provided in the community (Sch 9, para 9 to the ISG Regs 1987); see the discussion at **17.3**. For claimants who are in residential care, however, the rules are not consistent, but depend on the type of home occupied by the claimant, viz:

(i)   For temporary or respite placements of up to four weeks, either benefit may be claimed, and will not reduce the level of any income support which may be available to the resident (reg 8 of the Social Security (Attendance Allowance) Regulations 1991; reg 10 of the Social Security (Disability Living Allowance) Regulations 1991). Local authorities will, however, take either benefit into account when assessing a resident's contribution towards home fees (reg 15(1) of the National Assistance (Assessment of Resources) Regulations 1992). Although local authorities are not required to carry out a full financial assessment during the first eight weeks of a temporary placement in residential care, if they elect to do so the effect of reg 15 will simply be to increase an individual's contribution during the first four weeks because the disability benefit will be taken into account.

(ii) For permanent placements arranged by a local authority in the independent sector after 1 April 1993, neither attendance allowance nor DLA (care component) is available, and means testing is not, therefore, an issue. The same is true of placements in Part III accommodation.

(iii) Where residents purchase their own residential care, and claim income support, both benefits are disregarded income under para 9 of Sch 9 to the ISG Regs 1987. In addition, the basic level of income support will be raised in such cases because entitlement to either benefit will passport claimants on to the severe disability premium.

Generally speaking, however, it will not be feasible for residents who are in a position to claim income support, and whose capital is, by definition, very modest, to take this option except on a short-term basis (see the example at **19.3**).

(iv) Where residents have preserved rights, both attendance allowance and DLA (care component) will be taken into account against the enhanced levels of income support which this legal status attracts. In other words, such residents will gain nothing financially from pursuing a claim to either benefit once they begin to claim income support.

(v) Residents with substantial resources who make their own care arrangements may claim either benefit to help mitigate the loss to their estates.

19.3   Example

Mrs Ross has a house worth £90,000, a few other assets and a modest income. She can no longer manage at home and is looking for a suitable residential care home.

Mrs Ross has been advised that she will have to sell her house to fund the placement, but she is aware that it may take some time to sell it. She has also been advised that if her local authority makes the care arrangements they are likely to charge the house immediately in order to secure payment of the home fees (see **15.11.1**). The Benefits Agency, on the other hand, will continue to disregard the value of the house for at least six months and possibly for much longer after Mrs Ross enters the home (Sch 10, para 26 to the ISG Regs 1987). During that period, she may be able to fund the placement without involving the local authority provided that her son agrees to pay a top-up.

Accommodation charge		£250.00
Mrs Ross's resources:		
Retirement pension	£61.15	
Income support	£103.05	
(Personal allowance £47.90		
Higher pensioner premium £25.90		
Severe disability premium £36.40		
Residential allowance £54.00		
Applicable amount £164.20)		
Attendance allowance	£48.50	
	£212.70	
Top-up	£37.30	
	£250.00	£250.00

19.4   Practice points

(i) The financial option demonstrated by the above example may be worth considering in respect of clients who have a limited prognosis and wish to preserve their house for their family. Benefits paid out pending sale are not recoverable by the State, and the arrangement, in effect, buys time before the State begins to encroach on the capital value of a property.

(ii) It is always worth identifying entitlement to attendance allowance or DLA (care component) for clients who will be funding their own residential care. Over an extended period, the value to a client will be considerable, particularly if a claim for the DLA (mobility component) is also indicated. The claiming process itself is, however, not without difficulty since the application forms are long and complicated and entitlement rests, to a large measure, on self-assessment. Clients will benefit from hands-on assistance with claiming.

(iii) Given that attendance allowance or DLA (care component) is available to clients who make their own residential care arrangements, it may be argued that, by the same token, clients for whom the local authority makes arrangements under s 21 of the NAA 1948, but who in fact pay a full contribution towards their fees, should also be entitled to one of these benefits. The double funding argument referred to in **19.2.2** does not apply where the local authority is not *in fact* funding the placement and, consequently, regs 7 and 8 of the Social Security (Attendance Allowance) Regulations 1991 and regs 9 and 10 of the Social Security (Disability Living Allowance) Regulations 1991 should not be applicable. At the time of writing, the House of Lords is considering entitlement to attendance allowance in these and related circumstances and, hopefully, will clarify this issue (*Chief Adjudication Officer v Harris*, 15 April 1994, unreported).

APPENDIX

EXAMPLE OF CARE MANAGEMENT

Mrs Alice Baker is to be discharged from hospital following a stroke. The way her needs are addressed illustrate the seven stages of care management.

Stage 1
Publishing information

The ward sister ensures that she receives the information booklet on rehabilitation services for stroke victims and the leaflet on the volunteer 'Stroke Support Scheme', following discussion with her about her likely difficulties upon returning home.

Stage 2
Determining level of assessment

The ward sister completes a referral form to the hospital social work team, detailing Mrs Baker's concerns about managing at home, both immediately and in the longer term.

On the basis of that information, the social services team leader decides that Mrs Baker should receive a comprehensive assessment, co-ordinated by a social worker. This staff member attends the ward round; she has an initial interview with Mrs Baker and arranges for assessments to be completed by a physiotherapist and occupational therapist.

Stage 3
Assessing need

The social worker identifies that, although Mrs Baker is anxious to retain her independence, her confidence has been severely affected and she is unsure what level of support her daughter, who lives nearby, will be able to give her, because she has a large family of her own.

The physiotherapist confirms that Mrs Baker has suffered a significant loss of functioning in her right arm and leg; the prognosis is encouraging but uncertain and depends upon the patient's sustained commitment to rehabilitation.

The occupational therapist takes Mrs Baker on a visit back to her council home before advising her that she will initially have difficulty with most aspects of self-care. She will not be able to climb stairs, so sleeping and toileting facilities will have to be provided downstairs.

Despite her misgivings, Mrs Baker wishes to:

- return home as soon as support services can be arranged

- re-establish as much independence as possible
- review future options in six months in the light of progress.

Her daughter is supportive of this intention but limited in the amount of support she is able to give.

Stage 4
Care planning

The social worker clarifies the likely discharge date with the consultant; she refers Mrs Baker to the intensive discharge service and 'Meals on Wheels'. A care plan is devised in which:

- the discharge service covers getting up and going to bed for a maximum of six weeks.
- 'Meals on Wheels' are available five days a week and the daughter provides cover at weekends
- Mrs Baker agrees to meet the assessed charges
- the daughter undertakes to visit three times during the week at specified times, synchronised with contacts from the community nurse and social worker and the weekly outpatient physiotherapy.
- the occupational therapist undertakes to complete her initial assessment within one week of discharge and arrange provision of the appropriate disability equipment.

All visitors agree to complete a diary sheet to be kept by Mrs Baker and to review the situation after six weeks. Mrs Baker and all contributors receive a copy of the written care plan which spells out the primary objective of rehabilitating Mrs Baker and restoring her confidence.

Stage 5
Implementing the care plan

The ward sister confirms the date of discharge, so the social worker alerts all the relevant agencies and individuals. The daughter sets up the downstairs bedroom and takes delivery of the commode, ordered by the ward sister from the home loans service.

The social worker negotiates the budgetary allocation for the intensive discharge service and the 'Meals on Wheels' service. She also checks that all parties are able to honour their commitments.

Stage 6
Monitoring

One week after discharge, the social worker takes stock with Mrs Baker over how well the arrangements are working and makes some minor amendments to the programme of visiting, following consultation with the individuals affected. Those who have failed to complete the diary sheet are reminded of the importance of the record. Mrs Baker decides that she would like to make contact with the 'Stroke Support Scheme', so this is arranged by the community nurse. The social worker confirms that the daughter is able to continue with the agreed level of support. As Mrs Baker improves, the level of support is gradually reduced.

Stage 7
Reviewing

After six weeks, the social worker obtains feedback from all involved on the progress of the arrangements.

This is discussed with Mrs Baker at a meeting to which the daughter is invited, at Mrs Baker's request. Apart from a complaint about the unvaried menu of 'Meals on Wheels', there is general agreement that the arrangements have worked reasonably well and that Mrs Baker will be able to cope with the scaled-down input of the domiciliary care service after the intensive discharge service has been withdrawn. However, because Mrs Baker is disappointed with the pace of her rehabilitation, she requests that the social worker instigates an assessment by the Housing Department to explore alternative housing options.

A revised care plan is drawn up and re-distributed following consultation with all the contributors, setting the next review for a further six weeks' time. Mrs Baker's complaint about 'Meals on Wheels' is fed back into the quality assurance system. The budgetary allocation for the revised plan is re-negotiated by the social worker.

Note

This example is put forward in *Care Management and Assessment: Practitioners' Guide* (Social Services Inspectorate, 1991) as an example of best practice. It predates the new NHS guidance on hospital discharge procedures (HSG(95)8; LAC(95)5). Since it seems clear that Mrs Baker's physical condition would not require continuing nursing care, and she herself would not want it, the discharge is appropriate. Nevertheless, under the new guidance, Mrs Baker's care plan must identify a person to whom concerns may be referred in the first instance, and must also give Mrs Baker information about the new procedure for reviewing the decision on her eligibility for NHS continuing in-patient care. In addition, the social worker should provide Mrs Baker with written details of the prospective cost to her of her care package.

THE RESPONSIBILITY OF DIFFERENT ORGANISATIONS IN RESPECT OF CARE AND ACCOMMODATION SERVICES

AGENCY	FORM OF CARE	SERVICE	VARIATIONS
New Health Authorities (incorporating former DHAs and FHSAs)	Hospitals Residential Community Services	– In-patients – Day – Community units – Nursing homes – Nurses – Health visitors – Therapists	– Long-stay – Short-stay/respite – Qualified – Auxiliary – Physiotherapists – Chiropody
Purchasing functions	Primary Health Care	– GPs – Nurses – Dental and ophthalmic services	
Social Services (purchasers and providers)	Residential Accommodation Day Care Domiciliary	– Residential homes – Staffed group homes – Unstaffed group homes – Sheltered lodgings – Workshops – Day centres – Training centres – Drop-in centres – Social workers – Good neighbours – Home helps – Therapists	– Long-stay – Short-stay/respite – Occupational
Housing Authorities (providers)	Housing	– Sheltered housing – Hostels – Group homes – Flats/houses	– Wardens – Alarm systems – Improvement grants
Education	Training facilities for adults		

AGENCY	FORM OF CARE	SERVICE	VARIATIONS
Voluntary Sector and Housing Associations (providers)	Residential Housing Day Care Domiciliary	– Residential homes – Nursing homes – Group homes – Sheltered housing – Flats/houses – Luncheon clubs – Drop-in centres – Day centres – Care attendant schemes – Volunteers/good neighbours	– For special needs
Private Sector (providers)	Residential Housing Domiciliary	– Nursing homes – Residential homes – Sheltered housing – Domestic agencies	

BIBLIOGRAPHY

Age Concern *The Community Care Changes: Assessment and Care Management* (1992)

Age Concern *The Community Care Changes: Purchasing and Contracting* (1992)

Age Concern *The Community Care Changes: Community Care Plans* (1992)

Age Concern *The Community Care Changes: Quality and Inspection* (1992)

Age Concern *The Law and Vulnerable Elderly People* (1986)

Age Concern *No Time to Lose: First Impressions of Community Care Reforms* (1993)

Age Concern *Preserved and Protected? A Report and Recommendations about the Community Care Reforms and People with Preserved Rights to Income Support* England (1994)

Age Concern *The Next Steps: Lessons for the Future of Community Care* (1994)

Age Concern *Gold Standards: Professional Targets for the Care of Elderly People* (1994)

Allen, I. and Perkins, E. *The Future of Family Care for Older People* (HMSO, 1995)

Alzheimer's Disease Society *NHS Psychogeriatric Continuing Care Beds* (1993)

Ashton, G. *The Elderly Client Handbook* (Law Society, 1994)

Ashton, G. *Elderly People and the Law* (Butterworths with Age Concern, 1995)

Ashton, G. *Elderly People and Residential Care* (SJ, 27 October 1995)

Ashton, G. *Mental Handicap and the Law* (Butterworths, 1992)

Association of Directors of Social Services *Towards Community Care: A DSS Review of the First Year* (1994)

Association of Metropolitan Authorities *Review of Issues Relating to Charging for Community Care Services* (1992)

Association of Metropolitan Authorities *Guidance on Contracting for Residential and Nursing Home Care for Adults* (1994)

Association of Metropolitan Authorities *Guidance on Contracting for Domiciliary and Day Care Services* (1995)

Audit Commission *Making a Reality of Community Care* (1986)

Audit Commission *Community Care: Managing the Cascade of Change* (1992)

Audit Commission *Homeward Bound: A New Course for Community Health* (1992)

Audit Commission *Community Revolution: Personal Social Services and Community Care* (1992)

Audit Commission *Progress with Care in the Community* Bulletin (1993)

Audit Commission *Taking Stock: Progress with Community Care* (1994)

Baldwin, S., Parker, G. and Walter, R. (eds) *Social Security and Community Care* (Avebury, 1988)

Balloch, S. *A Survey of Social Services Charging Policies 1992/1994* (1994)

Bewley and Glendinning *Involving Disabled People in Community Care Planning* (Joseph Rowntree Foundation, 1994)

Bonner, D., Hooker, I., White, R. *Non-Means Tested Benefits: The Legislation* (Sweet & Maxwell, 1995)

Bull, J. and Poole, L. *Not Rich: Not Poor – a Study of Housing Options for Elderly People on Middle Incomes* (SHAC/Anchor Housing Trust, 1989)

Carers National Association *Community Care: Just a Fairytale* (1994)

Cassidy, P. 'Community Care and Benefits' (*Legal Action*, March 1993)

Centre for Policy on Ageing *Community Life: A Code of Practice for Community Care* (1990)

Centre for Policy on Ageing *Home Life: A Code of Practice for Residential Care* (1984)

Child Poverty Action Group *National Welfare Benefits Handbook (1995/6)*

CLAE Local Government Ombudsmen *Annual Report 1993/4* (1994)

Clapham, D., Monro, M. and Kay, H. 'Financing User Choice in Housing and Community Care' *Housing Summary* 6 (Joseph Rowntree Foundation, 1994)

Clapham, D. and Franklin, B. 'Housing Management, Community Care and CCT' *Housing Research Findings* 135 (Joseph Rowntree Foundation, 1995)

Clements, L. 'Duties of Social Services Departments' (*Legal Action*, September 1992)

Clements, L. 'Community Care: Definition of Need' (*Legal Action*, 1994)

Clements, L. 'Shifting Sands' (*Community Care*, 29 September 1994)

Clements, L. 'Community Care: Legal Structure' (*Legal Action*, July 1993)

College of Law *Law and the Elderly Client* (1992)

Commission for Local Administration in England *How to Complain to the Local Government Ombudsman* (CLAE, 1993)

Commission for Local Administration in England Annual Report, 1993/1994 (CLAE, 1994)

Common, R. and Flynn, N. *Contracting for Care* (Joseph Rowntree Foundation, 1992)

Counsel and Care *More Power to Our Elders* (1994)

Cox, B. 'Community Care: Top-Up Funding: R v Avon CC ex parte Hazell' (*Legal Action*, October 1993)

Dean, H. 'Social Care Provision: Problems of Redress' (*Legal Action*, December 1995, p. 8)

Department of the Environment and Department of Health, Housing and Community Care (DoE 10/92, DoH LAC(92)12)

Department of the Environment, Assistance with Minor Works to Dwellings (DoE 4/90)

Department of the Environment, House Adaptations for People with Disabilities (DoE 10/90)

Department of the Environment, Local Government and Housing Act 1989, House Renovation Grants (DoE 12/90)

Department of the Environment, Local Government and Housing Act 1989: Parts VII and VIII (DoE 5/91)

Department of Health *Community Care in the Next Decade and Beyond: Policy Guidance* (HMSO, 1990)

Department of Health Patient's Charter (1991)

Department of Health Hospital Discharge Workbook (1994)

Department of Health, Approvals and Directions for Arrangements from 1 April 1993 Made Under Schedule 8 to the National Health Service Act 1977 and Sections 21 and 29 of the National Assistance Act 1948 (DoH LAC(93)10)

Department of Health *Quality and Inspection* (1992)

Department of Health *Long-Term Care for Elderly People: Purchasing, Providing and Quality* (1992)

Department of Health *A Framework for Community Care Charters in England: Consultation Document* (1994)

Department of Health *Monitoring and Development: First Impressions, April–September 1993* (1994)

Department of Health *Implementing Caring for People. Impressions of the First Year* (1994)

Department of Health/Social Services Inspectorate *Houses are for Living In* (HMSO 1989)

Department of Social Security *The Way Ahead – Benefits for Disabled People* (Cmnd 917, 1990)

Dimond, B. 'How Far Can You Go?' (*Health Service Journal* 14 April 1994)

Disability Alliance *Disability Rights Handbook 1995/6.*

Eastman, M. *Old Age Abuse* (second edn) (Age Concern, 1994)

Eekelar, J. and Pearl, D. (eds) *An Ageing World: Dilemmas and Challenges for Law and Social Policy* (Oxford University Press, 1989)

Ellis, K. *Squaring the Circle: User and Carer Participation in Needs Assessment* (Joseph Rowntree Foundation, 1993)

Exchange on Ageing *Law and Ethics: A Study of Legislation Affecting Older People in Developed and Developing Countries*

Fordham, M. *Judicial Review Handbook* (Wiley Chancery Law Publishing, 1994)

Finch and Elam *Managing Money in Later Life* (DSS, 1995)

Fruin, T. *Finding and Funding Residential Care* (Kogan Page, 1995)

Glendinning *The Costs of Informal Care* (1992)

Gordon, R. *Community Care Assessments* (Longman, 1993)

Gordon, R. 'Challenging Community Care Assessments' (*Legal Action*, August 1993, p. 8)

Greengross, S. *The Law and Vulnerable Elderly People* (Age Concern, 1986)

Griffiths, R. (Chairman) *Community Care: Agenda for Action* (1988)

Griffiths, A., Grimes, R. and Roberts, G. *The Law and Elderly People* (1995)

Hardy, B., Wistow, G., Leedham, I. (Community Care Division Nuffield Institute for Health) *An Analysis of a Sample of English Community Care Plans 1993/94* (1994)

Henwood, M. *Community Care and Elderly People* (FPSC, 1990)

Henwood, M., Wistow, G. (Nuffield Institute for Health Care Studies) *Hospital Discharge and Community Care: Early Days* (1994)

Henwood, M., Wistow, G. (Nuffield Institute for Health Service Studies) *Monitoring Community Care: A Review* (1994)

Health Service Commissioner for England and Wales and for Scotland, *Annual Report for 1993–94 and 1994–95*

Health Service Commissioner *Report on failure to provide long-term NHS care for a brain-damaged patient* (HMSO, 1994)

Hills, J. *The Future of Welfare* (Joseph Rowntree Foundation, 1993)

Hinton, Cecil *Using Your Home as Capital* (Age Concern, 1994)

Housing Association Ombudsman Annual Report 1993–1994 (1995)

Kennedy, I. and Grubb, A. *Medical Law* (1994)

Johnson, E. (for Leeds CHC) *Getting the Message. Users' and Carers' Experience of Community Care in Leeds* (1995)

Jones, R. *Encyclopaedia of Social Services and Child Care Law* (Sweet & Maxwell, 1993)

Jones, R. *Registered Homes Act Manual* (second edn) (Sweet & Maxwell, 1993)

Joseph Rowntree Foundation *Housing Research Findings 123, Adaptations for Disability* (September 1994)

Joseph Rowntree Foundation *Housing Research Findings 135, Housing Management Community Care and CCT* (February 1995)

Joseph Rowntree Foundation *Housing Summary 6, Financing User Choice in Housing and Community Care* (October 1994)

Laing, W. *Financing Long-Term Care* (Age Concern, 1994)

Law Commission *Mental Incapacity* (1995)

Law Commission *Mentally Incapacitated Adults and Decision Making: A New Jurisdiction* (1983)

Law Society *Gifts of Property: Implications for Future Liability to Pay for Long Term Care. Guidelines for Solicitors* (1995)

Leat, D. *Re-development of Community Care by the Independent Sector* (Policy Studies Institute, 1993)

Leather, P. and Mackintosh, S. 'Adaptations for Disability', *Housing Research Findings* 123 (Joseph Rowntree Foundation, 1994)

Leeds Community Health Council *Getting the Message: Users' and Carers' Experience of Community Care in Leeds* (1995)

Letts, P. *Managing Other People's Money* (Age Concern, 1990)

Longley, D. *Public Law and Health Service Accountability* (Open University Press, 1993)

Mandelstam, M. with Schwehr, B. *Community Care Practice and the Law* (Jessica Kingsley, 1995)

Marks, L. *Seamless Care or Patchwork Quilt: Discharging Patients from Acute Hospital Care* (King's Fund Institute Research Report 1994)

McCafferty, *Living Independently, A Study of the Housing Needs of Elderly and Disabled People* (DoE, HMSO, 1994)

Mcdonald, A. and Taylor, M. *The Law and Elderly People* (Sweet & Maxwell, 1995)

McGlone, F. *Disability and Dependency in Old Age* (Family Policy Studies Centre, 1992)

McGlone, F. and Cronin, N. *A Crisis in Care?* (Family Policy Studies Centre, 1994)

Meredith, B. *The Community Care Handbook* (second edn) (Age Concern, 1995)

Mesher, J. and Wood, P. *Income Related Benefits: The Legislation* (Sweet & Maxwell, 1995/96)

McEwen, E. *Home Help and Care: Rights, Charging and Reality* (Age Concern, 1992)

Ministry of Housing and Local Government, Housing Standards and Costs: Accommodation Specially Designed for Old People (MHLG 82/69, Welsh Office Circular 84/69)

National Consumer Council *Charging Consumers for Social Services* (1995)

National House Building Council Sheltered Housing Code of Practice (NHBC 1990)

National Institute for Social Work *The Kaleidoscope of Care: A Review of Research on Welfare Provision for Elderly People* (HMSO, 1990)

Oldham *Moving in Old Age: New Directions in Housing Policies* (SPRU, HMSO, 1990)

Philpot, T. ed. *The Residential Opportunity?* (Reed Business Publishing, 1989)

Public Law Project *Challenging Community Care Decisions: A Briefing by the Public Law Project* (1994)

Royal College of Nursing *A Scandal Waiting to Happen? Elderly People and Nursing Care in Residential and Nursing Homes* (1992)

Schorr, A. *The Personal Social Services: An Outside View* (Joseph Rowntree Foundation, 1992)

Smith, C., Preston-Shoot, M. and Bradley, J. *Community Care Reforms: The Views of Users and Carers* (University of Manchester, Department of Social Policy and Social Work, 1995)

Schwehr, B. 'The Legal Relevance of Resources – or a Lack of Resources in Community Care' (*JSWFL*, 17, 1995)

Schwehr, B. 'Rational Rationing of Community Care Resources' (*Public Law*, 1995, p. 374)

Social Services Inspectorate *Caring for People: Progress on Implementation* (1993)

Social Services Inspectorate *No Longer Afraid. The Safeguard of Older People in Domestic Settings* (1993)

Social Services Inspectorate *Discretionary Charges for Adult Social Services* (1994)

Social Services Inspectorate *Inspection of Complaints Procedures in Local Authority Social Services Departments* (1993)

Social Services Inspectorate *Inspection of the Complaints Procedure: North Yorkshire* (1994)

Social Services Inspectorate *Inspection of the Complaints Procedure: North Yorkshire County Council, July 1993* (1993)

Social Services Inspectorate *Inspection of Assessment and Care Management Arrangements in Social Services Departments: October 1993–March 1994* (1994)

Social Services Inspectorate *Partners in Caring*, 4th Annual Report 1994/5

Social Services Inspectorate *Second Overview Report of the Complaints Procedures in Local Authority Social Services Departments* (1994)

Social Services Inspectorate *The Right to Complain: Practice Guidance on Complaints Procedures in Social Services Departments* (HMSO, 1991)

Social Services Inspectorate/NHS Executive *Community Care Packages for Older People* (1994)

Titmuss, R. *Commitment to Welfare* (Allen & Unwin, 1968)

Wagner, G. (Chair) *Residential Care: A Positive Choice* (1988)

Warner, N. *Community Care: Just a Fairy Tale?* (National Carers' Association, 1994)

White Paper *Caring for People: Community Care in the Next Decade and Beyond* (Cm 849, 1989)

Whiteford and Kennedy *Incomes and Living Standards of Older People* (DSS Research Report No. 34, 1995)

Wistow, G. *Inaugural Lecture University of Leeds November 1994*

LIST OF USEFUL ADDRESSES

Age Concern
Astral House
1268 London Road
London SW16 4ER
Tel 0181 679 8000

Alzheimer's Disease Society
Gordon House
10 Greencoat Place
London SW1P 1PH

Community Care Practitioners Group
c/o Professional Briefings
120 Wilton Road
London SW1V 1JZ

Department of Health Publications
PO Box 410
Wetherby LS23 7LN
Fax 01937 845381

Elderly Accommodation Council
46a Chiswick High Road
London W4 1SZ
Tel 0171 995 8320

The Family Policy Studies Centre
231 Baker Street
London NW1 6XE

HMSO Publications Centre
PO Box 276
London SW8 5DT
Tel 0171 873 0011
Fax 0171 873 8200

Housing Association Ombudsman
Palladium House
1–4 Argyll Street
London W1V 1AD
Tel 0171 437 1422

Housing Corporation
149 Tottenham Court Road
London W1P 0BN
Tel 0171 387 9466

Joseph Rowntree Foundation
The Homestead
40 Water End
York YO3 6LP
Tel 01904 629241

National Association of Community Health Councils
30 Drayton Park
London N5 1PB
Tel 0171 609 8415

National House Building Council
Chiltern Avenue
Amersham
Bucks HP6 5AP
Tel 01494 434477

The Public Law Project
Charles Clore House
17 Russell Square
London WC1B 5DR

Sheltered Housing Advisory and Conciliation Service (SHACS)
Walkden House
3–10 Melton Street
London NW1 2EJ
Tel 0171 383 2006

INDEX

References are to paragraph numbers.

Abbeyfield Homes   9.2.2, 12.4.4
Accommodation, *see* Means test for
    residential care; Part III
    accommodation; Residence,
    ordinary; Residential care
Adaptations to home   12.4.2
    complaint about   13.2.2
Addresses   App
Advice
    category of community care service,
        as   8.2
    legal, *see* Legal advice
    provision of, local authority
        duty   4.2.2
Advocacy services   4.2.5, 5.5.7, 5.6
Alcohol
    residential care for person with
        dependence on   10.3
Almshouses   12.4.4
Alzheimer's disease   1.2.2, 1.2.6
    disability living allowance for person
        with   19.1
    caring for sufferer   11.0
    examples   5.6, 7.7
    income support, and   2.4.3, 16.0
        example   16.4
Annuity
    capital value   15.3.5
    home income plan   15.4.1
    income from   15.4
        conversion to capital   15.4.3
Assessment of means   5.5.12, 14.4, *see
    also* Means test for non-residential
    services; Means test for residential
    care
Assessment of needs   5.1 *et seq*
    access rights   5.5.10, 5.5.11
    advice on   5.6
    carers, and   5.5.8, 11.1
    categories of people referred
        for   5.5.1
    challenge to   5.5.11, 5.6
    charge for, no power   14.3

charging for services separate
    from   14.4, 15.2
circumstances to be taken into
    account   5.1
collaboration between agencies,
    etc   5.5.9, 12.3.1
complaints procedure   5.5.1,
    5.5.13, 13.2, *see also* Complaints
comprehensive assessment   5.5.3,
    5.5.4
    information to be
        gathered   5.5.3
confidentiality   5.5.10
decision on   5.4.1, 5.5.11, 5.5.13
delay   5.5.5, 5.6
disabled people   5.5.3, 5.5.4–5.5.8
    duty of local authority   5.5.4, 6.3
    High Court decision on resource
        limitations   6.4
duty on local authority to
    make   2.5.1, 2.5.3, 4.1, 4.3
    'apparent need'   5.3
    limitations   5.3
    not absolute duty   5.3
    provision of services qualified
        by   5.3
eligibility   5.5.1
example   5.6
fund allocation, as gateway to   14.1
hospital discharge, prior to   7.2
housing needs, and   12.3.1, *see also*
    Housing
information on, duty   5.3, 5.5.1,
    5.5.2
    availability   5.5.3
    list of information   5.5.2
judicial review   13.2.1
levels of assessment   5.5.3
'needs-led' objective   5.1, 5.2
    inconsistencies   5.2, 6.0
place for   5.5.6
priority for   5.5.5, 5.6
procedure   5.5

Assessment of needs—*cont*
  procedure—*cont*
    complaint on   13.2.2
    explaining to service user   5.5.6
    flexibility needed   5.5.3
    reasons   5.5.11
    reassessment   5.5.13, 6.4
    refusal to make   13.2.1, 14.4
    relationship with service
      provision   5.4, 6.0
    representation at   5.5.7
    residential care, prior to   9.2.3,
      15.3.7
    review   5.5.13
    right to   5.3, 5.6
    simple assessment   5.5.3
    specialist assessment   5.5.3
    styles   5.5.6
    time for assessment   5.5.5, 5.5.6
    unmet needs   5.4.1, 6.0
    urgency   5.5.5
    written record   4.3, 5.5, 5.5.11
      usefulness   5.5.11
Assets   15.3.2–15.3.5
  see also Home
  disposal of   18.1
    recovery of, local authority
      powers   18.3
    setting aside   18.4
    see also Gift of property; Capital:
      notional; Planning for care
Attendance allowance   12.4.4, 17.3,
  19.1
  entitlement   19.1, 19.2.2
  income support premium
    with   19.1.1
  means testing   19.2.3
  rate   19.1
  residential care, for person
    in   19.2.2, 19.2.3

Bank account
  money in   15.3.2
Bankruptcy
  unpaid home fees, local authority
    power   18.4
Barrister
  review of complaint response, not to
    be at   13.2.3
Benefits, *see* State benefits

Blind person, *see* Disabled people
Bodily functions   10.3, 12.4.4
Breach of statutory duty   13.7, 13.7.1
Buildings   15.3.2

Capital
  deprivation of self of, *see* 'notional'
    below
  disregarded   15.3.5, 15.3.7, 18.2.8
  home-sharing, for, nature of   12.4.5
  non-residential services, and
    account of, approaches to   17.4
    limits   17.4, 19.1
    value of home, and   17.4
  notional   15.3.6, 18.1, 18.2
    calculation of   18.2.8
    circumstances of gift   18.2.6
    deliberate giving away   18.2.6
    deprivation, meaning   18.2.5
    disregard of   18.2.8
    effect of application of
      rules   18.3
    examples   18.2.8
    income support and   18.2–18.2.8
    inconsistency of approach
      to   18.2.7
    local authority rules   18.2.3–
      18.2.8
    purpose of gift   18.2.6
    reasonableness of gift   18.2.6
    time-limits for rule   18.2.7
  planning, and care services, *see*
    Planning for care
  residential care, and   18.2.3–18.2.8
    assessment   15.3.2–15.3.4
    knowledge of limit   18.2.6
    limit for   15.2, 15.3.1, 19.1
    see also Means test for residential
      care
Care by family
  see also Carer
  consideration for gift, as   18.4.1
Care home, *see* Residential care; Respite
  care
Care manager   6.5
  agent for health service commissioner,
    as   8.3
  example of care management   App
  purchasing for both health and social
    care services by   8.3

Care plan (individual)   6.5
   challenge to   7.8
   example   App
   review   6.5
Carer   2.3, 11.1–11.6
   assessment
      ability to provide care, of (piggyback
         right)   11.2
      own needs, of   5.5.8, 11.1
   assessment of recipient of care, role
      in   5.5.8, 11.1
   attitudes to care changing   11.6
   care plan for combined needs   11.2
   charges for services   11.4
      who has benefit   11.4.1
   complaints on behalf of user   11.5
   entitlement to involvement in
      community care, charter   11.1
   income support premium
      for   19.1.1
   local authority duties to   11.2
   meaning in new Act   11.2
   new Act for   11.2
   respite care, *see* Respite care
   review of service provision,
      seeking   11.3
   services of assistance to   11.2
   'substantial' care on 'regular
      basis'   11.2
Cash
   capital asset, as   15.3.2
   payments   5.2, 8.6
Challenge, *see* Complaints
Charge
   beneficial interest in land, on, power
      to create   6.6, 13.5.7, 15.11.1
Charges
   see also Payment for services
   carer, and   11.4
Charities   2.3.3
   assistance for preserved rights
      residents from   16.4
   income payments from, disregard
      of   15.4.1
Chiropody   2.3.2, 4.4, 15.5
Choice   6.6, 8.6
Christmas bonus   15.4.1
Cleaning, *see* Home help services
Client, *see* Legal advice
Cohabitees
   not liable relatives   15.6.3
   resources   15.6, 17.5

Commission of Local Authority
   Administration   13.4
Community care
   assessment, *see* Assessment of needs
   development of   2.2
   funding, *see* Finance
   meaning   2.0
   plan, *see* Community care plan
Community care plan   3.1, 3.2
   choice for consumer, and   6.6
   consultation by local
      authorities   3.1, 12.3.1
   duty to publish   2.5.2
   need for familiarity with local
      plan   3.2
   priorities   5.4
Community care services   4.1, 4.2
   assessment of needs necessary   5.3,
      see also Assessment of needs
   categories   8.2, *see also* Advice; Day
      care; Domiciliary services;
      Residential care
   checklist   4.4
   commissioning of, by local authority,
      see Contracting
   decision to provide, *see* Decision on
      service provision
   disabled person for, *see* Disabled
      person
   duty to decide on provision   4.1
   eligibility criteria   2.5.2, 4.3
      assessment, and   5.2
   identifying need of old for   4.2.2
   payment for   4.3, 14.1 *et seq*, 17.1 *et
      seq*, *see also* Payment for services
   provision   4.2, 4.3, 5.3
      discretion as to   5.4
      see also Decision on service provision
   withdrawal etc not possible where
      need   4.2.5, 4.3, 6.4, 6.7
Community health services   2.3.2,
   2.5.2, 4.2.3, 4.4
   list   2.3.2
   purchase by health authority for
      residential care   9.5
Compensation   13.2.4, 13.4.3
Complaints   4.3, 13.1 *et seq*
   carer may make on behalf of
      user   11.5
   choice of remedy   13.6.2, 13.8
   compensation   13.2.4, 13.4.3

Complaints—*cont*
  complaints procedure (local
      authority)   13.2
    formal stage   13.2.3
    group, use by   13.2.1
    independence of   13.2.4
    'informal' stage   13.2.3
    investigator, appointment
        of   13.2.3
    legislation   13.2
    Practice Guidance   13.2
    procedure, stages of   13.2.3
    'qualifying individual', complaint
        by   13.2.1
    recommendations of review
        panel   13.2.3
    'registration' of   13.2.3
    review stage   13.2.3
    scope   13.2.1, 13.2.2
    social services file,
        accessing   13.2.3
    time factor   13.2.3, 13.2.4
  formal remedies, list   13.1
  informal resolution methods   13.1
  judicial review, *see* Judicial review
  monitoring officers function   13.3
    report   13.3.1
  non-residential services, and   17.6,
    17.8
  ombudsman, to   13.4
    delay factor   13.4.3
    'How to complain' guide   13.4.2
    jurisdiction   13.4.1
    procedure   13.4.2
    time-limit   13.4.1
    uses of   13.4.3
  quality, relating to   13.1
  rationing decisions, relating
      to   13.1
  resources limitations as
      defence   6.4, 13.1
  Secretary of State, powers   13.5
    inquiry and order
        following   13.5.1
    judicial review, and   13.6.2
    limitations   13.5.2
  tort action   13.7
Confidentiality
  assessment information, of   5.5.10
Contracting   8.1–8.6

block contracts   8.2
call off contracts   8.2
categories of services   8.2
health authority, purchasing by   8.3
joint commissioning   8.3
legal advice, authority and provider
    must seek   8.4
local authority is lead authority   8.3
nature of the contracts   8.5
non-discriminatory, must be   8.4.1
quality of services   8.5
remedies, whether public or private
    law   8.5, 8.5.3
residential care contracts, *see*
    Residential care
selection methods   8.1
spot contracts   8.2, 8.5.1
tendering   8.1
terms and conditions of
    contracts   8.4
  carer and user involvement, need
      for   8.4, 8.4.2
  reasonableness of, cases   8.5.1,
      8.5.2
  service specifications   8.4.2, 8.5
  specific conditions   8.4.1
types of contract   8.2
user's rights   8.6
Contribution for residential care, *see*
    Means test for residential care
Costs, *see* Payment for services
Counselling   8.2
Court of Protection
  capital held by   15.3.2

Damages   13.7
Day and residential care
  category of community care service,
      as   8.2
  complaints on provision   13.2.2, *see*
      also Complaints
Day centres   4.3, 11.2
Deaf or dumb person, *see* Disabled
    person
Debt
  contribution from resident
      enforceable as   15.11, 18.4
  size of, for commencement of
      bankruptcy proceedings
      18.4.1

Decision on service provision   6.1–6.7
  care plan, setting up of following
      decision   6.5
  challenging   13.1 *et seq, see also*
      Complaints
  disabled people, for   6.3, 6.4
      absolute duty, when arises   6.4
      resource limits, High Court
          decision   6.4
  discretion   6.1
  factors to take into account   6.1
  Policy Guidance   6.2
  preference, order of   6.2
  reasons for   5.5.11
      failure to give   13.6.3
  resources, and
      disabled person   6.3, 6.4
      limitations arising from   6.2
      targeting of   6.2
Delay
  assessment of needs, as to   5.5.5, 5.6
  complaint to ombudsman,
      in   13.4.3
  complaints procedure of local
      authority, in   13.2.3, 13.2.4
  judicial review
      in seeking, effect   13.6.1
      process, in   13.6.4
Demographic statistics   1.2
  sources   1.2.6
Dental services   2.3.2, 4.4
  residential care, in   10.2
Directions   1.5.3, 4.1, 4.2
Disability living allowance   15.4.1,
      17.3, 19.1
  care component   19.1, 19.2.2
      means testing   19.2.3
  entitlement   19.1
      residential care, and   19.2
  income support premium
      with   19.1.1
  mobility component   19.1, 19.2.1
      proposed amendment   19.2.1
  rate   19.1
  residential care, for person
      in   19.2.1, 19.2.2, 19.2.3
Disabled Facilities Grant   12.3
Disabled people
  adaptations to home   12.4.2
  advocacy services   4.2.5, 5.5.7
  assessment of needs   4.2.5, 4.3, 5.5.4

  carer may request   11.1
  'comprehensive'
      assessment   5.5.3, 5.5.4
  duty to assess   5.5.4, 6.3
  prior representations as to
      needs   5.5
  benefits for, *see* Attendance allowance;
      Disability living allowance
  definition of 'disability'   5.5.4
  income support premiums   19.1.1
  mentally ill, *see* Mentally ill/disordered
  occupational and speech therapy for,
      see Therapists
  register of   4.3
  services for   2.3.1, 4.2.1, 4.3, 6.3, 6.4
      aids, etc, specified   4.2.5
      welfare services   4.2.5
  statistics   1.2.2, 2.1
  withdrawal of existing
      services   4.2.5, 4.3, 6.4, 6.7
Discharge from hospital   2.3.2, 5.5.9,
      7.1–7.9
  assessment of needs prior to   7.2
      critical interface between health and
          social care   7.1
  case study   7.7, App
  consultation prior to   7.3
  continuing care
      financing of   7.4
      plan, review of   7.6
      tests for   7.4
  eligibility criteria for continuing in-
      patient care, application
      of   7.6, 7.8
  legal advice, need for   7.8
  nursing home, into   7.4, 7.5
      pre-April 1993   14.2
  options, consideration of   7.4
  procedures   7.2–7.5, 7.9
  residential or nursing home, to, right
      to refuse   7.5
  review of decision to discharge   7.6,
      7.8
  flowchart   7.9
Discrimination
  contract for care service, and   8.4.1
District health authorities
  see also Health authorities (unified)
  provision of services by, and local
      authority provision   6.1

District health authorities—*cont*
  purchase of beds from private sector,
      power   2.3.2
  responsibilities   2.3.2, 4.2.3, 4.2.4
      after-care services   4.2.4, 7.4
Domiciliary services
  see also Home help services
  budget cuts, and   6.7, 14.7
  category of community care service,
      as   8.2
  choice as to   6.6, 8.6
  complaints on provision   13.2.2, *see
      also* Complaints
  home care assistance   4.2.2, 4.3, 6.5
  needs based, not payment
      based   17.8
  payment for   14.7, 17.1 *et seq*
      disparities   14.7
      flexible approach
          recommended   14.7
      post-April 1993   14.7
      pre-April 1993   14.3
      see also Means test for non-residential
          services; Payment for services
Drugs
  residential care for person with
      dependence on   10.3

Educational facilities   4.2.5, 4.4
Elderly persons home, *see* Residential
  care
Eligibility
  assessment, for   5.5.1
  criteria for provision of
      services   2.5.2, 4.3
  use in assessment   5.2
Enforcement procedures
  against local authority, *see* Complaints
  fees for residential care, and   18.3,
      see also Payment for services
Equipment
  adaptations to home   12.4.2
  complaint on provision   13.2.2
Equitable proprietary interest   12.4.5
Estoppel, proprietary   12.4.5
Eviction
  person with preserved rights, of, relief
      for   16.2, 16.3, 16.4
Expenses
  expenses allowance, personal
      (residential care)   9.6, 15.5

  amount of   15.5, 15.10

Family
  living with   12.4.5
  relative occupying home, effect on
      valuation   15.3.7, 18.2.8
  age/health of relative, relevance
      of   15.3.7
Fees, *see* Payment for services
Finance (public)   2.1 *et seq*, 14.1, 18.0
  see also Payment for services
  insufficient resources as defence to
      failure to provide service   4.2.5,
          5.4
      High Court decision
          examined   6.4
  post-1993   2.5
      allocation   2.5.3
      'mixed economy'   2.5.1
  pre-1993   2.4
      joint financing   2.4.1, 16.3
      see also Preserved rights
Financial assessment
  see also Means test for non-residential
      care; Means test for residential
      services
  spouse as liable relative, and   15.6.3
Financial difficulties
  see also Planning for care
  person in residential care,
      with   16.2–16.4
Financial services packages
  care fees, for   18.1

General practitioner
  access to services through   4.3
  assessments, involvement in   5.5.9
      discharge from hospital, on   7.2
  duties   2.3.2
Gift of property
  see also Capital: notional; Planning for
      care
  circumstances of   18.2.6
  consideration for, whether care
      is   18.4.1
  Law Society guidelines   18.1, 18.1.1,
      18.4.1
  solicitor's duty   18.1.1
  recovery by local authority from third
      party   18.3

Gift of property—*cont*
  setting aside, powers   18.4
  transaction at undervalue   18.4.2
Granny flat   12.4.5
Green form advice   5.6, 13.2.3
Griffiths, Sir Roy   2.5, 2.5.1, 12.3
Guidance (policy)   1.5.3

Health, *see* Community health services;
    General practitioner; Ill-health;
    National Health Service
Health authorities (unified)   2.3.2
  consent to nursing home
      placement   9.2.2
  creation of   7.6
  preserved rights, people on,
      and   16.3
  purchase of services by   8.3, 9.5
Health needs
  collaboration in assessment
      where   5.5.9
Health visitor   2.3.2, 4.4
Holidays   4.2.5
Home
  see also Housing
  care 'at home' keystone   12.1
  client wishing to remain in   6.6,
      6.7, 12.4.1, 12.4.2, 17.4
  discharge from hospital to   7.4, 7.5
  gift of, *see* Planning for care
  letting while in care   15.3.7
  people without, or in unreasonable, *see*
      Homeless people
  preserving   19.3, 19.4, *see also*
      Planning for care
  repairs, help with   12.4.2
  sharing with family, checklist for
      adviser   12.4.5
  value of, and non-residential
      services   17.4
  value of, and residential
      care   15.3.4, 15.3.7
    assessment of needs and
        arrangements following, effect
        on price   15.3.7
    Benefit Agency and local authority
        methods differ   15.3.4,
        15.3.7
    case studies   15.3.7
    co-ownership   15.3.4, 15.3.7

  discretion of local authority
      15.3.7
  disregard of value,
      circumstances   15.3.4,
      15.3.7
  effect of taking value into
      account   15.3.7
  'going private' option   15.3.7
  legal charge on   6.6, 13.5.7,
      15.11.1
  occupation by relative/third
      party   15.3.7, 18.2.8
  policy on   15.3.7
  sale being attempted,
      effect   15.3.7
  sale cannot be enforced   15.3.7
  temporary or permanent residential
      care, and   9.6, 15.3.7
  waiver of charges pending
      sale   15.3.7, 15.11
Home care assistance   4.2.2, 4.3
  see also Domiciliary services
  performance standards   6.5
Home help services   4.2.3, 4.3
  carer, assisting   11.2
  types of   8.2
Home improvement grants   12.4.1
Home income plan annuity   15.4.1
Homeless people
  cognitive ability test for
      rehousing   12.3.2
  definition includes unreasonable
      accommodation   12.3.2
  elderly as   12.3.2
  housing authority duty to
      rehouse   12.3.2
  'priority need'   12.3.2
  responsibility pre-1970s   9.1.1
Homeswap   12.4.3
Hospice
  benefit availability for person
      in   19.2.1
Hospital
  see also National Health Service
  benefits for in-patients   2.4.3, 2.4.4,
      19.2.1
  care beds   2.3.2, 6.2, 7.1
  cuts in, statistics   7.1
  discharge and social care implications,
      see Discharge from hospital
  funding   2.4, 2.5.2

Hospital—*cont*
in-patient care   2.3.2, 2.5.2
Housing   4.4, 12.1 *et seq*
adaptations   12.4.2
community care legislation has no
    clear duties   12.3.1
costs, income support for   19.1
council, move from owner-occupied
    to   12.4.3
government policies for
    elderly   12.3
'Housing and Community
    Care'   12.3.1
housing authority duty to homeless, *see*
    Homeless people
inter-agency collaboration   12.3.1
legal advice   12.4.4, 12.4.5, 12.5
marginalisation of   12.3.1
moving
    in with family   12.4.5
    smaller accommodation,
        to   12.4.3
    specialist housing, to   12.4.4
options   12.1, 12.4
profile of housing circumstances of
    elderly   12.2
renting   12.4.3, 12.4.4
repair grants   12.4.1
sheltered housing, *see* Sheltered
    housing
specialist, renting or buying   12.4.4
'staying put'   12.4.1, 12.4.2
supportive   12.4.4
Housing association   2.3.3, 12.4.4
Housing Association
    Ombudsman   12.4.4
Housing authority
adaptations for disabled
    occupant   12.4.2
allocation discretion   12.4.3
consultation by social services
    department   12.3.1
duties relevant to community
    care   12.3.1
provision of services by, and local
    authority provision   6.1
Housing benefit   12.4.4
Housing needs
collaboration in assessment
    where   5.5.9, *see also* Housing

Illegality   13.6.3, *see also* Judicial
    review
Ill-health
chronically ill   2.5.2, 4.2.5
needs arising from   2.1
prevention of   4.2.3
provision of care/after-care for ill
    people   4.2.3
residential care for people
    with   9.2, *see also* Residential
    care
statistics   1.2.2
Income
see also Means test for non-residential
    services; Means test for residential
    care
assessment   15.4
disregards   15.4.1
notional   15.4.3
Income support
applicable amount   19.1
capital disregards, and payment
    of   15.3.7, 18.2.8
capital limits   15.3.1, 18.2
chart   19.1
disregard as income,
    circumstances   15.4.1
housing costs, relevant   19.1
income of which claimant has
    deprived self   18.2.1
means tested   19.1
mortgage interest, and   12.4.4
notional capital rule   18.2.1,
    18.2.2–18.2.8, 18.3, *see also*
    Capital: notional
personal allowances   15.6.2
premiums   19.1, 19.1.1
    types of   19.1.1
preserved rights   14.6, 15.8, 16.1 *et
    seq, see also* Preserved rights
residential allowance   15.8
residential care, and   15.7, 15.8,
    19.1 *et seq*
couples, and   15.6
example   19.3
extra statutory concession   19.2.2
for person in   2.4.3, 14.1, 14.2,
    14.5, 14.6, 19.1, 19.2.2, 19.2.3
Part III accommodation, regime
    for   15.9
residential care means test separate
    from   15.1

Incontinence services 9.5.1, 9.6, 15.5
Independent Living Fund 8.6
Independent sector 2.3.3
  see also Charities; Nursing home;
      Residential care
  use increased 2.5.1, *see also*
      Contracting
Information
  access to, rights 4.3, 5.5.10
  assessment of needs, relating to
      confidentiality of information
          gathered 5.5.10
  duty to publicise 5.3, 5.5.1, 5.5.2
  importance of, for choice 6.6
  means test, for 15.2
Inquiry
  Secretary of State, by 13.5
Inspection, *see* Residential care
Institutions
  closure, policy of 2.2
Invalid care allowance 11.0, 11.2

Joint finance schemes 8.3
Judicial review 13.6
  alternative remedies, exhaustion of
      prior to 13.6.1, 13.6.2
  choice of, as remedy 13.6.2
  delay
    between leave and
        hearing 13.6.4
    in seeking 13.6.1
    discretionary 13.6.4
  eligibility criteria for continuing
      hospital care, of 7.8
  enforcement of order with directions
      by 13.5.1
  grounds 13.6.3
  inflexible housing policies,
      of 12.4.3
  leave, requirement and conditions
      for 13.6.1
  negotiating tool, use as 13.6
  refusal to make assessment,
      where 13.2.1
  role of court 13.6

'Laming' letter 5.4.1, 5.5.5
Land 15.3.2
  charge over, local authority
      power 15.11.1

valuation of co-owned 15.3.4
Laundry services 4.2.3, 11.2
Lease
  see also Rent; Tenant
  specialist housing, practical points
      on 12.4.4
Legal advice
  accessing services, on 4.3
  asset preservation, and 18.1, 19.4,
      see also Planning for care
  benefit claims, and 19.0, 19.4
  capital valuation, and 15.3.3,
      15.3.4, 15.3.7
  client, definition for book 1.2
  contracts for care, on 8.4
  financial matters, reference material
      for 14.8
  gifts, and, *see* Gift of property
  home, and 15.3.4, 15.3.7, 18.1
    case studies 15.3.7, 15.11.1
    gift of, and 18.1.1
    sale of home, and 15.11.1
  home-sharing with family, checklist
      on 12.4.5
  housing generally, on 12.5
  need for generally 18.1, 18.1.1
  non-residential care services,
      and 17.8
  range required for elderly 1.1, 1.4,
      3.2
  residential care arrangement,
      on 9.4, 9.6
    means test, at time of 15.1
    preserved rights, person
        with 16.4, *see also* Preserved
        rights
  role to client 3.2, 4.3, 6.7, 7.8
  sheltered housing, as to move
      to 12.4.4
  solicitor's duty as to gifts of
      property 18.1.1
  wishes of client 1.3
Legal aid
  Green form 5.6, 13.2.3
  review of complaint decision,
      for 13.2.3
Legislation 1.5
  availability of 1.5, 4.1
Letting
  home, while in care 15.3.7

Licensee   12.4.4, 12.4.5
Life policy   15.3.5
Local authority
  assessment by, *see* Assessment of needs
  breach of statutory duty   13.7,
      13.7.1
  charge over land, power   15.11.1
  community care plan, *see* Community
      care plan
  community care services, *see*
      Community care services
  complaints procedure, *see* Complaints
  contracting with independent sector,
      see Contracting
  co-operation with health
      authorities   4.2.3
    overlap, local authority has lead
        role   6.1, 8.3
  disabled people, services for   4.2.5,
      see also Disabled people
  duty of care   13.7.2
  funding   2.4, 2.5, *see also* Finance
      (public)
  illegal or irrational act, or procedural
      impropriety   13.6.3, *see also*
      Judicial review
  monitoring officer   13.3
  negligence   13.7, 13.7.2
  non-residential services, *see* Advice;
      Day care; Domiciliary services
  Part III accommodation, *see* Part III
      accommodation
  payment to, *see* Payment for services
  preserved rights, people on,
      and   16.2, *see also* Preserved
      rights
  purchasing role, *see* Contracting
  recovery of gift from third
      party   18.3
  remedies against   6.7, 13.1, *see also*
      Complaints
  residential accommodation, provision
      of   9.2
    charge for   15.7, *see also* Means
        test for residential care
    fee recovery   15.11, 18.3, 18.4
    homes managed by authority, *see*
        Part III accommodation
    see also Nursing home; Residential
        care
  review panel   13.2.3, *see also*
      Complaints

service provision by
  background   2.3.1, 2.5.1
  discretion   5.4, 6.1
  outline of duties   4.2
  'resources insufficient'
      defence   4.2.5, 5.4, 6.4
  time for provision   4.2.5
  see also Community care services;
      Decision on service provision;
      and specific services
  social services departments, *see* Social
      services
  tort action against   13.7
  vicarious liability   13.7.2
Local government ombudsman   13.4,
    see also Complaints
Local housing authority, *see* Housing
    authority
London
  residential care provision   2.5.1
  Part III accommodation   9.1.1

Mckenzie friend   13.2.3
Maintenance
  spouse, of other spouse,
      duty   15.6.3
Maladministration   13.3.1, 13.4.1, *see
    also* Complaints
Married couple   15.6, 17.5
Meals
  provision of   4.2.2, 4.2.3, 4.2.5
Means test for benefits   17.3, 19.1,
    19.2, 19.2.3
Means test for non-residential
    services   14.3, 14.7, 17.2
  see also Payment for services
  adaptation for home, for   12.4.2
  benefits, and
    charging practice for people
        on   17.3
    people on, not exempt from
        charges   17.3
    schemes may be based on   17.2
  capital, account of   17.4
  couples, assessment of   17.5
  example of charging scheme   17.2
  home, value of, and   17.4
  review or appeal of imposition of
      charge   17.6
  schemes for, variation in   17.2

Means test for residential care   5.5.12,
   9.3.1, 14.4, 14.5, 15.1 *et seq*
see also Payment for services
Benefits Agency link
   recommended   15.1
capital, assessment of   15.3
   co-owned assets   15.3.4
   disclosure and valuation   15.3.2
   disregarded capital   15.3.5,
     15.3.7
   home, valuation of   15.3.4,
     15.3.7, *see also* Home
   land   15.3.2, 15.3.4
   market value test   15.3.2, 15.3.4,
     15.3.7
   nil valuation of property   15.3.4
   notional   15.3.6, 18.1
   trust assets   15.3.3
capital limit   15.2, 15.3.1
complaints procedure, and   15.1
complexity of regulations   15.1
contribution from resident   15.7
   case studies   15.10
   charge over interest in land,
     power   15.11.1
   civil debt, as   15.11
   enforcement of   15.11
   statement of   15.2
couples, married or
     unmarried   15.6
   both going into care   15.6.2
   liability to maintain the
     other   15.6.3
   one going into care   15.6.1
guidance   15.1
income assessment   15.2, 15.4
   'available' income   15.4.3, 15.7
   benefits, and   15.4, 15.7
   capital-producing income
     15.3.7, 15.4.2
   common forms of income for
     elderly   15.4
   conversion into capital,
     effect   15.4.3
   disregarded income   15.4.1
   income of which resident has
     deprived self   15.4.3, 18.2.1
   notional income   15.4.3
   partial disregards   15.4.1
   rental income   15.4.2
   tariff income   15.4

topping-up payments by third party,
   effect of   15.4.3
   trust income   15.4.3
income support assessment separate
   from   15.1
legal advice, need for at time
   of   15.1
legal basis   15.1
operation of   15.2
personal expenses allowance   15.5,
   15.10
   amount of   15.5
repayment of cost required if
   possible   15.2
temporary placement in residential
   care   15.3.7, 19.2.3
withholding of information,
   effect   15.2
Medical services
   provision, duty   2.3.2
Mental nursing home   9.2, 10.3
   inspection   10.10.2
Mentally ill/disordered
   background to care of   2.3.1, 2.3.2
   care and after-care of   4.2.1, 4.2.3,
     4.2.4
   definition of 'mental
     disorder'   4.2.1
   residential and nursing care for
     person who is   10.3
   responsibility for provision
     for   2.5.2, 4.2
Minor works assistance   12.4.2
Monitoring officer   13.3, *see also*
   Complaints
Mothers
   expectant and nursing   4.2.3

National Health Service   2.3.2
   acute services   2.3.2
   care beds   2.3.2, 9.2, *see also*
     Discharge from hospital;
     Residential care
   community health services, *see*
     Community health services
   duty on Secretary of State to
     provide   2.3.2
   'free', erosion of   6.1
   funding   2.4, 2.5
   hospitals, decline in use by
     elderly   2.2, 7.1 *et seq*

National Health Service—*cont*
  joint work with local
      authorities   2.5.2
  residential care home, medical etc
      provision in   9.5
  services for which responsible   2.5.2
  transfer of services to   2.3.1
National insurance
      contributions   18.0
Natural justice   13.6.3, *see also* Judicial
  review
Need, *see* Assessment of needs
Negligence   13.7, 13.7.2
Night sitter   11.2
Non-residential services, *see* Domiciliary
  services
Nursing care
  meaning   10.3
Nursing home   1.2.5, 2.5.2
  see also Residential care
  benefits, and   19.2.2
  community health provision in   9.5
  contract for beds   9.2
  discharge from hospital to   7.4, 14.2
    right to refuse   7.5
    see also Discharge from hospital
  distinguished from residential care
      home   9.1.4, 9.1.5, 10.3
  emergency placement   9.2.2
  eviction or closure threat   16.3, 16.4
  financing   2.5.2, *see also* Payment for
      services; Means test for residential
      care
  health authority consent for placement
      by local authority   9.2.2
  inspection   10.10.2
  local authority responsibility   2.5.2
  medical and health services, purchase
      for   9.5
  nursing services, purchase of   2.5.2
  personal care, providing   10.8
  preserved rights to enhanced income
      support, *see* Preserved rights
  private, contracted beds   2.3.2
  registration   10.1, 10.3, 10.5
    cancellation   10.9
    conditional   10.6
    dual, as residential care home as
        well   10.8
    'fitness'   10.6

    personal registration   10.5
    qualifications for   10.5
    refusal   10.6
    size, and   10.7
  responsibility for provision   2.5.2
  sick person, placement for   2.5.1,
      2.5.2, 9.2
  standards   10.2
Nursing services (community)   2.3.2,
  4.4
  purchase of   2.5.2, 8.3

Occupational pension   15.3.5, 15.4
  disregard of half where paid to spouse
      at home   15.6.1
Occupational therapist
  see also Therapists
  assessment for home
      adaptation   12.4.2
  no charging power for   14.3
Ombudsman
  housing association   12.4.4
  local government   13.4, *see also*
      Complaints
Optical services   2.3.2, 4.4
Order
  payments from liable relative,
      for   15.6.3, 15.11
Ordinary residence, *see* Residence,
  ordinary

Para-medical services   2.3.2, 4.4, *see
  also* Therapists
Part III accommodation   9.1.1,
  10.10.3, 14.2, 15.9
  benefits, and   19.2.2, 19.2.3
  charge for   15.9
  financial disincentives of   15.8, 15.9
  gift of asset, local authority recovery
      powers   18.3
  time-limit   18.3
  income support in   15.9, 16.0
Partner
  occupying home   15.3.7, 18.2.8
  unmarried   15.6
Payment for services   4.3, 14.1 *et seq,*
  15.1 *et seq,* 17.1 *et seq*
  complaints as to, *see* Complaints
  domiciliary services   17.1 *et seq*
    collecting charges   17.7

Payment for services—*cont*
  domiciliary services—*cont*
    decline of services for inability to
      pay   17.6
    fees, increase post-1993   17.0
    means-testing, *see* Means test for
      non-residential services
    post-April 1993   14.7, 17.1 *et seq*
    power to charge   14.3, 17.0,
      17.1
    pre-April 1993   14.3
    'reasonable' charges   17.1, 17.2,
      17.6
    review of charge   17.6
  legal adviser, and   14.8, 17.8
  non-residential services, *see*
    'domiciliary services' *above*
  policies post-April 1993,
    general   14.4
  preserving assets from State, *see*
    Planning for care
  provision and ability to pay   14.4,
    17.6
  residential care   15.1 *et seq*
    benefits, use to fund   19.2.2, 19.3
    contribution calculation   15.7
    fee payment methods   9.3.1,
      9.3.2, 15.7
    means-testing, *see* Means test for
      residential care
    post-April 1993   14.5, 14.6
    pre-April 1993   14.2
    preserved rights to enhanced
      benefit   14.6, 15.8, 16.1 *et*
      seq, see also Preserved rights
Pension
  income, as   15.4
  occupational, disregard of   15.3.5,
    15.6.1
Pensionable age
  clients as people of   1.2
Personal care
  benefits for person needing   17.3,
    19.1, 19.2
  meaning   10.3
  nursing home providing   10.8
Personal expenses allowance   9.6,
  15.5
  case studies   15.10
Personal injury trust   15.3.5
Pharmaceutical services   2.3.2

Physiotherapy   9.5, *see also* Therapists
Placement, *see* Residential care
Planning for care   18.1 *et seq*
  'cradle to grave' care, and   18.0
  'deprivation' of self of
    capital   18.2.5
  disposal of assets to avoid sale to
    finance care
    ethics   18.1
    recovery   18.3, 18.4
    see also Capital: notional
  Law Society guidelines   18.1,
    18.1.1, 18.4.1
  local authority power to recover
    property   18.3
  notional capital, local authority
    approach to   18.2, 18.2.3,
    18.2.4–18.2.8
    discretion on application
      of   18.2.3
    disregards, client taking advantage
      of   18.2.8
    see also Capital: notional
  notional capital rule, and income
    support   18.2, 18.2.1, 18.2.2
    Adjudication Officers' Guide
      on   18.2.4–18.2.8
    reduction on expenses
      etc   18.2.2
  setting aside disposition   18.4
Policies
  see also Finance (public)
  background   2.2
Possessions, personal   15.3.5, 18.2.8
Pregnant women   4.2.3
Preserved rights   14.6, 15.8, 16.1 *et seq*
  attendance allowance and disability
    allowance for person
    with   19.2.2
  income support claim,
    and   19.2.3
  duration   16.4
  effect in practice   16.0, 16.1
  entitlement and categories
    having   16.0
  eviction, or threatened eviction, of
    people with
    local authority relief for   16.2
    health authority powers   16.3
    other options   16.4
    representations to Secretary of State
      for   16.4

Preserved rights—*cont*
    income support payment and home
        fees, gap between   16.1
    local authority general prohibition
        from assisting people
        with   16.2
    loss of   2.4.3, 16.3, 16.4
        advantage of   16.3, 16.4
    options for people on, outside local
        and health authorities   16.4
    top-up payments, reliance on   16.1
Private sector   2.3.3
    checklist of services   4.4
    delegation of services to   4.2.2
    purchase of services from, *see*
        Contracting
Property, *see* Assets; Home; Gift of
    property
Public law contract, concept of   8.5.3
Publications   1.2.6, 1.5.3
Purchase of services, *see* Contracting

Quality
    assurance   9.1.5, 10.1 *et seq, see also*
        Residential care: registration
    complaints about   13.1 *et seq, see
        also* Complaints

Rationing, complaints on   13.1,
    13.6.4, *see also* Complaints
Receiver   15.3.2
Recovery
    local authority, by, of asset disposed
        of   18.3
Recreational facilities   4.2.3, 4.2.5,
    11.2
Registered Homes Tribunal   10.9
Registration, *see* Nursing home;
    Residential care
Relative,
    see also Family; Spouse
    care provided by, scale of   18.0
    liable   9.2.5, 15.6.3
Renovation grants   12.4.1
Rent
    income from   15.4.2
    right to receive for life under
        trust   15.3.5, 18.2.8
Rented accommodation   12.4.3,
    12.4.4, *see also* Sheltered housing

Repair
    housing, of   12.1, 12.3, 12.4.1
    grants   12.4.1
Representation
    review of complaint decision,
        at   13.2.3
    right to   5.5.7, 5.6
Residence, ordinary   5.3, 9.2.1
    meaning   9.2.1
    in-patient, of   9.2.1
    placement etc in area of another
        authority, and   9.2.1, 9.6
Residential accommodation   9.1, 9.2,
    see also Residential care
Residential allowance   15.8
Residential care
    assessment of need prior to
        arrangement for   9.2.3, 9.2.4,
        14.5
    benefits during
    entitlement   19.2, *see also*
        Attendance allowance;
        Disability living allowance
    finance, and, *see* Payment for
        services; Preserved rights
    financing placement out
        of   19.2.2, 19.3
    'board and personal care', and
        registration   9.2.2
    checklist   4.4
    choice as to   6.6, 9.2.4, 9.2.5
    closure   10.9, 10.10.1
    Codes of Practice   10.1
    complaints on provision   10.11,
        13.2.2, *see also* Complaints
    contract for, by individual   9.4, 9.6
    contract for services   9.2, 9.3
    cases on 'reasonableness' of
        demands   8.5.1, 8.5.2
    conflict of interest
        safeguards   9.3.2
    contract type most used   8.2
    linked contracts, use of   9.3.1
    service specifications   8.5, 9.2.4,
        9.3.2, 10.11
    terms and conditions   9.3.2
    contribution from resident   15.7,
        15.10, *see also* fees *below,* Means
        test for residential care

Residential care—*cont*
  cost as factor   9.2.4
    topping-up arrangements   9.2.5
  discharge from hospital to   7.4
    right to refuse   7.5
    see also Discharge from hospital
  duty to arrange   4.2.1, 9.2, 9.2.3
    client group, new definition   9.2
    historical background   9.1
    ordinary residence
      requirement   9.2.1
    persons in 'relevant
      accommodation', exclusion
      for   9.2.2
    registered premises, restricted
      to   9.2.2
  eviction of person resident prior to
    April 1993   16.2–16.4
  expenses allowance, personal   9.6,
    15.5
    amount of   15.5, 15.10
  'extras'   9.3.2, 9.6
  facilities and services,
    minimum   10.2
  fees
    civil debt, as   15.11, 18.4
    gift of property to avoid   18.3
    notional capital reflected in   18.3,
      see also Capital: notional
    payment of   9.3.1, 9.3.2, 15.7
    review frequency   9.6
  financing   14.5, 14.6, 15.1 *et seq, see
    also* Payment for services
  hairdressing, laundry, etc   9.6
  inspection   9.2.2, 10.10, 10.11
    contract clause as to   9.3.2
    joint inspection units   10.10.2
    lay assessors   10.10.3
    power of social services
      departments   10.10
    purpose of   10.10
    suspicion that not
      registered   10.4
    units   10.10.1
  'liable relative' obligation   9.2.5,
    15.6.3
  means testing   9.3.1, 14.4, 15.1 *et seq,
    see also* Means test for residential
    care
  medical and health needs   9.5, 10.2
  need of individual for   9.2.3, 9.2.4,
    14.5

  need for (general)   2.1
  nursing and social care,
    overlap   9.1.4, 9.1.5, 10.3
    use of residential care where nursing
      home appropriate,
      trend   9.2.4
    see also Nursing home
  nursing care in   10.8
  offences relating to provision   9.2.2,
    10.4
    conviction, effect of   10.4, 10.9
    sanctions   10.1
    termination of contract, clause
      for   9.3.2
  Part III accommodation   9.1.1,
    10.10.3, 14.2, 15.9
  pre-1993 regime   9.1
  preserved rights, people with, *see*
    Preserved rights
  private
    arrangements   9.4, 9.6
    benefits for person
      making   19.2.3, 19.4
    purchase of   2.3.3, 9.1.3, *see also*
      'contract for services' *above*
  quality of life of residents   10.2
  quality of services   10.1–10.11
    inspection, use for enhancing
      10.11
  registration   9.2.2, 10.1, 10.3, 10.4
    appeal against decision   10.6,
      10.9
    cancellation   10.4, 10.9
    conditional   10.6
    dual, as nursing home as
      well   10.8
    'fitness'   10.6
    operation of home without   10.4,
      10.9
    owners and managers   10.4
    person carrying on must
      register   10.4
    refusal   10.6
  residential allowance   15.8
  respite care, as   9.6
  size   10.2
  small homes   9.2.2, 10.7
  statistics   1.2.5, 10.1
    spending on   2.4, 2.4.2, 2.5.3
  temporary placement in
    benefits means test, and   19.2.3

Residential care—*cont*
  temporary placement in—*cont*
    house value, and   9.6, 15.3.7
    third-party contributions   9.2.5,
      9.3.1
      failure to pay   9.3.2
    use of, background   2.2, 9.1
Respite care   4.3, 9.6, 11.1, 11.2, 11.3
  breach of Guidance unlawful   11.3
  charges   11.4.2, 17.8
  enforcement of claim for by
    carer   11.3
  integral part of NHS provision   11.3
  legal adviser, and   17.8
  means test discretion   11.4.2
  uses of   11.3
Retirement housing   12.4.4, *see also*
  Housing; Sheltered housing; Warden
  services
Retirement pension
  income, as   15.4
Review
  see also Complaints
  charge for non-residential service,
    of   17.6
  complaint response by local authority,
    of   13.2.3
  hospital discharge decision, of   7.6

Sale of home
  see also Home
  charging order for   15.11.1
  person in care attempting, effect and
    case studies   15.3.7
  waiver of charges pending   15.3.7,
    15.11
Secretary of State
  approval   4.1, 4.2
  complaints, power as to   13.5, 13.6.2
  directions   1.5.3, 4.1, 4.2
  guidance   1.5.3
  judicial review of actions   13.6.3
  representations to, for resident facing
    eviction   16.4
Service charges   12.4.4
Services, *see* Community care services;
  Community health services
Setting aside disposition   18.4
  time-limit   18.4.1
  transaction at undervalue, court
    power   18.4.2

use of power by trustee in bankruptcy,
  considerations for   18.4.1
Sharing home   12.4.5
Sheltered housing   4.4, 12.3, 12.4.4
  categories   12.4.4
  council-run   12.4.4
  financing   12.4.4
  lease or management deed, practical
    points   12.4.4
  private sector   12.3, 12.4.4
    Code of Practice   12.4.4
  statistics   12.4.4
  'very sheltered'   12.4.4
  waiting lists   12.4.4
  warden services   4.2.2, 12.4.4
Sheltered Housing Advisory and
  Conciliation Service   12.4.4
Social services
  see also Local authority
  access to personal files   4.3, 5.5.10,
    13.2.3
  adaptations to home, overlap of duties
    with housing authority   12.4.2
  care manager   6.5
  county, consultation duty with district
    housing authority   12.3.1
  creation of departments   2.3.1
  service provision   4.2.3, 4.2.4
    accessing services   4.3
    after-care services   4.2.4
    changes to   2.3.1, 2.4, 2.5
    checklist   4.4
    purchaser and provider split   6.5
  social work support,
    providing   4.2.2
Social work services
  complaint on provision   13.2.2, *see
    also* Complaints
Solicitor, *see* Legal advice; Representation
Sources
  demographic information   1.2.6
  know-how   1.4.1
Spouse
  contribution to cost of residential
    care   9.2.5
  liable relative, as   9.2.5, 15.6.3
    no liability to income
      assessment   15.6.3
  non-residential charges, and   17.5,
    17.8

Spouse—*cont*
  occupying home   15.3.7, 18.2.8
State benefits   19.1–19.4
  see also Attendance allowance;
      Disability living allowance;
      Income support
  arrears or compensation for non-
      payment, disregard of   15.3.5
  Benefits Agency, disregard of capital
      value of home by   15.3.7
  charge for non-residential services,
      and people on   17.3, 17.8
  income assessment, and   15.4
  information on, prior to hospital
      discharge   7.3
  legal advice on interface between
      residential care, and   19.0,
      19.4
  means tested/non-means
      tested   17.3, 19.1, 19.2, 19.2.3
  residential care, during
      availability   19.2, *see also*
          Attendance allowance;
          Disability living allowance
      background to   2.4.3, 2.4.4, 2.5.3
      effect of entering home   19.2
      financial issues, *see* Payment for
          services; Preserved benefits
      own arrangements, for person
          making   19.2.3, 19.4
Statistics   1.2, 7.1
Statutory duty
  action for breach   13.7.1
Statutory instruments   1.5.2
Stocks and shares   15.3.2

Telephone
  provision of   4.2.5
Tenant   12.4
  council, moving to another council
      property   12.4.3
  home shared with relative,
      of   12.4.5
  property held subject to tenancy, and
      disregarded capital   18.2.8
  service charges   12.4.4
Tendering   8.1
Therapists   2.3.2, 4.4, 8.3
  no power to charge for   14.3
  residential care, purchase of services
      for   9.5

Third party
  contributions to residential care
      by   9.2.5, 9.3.1
      failure to pay   9.3.2
  occupation of house by   15.3.7,
      18.2.8
  payment made to for claimant,
      treatment of   18.2.1
  recovery of gift from   18.3
  topping-up payments for residential
      care by   15.4.3
Topping up   9.2.5, 15.4.3
  lump sum payments 'belong' to
      claimant   18.2.1
  preserved rights, and   16.1
Tort action   13.7
Transaction at undervalue   18.4.2
Trust
  assets held in   15.3.3
  creation as 'deprivation' of
      settlor   18.2.8
  discretionary   15.3.3
      use in care planning   18.2.8
  income from   15.3.3, 15.4, 15.4.3
  life interest   15.3.5, 18.2.8
  reversionary interest   15.3.5, 18.2.8
  meaning   18.2.8
Trustee in bankruptcy
  setting aside voluntary
      disposition   18.4

Undervalue, transaction at   18.4.2, *see
    also* Gift of property
Unified health authorities, *see* Health
    authorities (unified)
Unit trust   15.3.2
Unitary authorities   12.3.1
Urgent need   5.5.5

Valuation, *see* Home; Means test for
    residential care
Vicarious liability   13.7, 13.7.2
Voluntary disposition, *see* Gift of
    property
Voluntary sector   2.3.3
  see also Charities
  checklist of services   4.4
  purchase of services from, *see*
      Contracting

Voluntary sector—*cont*
  use by local authority to provide
      services   4.2.2

Wagner Report   10.8
War disablement pension   15.4.1
War widow's pension   15.4.1
Warden services   4.2.2, 12.4.4
  arrangements for   12.4.4

Welfare, promotion of   4.2.2
Welfare services, *see* Community care
      services; Community health services;
      Local authority; National Health
      Service; State benefits
White Paper 'Caring for People'   2.5,
      3.1, 5.1, 10.10
  housing as component in community
      care   12.3